GUIDE FOR
THE CHRISTIAN ASSEMBLY

THIERRY MAERTENS – JEAN FRISQUE

GUIDE FOR THE
CHRISTIAN
ASSEMBLY

REVISED EDITION

22nd to 34th WEEKS

Notre Dame, Indiana 46556

TRANSLATED FROM THE FRENCH BY JOHN W. LUNDBERG

Nihil Obstat: V. Descamps
can. libr. cens.

Imprimatur: J. Thomas, *vic. gen.*
Tournai, July 16, 1970

LCCCN: 72-114245

ISBN: 0-8190-0008-6

1773

Translated from the original French edition,
Guide de l'assemblée chrétienne, Casterman, 1970.
An edition of St. Andrews Abbey, Bruges.

CONTENTS

TWENTY-SECOND WEEK

I. 1 Thessalo-
nians
4:13-18
1st reading
1st cycle
Monday

Paul tries to calm the anxieties of his readers about the events surrounding the end of the world. In fact, their question calls to mind one which the Jews themselves frequently asked: will those already dead be present for the inauguration of the Kingdom? Many believe in a restoration of the people, but do not see clearly the relationship between this restoration and individual resurrection.

a) Like the Jews of his day, Paul answers that the dead will be present at the time of the restoration of the people, for they will be raised up first of all. But this *resurrection* is seen as a new day; it will be brought forth "with Jesus" (v. 14): God who raised Jesus from the dead will likewise raise up those who have died "in Jesus." Paul next appeals to "what the Lord himself had said" (v. 15): undoubtedly a special teaching of Jesus (and not an idea of the apostle) according to which the dead and the living (without any special advantage for these latter) will join Christ the very moment of the Parousia and accompany him in the events which will set the stage for the definitive coming of the Kingdom.

b) To the Jewish scheme: the resurrection of the body, the coming of the Kingdom, Paul adds something new: resurrection, Parousia, being "with" the Lord, the definitive coming of the Kingdom. The expression "with me" (cf. Jn 14:3; 17:24) is to be taken in a strict sense: it is not simply living "in the company" of the Lord, but sharing his privileges. Parallel expressions are: "to sit with me on my throne" (Rv 3:21; 20:4-6; 5:10; 2 Tm 2:12), "to have supper with him" (Mt 26:29; 25:10; Rv 3:20) or again a "share in my heritage" (Jn 13:9), "with me in paradise" (Lk 23: 42-43).

St. Paul's idea, then, is that the dead will not be raised simply to be inhabitants of a marvelous kingdom but to share the reign of the Lord. Christ assumed the lowly and mortal situation of man. In return he will share his glory and his lordship with the resurrected. The Christian will not only have access to the future glory, but he will really share this special glory which the God-man enjoys since his resurrection.

II. 1 Corinthians 2:1-5
1st reading
2nd cycle
Monday

After he pointed out the superiority of the gospel to philosophical systems (1 Co 18-25), Paul then explains why he did not preach such a doctrine. He did far better once he disclosed the living source for the attitude of the faithful.

Paul does not preach a philosophical system; he proclaims a *testimony* (v. 1). Now the testimony is of value only because of the quality of the event and not because of the rhetoric involved. In contrast to philosophical discourses, that of the witness is basically relative; its value is found outside itself. Paul seems, however, to have made a choice in the events to which he witnesses. He dwells more on the cross than on the Lordship of Christ (v.2), more on the humility of Jesus than on his wisdom. He does not necessarily make the same choices in all the communities he evangelized, but he does so at Corinth ("among us"), to avoid, no doubt, the ambiguities which another position would have created in a milieu so open to gnosis and syncretism.

Moreover, since the teaching has value because of the quality of the events it reports and not because of the quality of the speaker, Paul is not afraid to speak despite a weak and faltering speech which already cost him defeat at the Acropolis in Athens (Ac 17:16-34).

A witness must however base his statements on a minimum of proofs. The apostle does not supply them by way of precise oratorical technique, but by a show of spirit and power (v.7). This does not necessarily involve miracles but probably charisms suddenly poured out on the community at Corinth and especially the changes brought about in the lives of his converted listeners.

Paul vigorously defends his witness to Christ crucified (v.2) because for him the cross had long been an incomprehensible phenomenon. He could not admit that the expected Messiah would be a crucified Messiah. The vision on the road to Damascus caused him to discover that the crucified is truly Lord and that he lives among men, persecuted in their turn, so they can be joined to his glory.

Is Paul saying that if God was able to convert him, a Pharisee, by revealing to him that the glory was passing as a madness as incomprehensible as the cross, then the best way to convert men consists in taking up anew that experience on the road to Damascus and in presenting it with the folly of the cross as the road to glory?

Thus the witness which the apostle brings to the world is accepted as a definite existential experience: the missionary converts others because he himself is converted. Otherwise he is only a propagandist and his speech is not a witness.

III. Luke
4:16-30
Gospel
Monday

Although Matthew presents Christ as an itinerant rabbi (Mt 4:12-17), Luke, more the liturgist (he begins and ends his gospel in the temple: Lk 1:5-23; 24:50-53), has Christ's ministry begin with the synagogue liturgy for the Sabbath.

At that period the synagogue liturgy evolved around two readings. The first, taken from the law (Pentateuch), was read and explained by a doctor of the law; the second, of later origin, was taken from the prophets and could be read and explained by anyone who was at least thirty years of age. Now, Jesus had just celebrated his thirtieth birthday and so lays claim to the right to present and explain the second reading. His first public speech, therefore, is a liturgical homily.

a) Luke has not preserved the exact words of Jesus, but he does sum up their essence in a single verse: "Today this Scripture passage is fulfilled" (v.21). All the *rules of the homily* are evident in this speech. Thanks to him, the synagogue liturgy of the Word is no longer a simple catechism lesson like the Scribes and the doctors of the law provided, nor the affirmation of the eschatological hope kept alive by the prophets; it becomes the announcement of the Father's plan now accomplished this day and for this assembly. No longer does one contemplate former times, be it a golden age or the occasion of a defeat; no longer does one dream of an extraordinary future; rather one lives the present time as the privileged locus for the coming of the Lord.

The apostles will often use this homiletic procedure as a new style which Jesus proposes for the first time in the history of Israel (cf. Ac 13:14,42; 16:13-17; 17:1-3; 18:4). The Christian liturgy of the Word is thus a daughter of the synagogue, but it moves beyond with the celebration of the today.

At times we wonder if the sermons preached in our times in Christian assemblies are faithful to that of Christ at Nazareth or to those by the doctors of the law.

b) Christ (or St. Luke) seems to have purposely halted his reading at the place where the prophecy of Isaiah 61 proclaims a "year of grace." By skipping the following verse which announces the judgment of the nations: "And a day of vengeance for our God" (Is 61:2), Jesus stresses the grace of God and leaves in the background the condemnation of the nations. His words of "grace" moreover, cause astonishment in the assembly (v.22) and this manner of suggesting a *universal* divine grace provokes the incidents related in vv. 25-30. Besides, to reinforce the idea that his mission is entirely one of grace and not of condemnation, Christ (or Luke) joined to the citation from Is 61:1-2, a verse borrowed from Is 58:6 about the liberty offered to prisoners.

At the very start, therefore, Christ defines his mission as a proclamation of the love and grace of God to every man. Such a revelation could only be a scandal for the Jews who awaited eschatological times with all the drive that hatred could breath into them.

c) Verses 23-30 do not seem to be in the right position: they probably come from another of Christ's speeches. There is, in fact, a certain lack of unity between the simple astonishment of the crowd in v.22 and the violence of Christ's words in vv. 23-27. No doubt Luke joined the two speeches around the key-word "grace" which appears successively in v. 19, in the quotation from Isaiah in v. 22 where he describes the words of Christ and in v. 24 where he describes the *prophet*. In fact, instead of translating as is usually done: "No prophet has received," it would seem more exact, since the word is the same as in vv. 19 and 22 *(dektos)*, to translate: "a prophet is not acceptable in his own country," which would indicate the will of Jesus to depart from his surroundings in order to fulfill his mission.

The missionary is challenged both from within and without. Paul suffered affronts from "false brethren" as well as from the pagans. The power of Eliseus was challenged by the pagan Naaman, that of Jesus by his countrymen.

By definition, in fact, the missionary is bound to the Church. But at the same time he must be completely concerned with evangelizing the world. This twofold belonging provides him with the starting point for an unlimited love. This position is inevitably uncomfortable. The non-Christian world does not recognize him as one of its own, especially when its culture is different from his own; the Christian world does not always recognize him either, for his style of life, his challenges and the questions he asks, disturb the firmest position. The missionary questions the values that they prized as sacred. He unsettles things, at times even instilling fear. When the authorities of the Church are themselves uneasy, the missionary is sometimes drawn to bring about shattering revisions.

But by separating himself from his original milieu he is invited to an unexpected enrichment. For if it is true that he has given his life to Christ, it is equally true that the challenge purifies him and makes him more and more like Christ crucified and savior.

IV. 1 Thessalo- **nians 5:1-6,** **9-11** *1st reading* *1st cycle* *Tuesday*	Once returned from Thessalonika, Timothy informs Paul that the community is eager to have some clarification on the Parousia, the how and when of it. The apostle here deals with the question about the moment of the Lord's coming, a question which the Christians of that time ask rather frequently (v. 1;

cf. Ac 1:6-7; Mt 24:36).

a) The Jewish heritage brings them to consider the *Day of the Lord* as a day of vengeance and of triumph over the enemy. But, by referring to the theme of light and darkness—for a long time linked to the theme of the day of Yahweh (Am 5:18-20; Sg 1:15)—Paul underscores the moral aspect (vv. 4-5; cf. Rm 13:12-13). Moreover, the "son of light" is well placed so as not to be surprised when the day of the Lord comes. For as "child of the day" the coming of the Day cannot surprise him.

b) The antithesis *light* and *darkness* often designate, in the Scriptures, the opposition between the world of the just and that of the impious (Am 8:8; Jr 4:23-24; Is 3:20) or yet, the opposition between the actual world and the eschatological future (Is 60: 19-20; 30:26). When someone who is a son of the night is converted and becomes a son of the light, he prepares himself for the Day of the Lord.

c) As for the antithesis *sons of light* and *sons of darkness,* it derives no doubt from those who considered the monastic life as the assembling of the sons of light and the sharp separation from the sons of darkness. In any case, a treatise just recently discovered and belonging to the library of the Qumran monastery contains this significant title: "The war of the sons of light against the sons of darkness."

d) The sons of darkness are spoken of as asleep while the sons of light remain awake and sober (v. 6): the first group in fact are insensitive to the meaning of the events, while the second group are vigilant and have mastery over themselves, which is necessary in order to know God (cf. 1 Co 15:34; Rm 13:13).

By complying with the rule of faith, Israel valued the event and became the privileged ground for the encounter with God. But, when she imagined salvation, that is, the decisive intervention of Yahweh in favor of his people, she links it to a day which no longer belongs to the unfolding of time, a day which had to halt the course of history: the "Day of Yahweh." A sort of dichotomy was maintained between profane time and sacred time, the time of man and the time of God.

Jesus of Nazareth significantly altered these traditional values. The Kingdom which he brings is built here below, in the ordinariness of existence. In his eyes there is only one time for man: secular time, which must be lived in its fullest as the dimension in which God intervenes to save us.

Such is Paul's thesis: in place of desperately waiting for a "Day of Yahweh," it is better to live with God in the light each day that is given to us. This is also the thesis of Matthew who answers questions concerning the coming of the son of man with parables about daily vigilance (Mt 24:25).

V. 1 Corinthians Here Paul contrasts the "natural" man who re-
    2:10-16 lies solely on his own powers—were these
    1st reading intellectuals—with the "spiritual man who has
    2nd cycle the presence of God in him."
    Tuesday

                In this passage the *spirit* of God is not yet personalized. There is only a participation in the divine intelligence and hence a manner of knowing the plan of God and more particularly the gifts which he gives to men (v. 12). This spirit, then, is necessary for the Corinthians to discern the charisms which come from God and those which come from man.

The spirit of God supplies as well the thought and vocabulary which make it possible to speak about God in a suitable manner, without the aid of secular wisdom (v. 13). That amounts to saying that a charism of tongues, for example, could very well not come from God if it does not aid in the understanding of his plan or cast light on his presence in the Church.

A final result of the action of the spirit of God in the heart of the Christian is the facility which it bestows for judging all things. Considering the world and the events of more importance than purely natural faculties, the Christian enjoys a certain superiority over the supporters of gnosticism or of asceticism. For if it is true that human intelligence cannot rise to the divine intelligence, it is likewise true that no one can judge someone who consciously places himself under the movement of the spirit of God (v. 16).

Paul makes an answer of sorts to the reproach of the Corinthians who claim that he did not instruct them in a sufficiently learned manner. They themselves could by-pass in knowledge all the philosophies of the earth if they had enough humility to give ear to the understanding of God which is superior to everything and places the Christian above all. But a serious desire for humility and an openness to God is needed if one is to arrive there.

VI. Luke
4:31-37
Gospel
Tuesday

The first part of this gospel (vv. 31-33) shows how the young rabbi proceeds to make his message known and it underscores the authority which emanates from his person. The second part (vv. 33-36) relates the first miracle of Jesus, at least according to the synoptic tradition. Successively there is a description of the state of sickness (v. 33), the supreme authority of Jesus (v. 35) and the reaction of the crowds (v. 37).

A common theme unites the two parts of the gospel: the *authority* of the word of Jesus in his teaching and in his miracles alike.

For the contemporaries of Jesus, the world is subject to the influence of demons, catastrophies and death. One day, God will make an end to their empire by sending a "holy one of God" (v. 34; a term which implies belonging to the divine world as opposed to the "impure" which designates belonging to the world of demons). Jesus' first miracle is not as such an interpretation of the faith but the unique weapon of the envoy of God against the imperialism of the spirits. This is a very primitive way of speaking about redemption and salvation, but it has the advantage of stressing the power with which Jesus is revealed as the envoy of God.

But the Jewish world is still oppressed by the influence of the Scribes whose mentality entrusts to the law an import which they themselves cannot fulfill. Contrary to them, Jesus uses his authority to teach in a new way (v. 32). Instead of appealing to the text of the law or the traditions of the schools, he appeals directly to his own judgment and conscience. To speak with authority is to speak in such a way that the speaker answers by placing himself on a different level of personal relationship and that he desires not to argue but to encounter the person of the master and to love him faithfully.

VII. Colossians The Phyrgian town of Colossae was not evan-
    1:1-8 gelized by St. Paul but by some of his dis-
    1st reading ciples, among whom was Epaphras (Col 1:7;
    1st cycle 4:12-13). Paul is in prison when Epaphras
    Wednesday visits him about 61-62 A.D. (Col 4:12; Phm 23)
to bring him up to date on the difficulties in

the community at Colossae, then struggling with the temptation to syncretism.

After the regular greeting (vv. 1-3), the apostle makes an *act of thanksgiving* which he traditionally addresses to the Father at the beginning of most of his letters.

The purpose of this praise is to carry forward the progress of the Kingdom, both by the inner transformation of man (faith, hope and charity: vv. 3-5a) and by the external spread of the gospel and its rapid bearing of fruit (vv. 5b-7).

The act of thanksgiving in the Eucharist repeats the same themes found in St. Paul; it is a profession of faith for an assembly eager to attain the good things promised by God, in fraternal love and the presence of the gospel at the heart of earthly realities.

VIII. 1 Corin- The beginning of Paul's conclusions to his
thians statement on the factions created at Corinth
3:1-9 because of teachers more concerned with their
1st reading originality than with the transmission of reve-
2nd cycle lation (cf. 1 Co 1:12). The apostle sets forth
Wednesday the resulting superiority of divine wisdom over
human wisdom (1 Co 1:26-31; 1 Co 2:6-10)
and brings a judgment to the whole situation.

The *teachers* are servants and collaborators with God. They may not act in their own name (vv. 10-23) and they will have to render an account to God (1 Co 4:1-5).

Paul and Apollos are servants of God just as much as they are of the Corinthians. This concept of service involves the idea of collegiality (v. 6): if each one has his function and his special charisms, all, nevertheless, must work together at the same task. What a mockery to see this collegiality questioned by the spirit of clannishness and partisanship (vv. 2-3). All this transpires at

Corinth as if the teachers had the initiative in the work of the mission, whereas they are only the middlemen of God who himself brings to completion his work (v. 7).

The fact that they work together does not dispense the teachers from individually rendering an account to God (v. 8). Each one is responsible for the part he plays in the common task; responsibility for the doings and deeds which could engender a clannish and factional spirit.

IX. Luke   This gospel relates the first healings performed
4:38-44   by Jesus at Capharnaum: the healing of the
Gospel   mother-in-law of Peter and of various demon-
Wednesday   iacs. The theme of *threat* forms the unity of
the account. Contrary to Mt 8:14-17 and to
Mk 1:29-34, Luke stresses that Christ "threatens" the fever of Peter's mother-in-law (v. 39) and "threatens" the demons. In Luke 4:35, this "threat" already cured a demoniac and it is not impossible that in the primitive source this account was followed by that of the calming of the storm—where Jesus "threatens" the winds and the sea. Matthew effectively relates it to the sequel of texts which form the subject matter of this gospel (Mt 28:23-27).

This theme of the *threat* is rather revealing as to the spirit of the source used by Luke. Although Mt 8:17 interprets these healings as the fulfillment of the prophecy about the Suffering Servant (Is 53:4), Luke sees them as a manifestation of eschatological power and authority (Lk 4:32, 37).

The threat of God is one theme of the ancient cosmologies where creation appeared as the result of a battle between the creator God and rebellious elements (Pss 103/104:5-9; 73/74:13-14; 88/89:9-11; Jb 26:11-12). The biblical traditions revived it to describe the marvels in the victory at the Red Sea (Ps 105/106:9; Is 50:2). They have likewise used it in the eschatological era (Hab 3:8; Na 1:4) which will witness the definitive deliverance of God's people.

By so patently threatening the elements of evil, Christ announces the imminence of the final struggle: as a warrior who is prepared to fight, he begins by threatening the enemy whom he will not delay in destroying. He thus announces the preparation of a new universe that already possess a new Adam at its center.

X. Colossians The letters of St. Paul usually begin with a
1:9-14 prayer inscribed by the pattern and formulas
1st reading of Jewish "blessings" (acts of thanksgiving:
1st cycle Col 1:3-8 and intercessory prayers: Col 1:9-
Thursday 14). Verses 12-14 probably reproduce a liturgical formula, for it is found in more or less
identical words in Ephesians 1:11-13; 1 P 2:9; Ac 26:18 etc. Paul bases himself on a text already known to his readers so as to show them that his teaching is not a fabrication of his intellect as with gnosticism, but the common possession of the Church.

a) Paul hopes that the Colossians come to the *knowledge* of God (cf. vv. 9-10). He is undoubtedly nervous about the influence on their community of gnostic teachings which claimed to bestow on those initiated into such teachings the divine "fullness." For the apostle the sole access to this fullness is faith or "knowledge" of God (cf. Is 19:20-22) which must be translated into real life (Hos 6:6; Is 1:17; Jr 22:16; Mt 7:22-23) and which is acquired by submission to the divine will.

This knowledge of God is made real in "good works" or "leading a life worthy of the Lord" (v. 10). These expressions are commonplace but Paul insists especially on the importance of involvement. The Christian knowledge of God is not something speculative, it is communion with life.

b) By linking *patience* to this knowledge of God (v. 11), Paul stands in opposition to the gnostics who believe they know God without submitting to the natural laws of belief. The adherents of gnosis were victims of their immoderate desire to know everything. But true knowledge is not linked with the discovery of secrets but to the progressive conversion of one's whole life.

That the Colossians, then, thank God for the knowledge which he already gives them (v. 12) thanks to the death and resurrection of Christ and to the redemption which remits sins (vv. 13-14), gives hope for the fullness of knowledge and permits one to live a life worthy of the Lord (v. 10).

The "last days" which we live in measure the slow passage to the age of the adult from a still infant world. The Christian must accept the delays imposed by his littleness and assume the trouble of atuning his life with his knowledge of God. Convinced that man can say nothing about God "in himself," and that he can attain only a God "for him," he seeks in all things that which makes communication with him possible. He profits from the eucharistic happenings during this slow progress towards fullness.

XI. 1 Corin- thians 3:18-23 *1st reading* *2nd cycle* *Thursday*	Eager for wisdom and thirsting for gnosis, the Corinthians reproach Paul because of the simplicity of his teaching. The reading from 1 Co 3:9-17 has already supplied one of the arguments which Paul uses to refute this accusation. The reading for today presents two more.

a) The first of these arguments relates to Scripture (vv. 19-20; cf. Jb 5:12-13 and Ps 93/94:11). God is not found by way of a philosophical search. On the contrary he confounds the *wise* by revealing himself to men who do not expect their own search to succeed and by disclosing who he is in Jesus Christ crucified.

b) The second argument is particularly original (vv. 21-23). Why do Christians entrust themselves into the hands of a philosopher and become intoxicated with such slavery whereas their allegiance to God makes them masters of everything and every-body?

One senses here the dawning of the Christian idea of the hierarchy which is above all *service* (1 Co 4:1; Lk 22:24-27), an idea that is in contrast to the master of wisdom ideal among the Stoics and the Jews with its right to demand all from its disciples.

To promote the authentic wisdom of God is not to deny the value of man's search. On the contrary it seeks to further it, to purify it and to cause it to reach the God of Jesus Christ. In final analysis man must recognize that the God of Jesus Christ escapes all intellectual search and every moral or mystical ascent; faith alone allows access to him.

XII. Luke   This passage joins together two distinct tradi-
    5:1-11   tions: the calling of the first disciples (as in Mk
    Gospel   1:16-20) and the account of the miraculous
    Thursday   catch of fish (as in Jn 21:1-11).

In Mark 1:17 and Mt 4:19, Christ, making an allusion to the profession of his disciples, announced to them that he would make them *fishers of men.* There is an obvious play on words here evoking their vocation in the light of the profession they were working at. In St. Luke the title is awarded after the miracle of the abundant catch of fish. Beyond the play on words, the writer of the third gospel attempts to describe the apostle's function himself and to appraise its efficacy.

We can appreciate more the importance of the episode about the miraculous catch of fish if we recall that the Jews considered water, especially the sea, as the abode of Satan and the forces opposed to God (Gn 1:7, 17-34; Pss 73/74:13; 23/24:2; Jb 38:16-17; Jon 2:2-4; Rv 9:1-3; 13:1; 20:3). Until the arrival of the savior, nothing could be attempted—except a miracle like that of the Red Sea—to save those whom the hostile sea engulfed. But when he comes, men can be fished in abundance and lifted from the empire of evil. Such is, moreover, the meaning of the descent into hell (*inferi*—the water below) in 1 P 3:19, where Christ descends to save man engulfed by the waters of the deluge. To be a fisher of men is to share in that enterprise of rescuing all those whom evil engulfs. Jeremiah 16:15-16 already foresaw that role.

St. Luke, then, considers the Church as the institution charged with saving humanity from the engulfing waters which threaten it. To insure the realization of this mission, some men are entrusted with a special function; but they owe to Christ alone the power which they have at their command to guide to a successful conclusion their "fishing" and the devotion involved in following it.

In the preceding centuries, the missionary was considered a fisher of men to the degree in which he introduced individuals to the Church through baptism. But this individualistic approach does not suit either the mentality of Luke or that of our age. Under mythical appearances, the account of the miraculous catch presents quite a different abundance. Humanity is the prize for the powers and forces which engulf and submerge it. Christ envisages for himself and his disciples a liberating role which brakes and thwarts that descent into the abyss.

Now, actual humanity is not far from being engulfed and the demonic forces which work in it are called egoism and the thirst for power. To be a fisher of men today, one needs to participate in all the enterprises which try to draw humanity from the ocean which submerges it, by seeking to advance peace and development among people. To stand outside these movements is to condemn the Church to powerlessness in unveiling its identity and mission among men.

XIII. Colossians 1:15-20 *1st reading* *1st cycle* *Friday* — This passage draws attention to the preeminent lordship of Christ, proclaimed in a hymn of two couplets conjuring up, on the one hand, his royalty over the created world (vv. 15-17) and on the other hand, his royalty over the re-created world (vv. 18-20). The two strophies are built on a scheme that ensures their harmony:

v. 15: He is ... first born of all creatures.	v. 18b: It is he ... the first born of the dead.
v. 16: In him everything	v. 19: ... absolute fullness resides in him
v. 16: in heaven and on earth	v. 20: both on earth and in heaven
v. 16: were created ... for him	v. 20: to reconcile ... in his person

a) These verses, 15-17, are no doubt a paraphrase of an ancient liturgical hymn (perhaps baptismal). To start with, notice that the first strophe is completed by the enumeration of the powers of creation: thrones, dominations, principalities; whereas the second ends with the mention of the cross which is the sign of the new dominion. The earth and the sky are cited in the two strophies, implying the idea of totality or universality.

Furthermore, each phrase has as its object the incarnate Word, not the divine Word:—he is the first born of all creation, not on the chronological plane but on the plane of causality: in creating the world, God made use of Christ as a model (cf. Pr 8:22 in reference to wisdom).

—He is also the first born on the supernatural plane (and this chronologically as well as causally). Thus he is dealing with the preexisting Christ, but possessed in the historic person of the Son of God made man.

Finally, the *primacy of Christ* is presented through three images, firstborn, head of the body, fullness. These themes, dear to St. Paul, express the fact that the resurrection of Christ has placed his human nature at the head and source of regenerated humanity and creation itself (Rm 8:19-22; 1 Co 3:22; 15:20-28; Ep 1:10; 4:10, etc.).

b) This christological hymn should be read less as a doctrinal pronouncement than as a passionate *profession of faith*, declared in the context of gnosis. For a Christian the primacy of Christ is the chief point of his religion; all else is fancy! The gnostic discussions on the existence of a creator God are a mockery: Christ made all. Even Adam is deprived of his title as first man because of Jesus. The comments on the existence of angels are also quite useless since Christ is here. Paul thus struggles with the difficulty gnosticism has with its own vocabulary.

The risen Lord is head of the faithful who desire to follow him by participating in the life of the Church. But his resurrection establishes and confirms him in an absolute preeminence in the universe. He becomes its Lord. Paul affirms in effect that the powers and angelic dominations have usurped a power over creation which Christ recovers by his resurrection.

But the lordship of Christ need not be conceived in the same way as that of the angelic powers, as a reign which granted man the free choice of his destiny. This is not the case. Of every lordship, only that of Christ alienated neither man nor creation. Jesus in effect had won it in the depth of his life as man. By working towards a progressive spiritualization of creation, man participates in the reign of Christ over all things.

Christ acquires his lordship in the mystery of his resurrection because it is the foundation for the reconciliation of body and soul, of matter and spirit, of heaven and earth. The meaning of the Eucharist is to realize the victory of the spirit over matter and over the "flesh."

XIV. 1 Corin-   In their conversion the Corinthians accepted
thians 4:1-5   not only the teachings of the Lord but also the
1st reading   direction of various schools of thought. Thus
2nd cycle   the Good News is often found infiltrated with
Friday   personal ideas which involve various options
          in the mind of the faithful, though there is no
thought of forming clans and factions. The universality of the
message is thus jeopardized. Here Paul ends his argument.

The author first of all reminds teachers that they are the
"repositories" of the gospel, "stewards" who do not have the right
to alter the possession they administer. They ought to be "faithful" servants. This theme of service to the mysteries of God is very
important in the first Christian theology of the priesthood. Several
of the Lord's parables on the role of the apostles after his departure are inspired by it; they must administer the possessions of
the Father as confidential servants and they will be servants of his
family during his absence (Mt 24:45-51; 25:14-30; 20:24-28).

The second declaration of the apostle bears on the judgment
that the servant will undergo when the time for rendering an account comes. Here Paul adopts the perspective of the parable of
the stewards (Mt 24:45-51). All "service" is performed not because
of the support which can be created or the success that can be
experienced, but basically because of the appreciation which the
master of the family will show at his return.

XV. Luke   The discipline which the young rabbi places
5:33-39   upon his disciples, scandalizes the crowds, for
Gospel   it had nothing in common with that which
Friday   other rabbis impose on their disciples. Al-
          though the disciples of the Baptist and the
Pharisees observe certain fast days, those of Christ seem to be
dispensed from them (v. 33). It is the problem of the independ-
ence shown by Jesus and his disciples in the matter of traditional

observances that is set forth here. Jesus justifies this attitude by a declaration about the presence of the Spouse (vv. 36-37).

a) In the Old Testament and in Judaism the practice of fast was linked to the expectation of the coming of the Messiah. The fast and abstinence from wine, the special practice of the Nazirite (Lk 22:14-20) expressed dissatisfaction with the present time and expectation of the consolation of Israel. John the Baptist used this attitude as a fundamental law of his conduct (Lk 1:15). Since then, when the disciples of Jesus are dispensed from the prescribed or freely-chosen fasts, they give the impression of being disinterested in the coming of the Messiah and of refusing to share the messianic hope. The response of Jesus is clear: the disciples do not fast because they no longer have anything to wait for; *messianic times* have arrived: they no longer have to urge on, by ascetical practices, the coming of a Messiah, for they already live in intimacy with him. This intimacy will be innterrupted by the passion and death of their master: at this time they will fast (v. 30, cf. Lk 22:18) until the time when the Spouse is returned to them in the resurrection and in the definitive Kingdom.

b) The parables about the garment and skins supply another response to the astonishment of John's disciples and of the Pharisees. As inaugurator of messianic times, Jesus is conscious of bringing to the world a reality without precedent in all that man possessed until that moment (cf. Lk 16:16, or the miracle at Cana, Jn 2:10). The two parables do not make a value judgment when they state that old wine is better than new wine or that new clothing is preferable to old clothing. They do not make a comparison but simply stress an *incompatibility*: we must not join the old and the new for fear of doing harm to one or the other, for the patched clothing will be badly matched and the old skins irretrievably lost, and the wine with it. The lesson which is gained from Christ's reply is thus clear: we must choose in renouncing compromises that lose all.

Luke is particularly sensitive to this incompatibility between the two orders of the covenant. He modifies for this reason the parable of the garment (v. 36) and adds a rather odd verse, verse 39. Mark and Matthew stress that to patch an old garment does not prevent its loss. Luke, on the contrary, points out that to remove material from a new garment (which no one does) to repair an old one damages both of them. The first two evangelists retain only the loss of the old garment, while Luke stresses that of the old and the new. He does not make a value judgment; he simply states the incompatibility. The same judgment explains v. 39a (verse 39b seems to be only a rather clumsy explanation, poorly certified moreover from a literary point of view). The drinker of old wine does not say that the new wine is bad; he only states that one does not drink it after having tasted the old, their bouquet being incompatible.

One who has known the spouse and wishes to share his love cannot at the same time live as if he did not exist! The gospel excludes compromise.

XVI. Colossians   The letter to the Colossians is often considered
1:21-23   a rough draft of the letter to the Ephesians.
1st reading   The text for today seems in fact an outline for
1st cycle   the passage in Ephesians 2:17-22. We recog-
Saturday   nize there the idea that Christians came from
paganism and "strangers to Israel" are in-
cluded, even these, in the universal reconciliation by the mediation of Christ (vv. 21-22). The same themes are treated in each of
them: the alienated situation of the pagans (v. 21; cf. Ep 2:11, 12,
19), reconciliation (v. 22; cf. Ep 2:16), foundation (v. 23; cf. Ep
2:20), holiness (v. 22; Ep 2:21), etc.

a) Some nuances differentiate the two passages, the most important of which is concerned with the way of envisaging *recon-*

ciliation. In the letter to the Ephesians Paul declares that Christ won reconciliation for men with God and reconciliation for Jews and pagans among them. The letter to the Colossians leaves the latter in the background in order to stress that God reconciles men to himself in the death of Christ before he is even conscious of it. They have only to accept this reconciliation with faith (v. 23) and by baptism which "presents you to God holy" (v. 22).

b) This notion of a God who reconciles men even before they grasp the divine action gives to the image of *foundation* (v. 23) a nuance which is not so apparent in Ep 2:17-22. It is no longer a question of the messianic foundation foreseen by Isaiah 28:16-17 or of the institutional or apostolic foundation of Ephesians 2:17-22. The theme conjures up especially just now the priority of the divine initiative in reconciliation: God has already done all, and this priority assures the Church and each Christian invulnerability as long as he respects the faith, the necessary stability. It is on this foundation that Christian hope rests. If God has taken the initiative in reconciling men, he will also take it in crowning his work at the desired time.

XVII. 1 Corin- The conclusion to the apology of the Christian
thians apostle begins here. The Church at Corinth
4:6-15 was unsettled by the presence of apostles who
1st reading mingled along with the message of the Good
2nd cycle News some very human considerations. Paul
Saturday has already explained how the true apostle
distinguished himself by his service. He expresses now a new criterion for discerning the true apostle.

a) In the eyes of Paul, it is in suffering and persecution that an apostle can truly lay claim to the title of minister of Christ (2 Co 6:4-10; 11:23-33; 2 Tm 3:10-11). Paul even pushes this exigency as far as a *paradox:* when the world awaits wise men, the apostle will be a fool (v. 10, cf. 1 Co 1:18-25; 2 Co 12:11); when they await the strong and the powerful, the apostle appears in the most extreme weakness (v. 10; cf. 1 Co 2:1-5; 2 Co 11:30).

Thus the life of the apostle is revealed within the paradox: he brings the blessing of the gospel at the cost of curses of which he is the object; he announces consolation and undergoes calumny; he initiates into true wisdom and is treated as a fool.

b) The second criterion of the true apostle is his fidelity to the *Scriptures* (v. 6). Paul preaches Christ "in accordance with the Scriptures" (1 Co 15:3-4), and the passages to which he refers (Jb 5:13 in 1 Co 3:19; Ps 93/94:11 in 1 Co 3:20 and Is 29:14 in 1 Co 1:19) recall that the wisdom which did not take account of God's plan revealed through the Scripture is sworn to failure.

c) The apostle comes to a conclusion by alluding to his *spiritual fatherhood* (v. 15). The Old Testament often used this image to express the relations between masters of wisdom and their disciples (Gn 45:8; 2 K 2:12; 6:21; Pr 1:8; 2:1; 3:1; Mt 23:9; etc.). There is no doubt that this image is especially developed in a context where the concern is to show the power of the Word of God, its efficacy, its vitality (1 P 1:22-25; Jm 1:17-27; 1 Jn 3:9). In Judaism the metaphor is used not only to designate the rabbi-disciple relation but also the "converter-convert" relationship.

Paul willingly gives the name children to the members of the churches he founded (1 Co 4:14; 2 Co 6:13; Ga 4:19; 1 Th 2:7-11) and he does the same for all those to whom he has brought the faith (1 Co 4:17; 1 Tm 1:2; Tt 1:4). Childbirth happens "through the gospel," that is to say, it consists in introducing Christians into a new life characterized by union in Christ, life in the Spirit, the glory of the Father (cf. 2 Th 2:14; Ep 3:6; 1 Co 15:1-2).

But the apostle reserves the title father to the first who sowed (1 Co 3:5-10; 4:14-15). Every man can have several teachers, he never has but one father. So Paul sees the apostolic charism proper with that which is intransmissible; the charism of fatherhood because it is the bearer of the Word of God which produces children of God.

XVIII. Luke   All the synoptics relate this account which is
6:1-5   followed by the episode of the healing of the
Gospel   man with the withered hand (Lk 6:6-11). In
Saturday   both of them, there is a violation of the Sab-
             bath by the disciples of Jesus, and by Jesus
himself, and the reaction which it drew from the legitimate authorities. But Luke who deals with a public less smitten by legalism, summarizes the episode. He does not take up again all the arguments of Jesus (e.g., Mt 12:5-7) and he is not as solicitous as the other evangelists are to extract conclusions of the ethical order (as does Mark 2:27).

In reality the disciples have not violated the Mosaic law by picking grains of wheat on the Sabbath for no text of the Penta-teuch condemns this practice. It is solely a violation of one of the thirty-nine activities forbidden on the Sabbath by the Mischna (Sabbath 7:2).

In other respects there is so much less transgression of the law of Moses because there is a scriptural precedent (v. 3-4; cf. 1 S 21:2-7).

By calling himself "master of the Sabbath," Jesus claims to possess the right to question the preciseness of the commentators on the law when they violate the original intention of the legis-lator.

When man wishes to achieve his salvation by himself, he sacralizes the means which in his eyes can lead there and he suppresses those which threaten his security.

Jesus Christ accepted the gift of the Father and responded to it with an unconditional yes. His salvation did not then depend on external means but on the encounter between his faith and the initiative of God.

In his turn, any man able to perceive the gift of God and anxious to respond to it with total fidelity participates in this mastery over the Sabbath which then loses its absolute value to become only the time of the free and faithful encounter between the believer and his Father.

TWENTY-THIRD WEEK

1. Colossians
1:24-2:3
1st reading
1st cycle
Monday

About 65 A.D. Paul was in prison, probably at Rome. When he learned that strange doctrines were circulating at Colossae and Ephesus, he immediately sent letters, two of his most important, to these communities. As was his custom, the apostle adds an ardent personal appeal to his epistolary teaching.

a) The apostle considers his sufferings in the same way as his preaching, a valuable instrument for bringing growth to the Church, especially the community at Colossae (v. 24). The suffering of the minister "completes" in fact what is lacking to the sufferings of Christ which in no way means that the work of Christ is incomplete (cf. Col. 1:12-14, 19-22). To say that redemption awaits completion, would amount to denying its efficacy and to leading believers to that religion of works which was precisely what Judaism wanted to propagate at Colossae (Co 2:14-23).

In fact, Paul sees in the sufferings of Christ and in his own, the trial foreseen by the Jews as a preliminary element for the coming of the last days. For the apostle thinks these will be characterized by the conversion of the pagans (vv. 27-28; cf. Rm 11:25-26); his sufferings then hasten the latter and at the same time the arrival of the Kingdom. In this sense his sufferings complete those of Christ by bringing them closer to their ultimate goal: the establishment of the reign of the Lord. Likewise he does not hesitate to call himself not only a minister (1 Co 3:5) or a minister of God (2 Co 6:4; 11:23) but a minister of the Church, the growth of which he is effectively hastening.

b) Paul did not usurp this rank of minister of the Church. On the contrary it belongs to the economy of God who willed that his plan (the "mystery" of salvation for the Gentiles: v. 26; cf.

Ep 3:1-13) be revealed to the world by the ministry of the Word (v. 25) and by the "announcement of Christ" (v. 28).

To proclaim Christ is to "inform" and "to instruct" all men. The ministry of the Word begins then by the proclamation of the redemptive event and is continued by the teaching which cautions against heresy by revealing the way of God that leads man to adulthood (v. 28; cf. 1 Co 2:6; 3:1; 14:20).

c) In this brief personal apology Paul insists on his title as *apostle of the nations.* This charism authorizes him to take care of the communities he did not himself found, such as Colossae and Laodicea (v. 1). His apostleship rests then on an unlimited call from God (Co 1:25) and every community coming out of paganism is strengthened in some way by this solicitude.

Once he justifies his apostolic mandate and his responsibility, Paul could oppose underground movements and false apostles who wish to draw Colossae to syncretism (v. 4).

The apostle is the only minister of Christ to reveal "the knowledge of the mystery of God" (v. 2), to understand the admission of Gentiles to salvation, the keys to which belong only to Christ. The Colossians cannot then claim these for occasional preachers: only the minister of Christ can claim them.

II. 1 Corinthians Paul finds himself faced with a public case of
5:1-8   incest. A Christian from the community at
1st reading   Corinth is living with his father's wife, his
2nd cycle   stepmother (v. 1). From afar and without even
Monday   waiting to study the case more closely, the
                  apostle demands excommunication for the in-
dividual (v. 4), before the approaching feast of Easter (vv. 7-8).

a) The Jewish law punished *incest* (Lv 18:29). However, this unnatural act was not as severely sanctioned in the Greek culture and one could understand that the Christian envisaged by

St. Paul did not consider his union with his stepmother a positive fault contrary to the law.

b) But Paul is too imbued with the law of Moses to tolerate such scandal and he pronounces sanction without hesitation: the offender will be gotten "rid of" (v. 2; cf. Lv 18:29; Dt 13:6); he will be *excommunicated*.

The apostle however can no longer decree the penalty of death as the elders of Israel did. The Church is not a definitive reality already complete; it is only making its way towards the judgment of God; it does not then possess the right over life and death. Hence, there is no question of condemning the offender to death, either physical or spiritual, but of excluding him from a community which wants to be the sign of life (for "outsiders"; vv. 12-13). He will then face the judgment of God as well as that of every man, and nothing allows one to say that he will not be saved (v. 5). Furthermore he will know material affliction (the meaning of the expression "hand him over to Satan") since he will be deprived of the support of his brethren. This affliction will aid him perhaps in gaining salvation.

Excommunication then is not a measure which anticipates the judgment of God. This latter remains reserved and Paul refrains from implying otherwise. It involves only an opportunity for the community to give a witness to the divine life in man and to reject the obvious countersigns. The apostle affirms that the excommunicated remains on the road to salvation (v. 5) but that they are unable to be signs of it and saviors of the world.

Excommunication regulates the status and the appearance of the community, but it does not encroach on the final lot of the offender or on the attitude of God towards him. The demand for charity from the Christian towards this man remains intact.

c) St. Paul compares this practice of excommunication of a member of the community to the Jewish practice of throwing out the old *leaven* on the vigil of the Easter feast (Ex 12:15). His argument is based then on a prescription for the paschal ritual which demanded that one eat the lamb using bread without leaven, after having thrown out the leavened bread of the previous year. For the paschal lamb is now spiritual and is named Jesus Christ (Jn 13:1; 18:28; 19:14; 31:42). Since then the eating of the paschal lamb was done in purity and truth (v. 8) and the rejection of the old leaven becomes the struggle against perversity and malice. Thus Christians become the "unleavened loaves" (v. 7) and Paul can present a desacralized idea of the feast of Easter in which Christ and Christians are together food for the meal and signs of the mystery of Easter offered for the manducation of men. All that is demanded from Christians is that they be as conformed as possible to the lamb by being as much as possible spiritual "unleavened loaves."

III. Luke 6:6-11 Luke and Mark report this episode about the
  Gospel   healing of the withered hand on the Sabbath.
  Monday   Each of them places it in the context of the
            polemics created by the young rabbi Jesus
over the sclerotic institutions of religion: rules about cleanliness at meals (Lk 5:29-32), fasting (Lk 5:33-38) and Sabbath rest (Lk 6:1-11). But Luke does not attach great interest to these discussions that are hardly comprehensible to readers of Gentile origin. He is satisfied with relating the facts without matching them with personal reflections or doctrinal conclusions. Thus he does not retain the remarks of Mark 3:5 on the callousness of the Pharisees and he suppresses every allusion to the anger of Jesus (Mk 3:5).

a) Luke recalls nevertheless the *understanding* that Jesus possesses of the human heart (v. 8; cf. Jn 1:48; 2:24-25; 4:17-19; 6:61-71, etc.). Thus Christ not only has an understanding more profound than other rabbis of the law which he teaches, but he knows men better. There is the secret of the authority with which he teaches and which places him over all others (cf. Lk 4:32).

b) At the time of the Lord, the practice of medicine and corporal works were strictly curtailed on the *Sabbath* day. Far better for the sick man to suffer than the Honor of God! Knowing that the glory of God is above all served by goodness towards the unfortunate (v. 9), Jesus does not hesitate to practice it in order to honor the Sabbath. But to liberate some unfortunate person from the chains of evil, is this not a more profound way of sanctifying this anniversary day of the liberation from Egypt than to keep him in bondage for the supposed honor of God?

The Sabbath was observed because it was ordered by the law of God and constituted a characteristic by which the Jews were distinguished from the surrounding Gentile world. Therefore there was great scandal when the young rabbi Jesus dared to question not the law but the way of obeying it; he was suspected of preferring man to the glory of God! In general Judaism placed all the decrees of the Old Testament on the same plane, since they were equally the commands of God, but it granted a certain preference to the cultural decrees in which man is obliterated still more before the honor of God. So it was with the Sabbath and circumcision.

Jesus acknowledged that the law represents the will of God, but he denies it any purely formal and external authority. Man must interpret the Scripture in order to recognize the commandment of God there. On the other hand there is no true obedience except where man recognizes that the mandate relates to him. It is moreover because of this that he can accomplish deeds in communion with God even where there is no precise commandment. This is the meaning, it seems, of the question Jesus asks in v. 9: in each case it is that of true obedience. Christ scorns the Pharisees who believe themselves perfect because they are faithful to the law, but who basically are unfaithful because they have smothered every notion of brotherhood and fellowship.

There exists therefore an obedience more radical than submission to the law: that which fulfills the deepest me where God is present, beyond the anxieties which casuistry create, beyond the fear of having failed in one's duty, beyond the scorn of those who judge the other on externals without knowing his heart.

IV. Colossians 2:6-15 *1st reading* *1st cycle* *Tuesday*	Paul gets to the heart of the matter. In their search for God the Colossians do not accept the mediation of Christ because they have turned to "philosophy" and give in to the temptation of syncretism.

a) Paul distinguishes the primordial and exclusive mediation of Christ from all others. He recalls in four complimentary images the *primacy* of Christ in the life of the Christian: Christ, the root of the tree, humanity (v. 7); the foundation of the temple formed by Christians and in the course of being built (v. 7); the dwelling place of the fullness of the divinity (v. 9) in the sense that in him is found all that which the Colossians can seek and desire; and head of the angels (v. 10) because he has "despoiled" them of their domination over men and over creation (v. 15). This last image is an allusion to the mythical beliefs of the period according to which the angels were masters of the universe and mediators of the law (v. 14). Paul thus rejects the pretensions of Judaizers who still wanted to hold fast to the law proposed by the angels, and he objects to the gnosis which invented a series of intermediary beings between God and man.

b) The Christian shares in the primacy of the Lord over the world by *baptism* (vv. 11-13) which binds him to the death and the resurrection of Christ, that is to say, at that precise moment when Jesus obtained his primacy. He profits then from numerous benefits that render circumcision unnecessary. What would it add in fact to those who are circumcised in their entire body (that is to say, who profit from a fullness of conversion) and for whom sins are radically pardoned (v. 13)? Baptism then exempts the Christian from having recourse to other ritual practices whatever they may be.

The "primacy" of the Christian over the world is not superiority over others but service by way of understanding things and persons.

The starting point for our reflection is humanity. Its progressive control over itself and over nature has meaning (for example: the spiritualization of matter). It draws upon a series of roles (political, technical etc.) in order to be effective and to destroy the obstacles which stand in the way of this design.

But faith consists in believing that God gives a still more decisive meaning to this mastery of man over himself and over all things: that of the assembling of everything and everyone in the divine life itself. It believes that a new function is practiced in humanity to attain this meaning: that which the Man-God exercised among men. In him the primacy of man over all things receives a new and unheard of meaning and all the obstacles raised against it, evil, sin, death and the angels, collapse before the role of Jesus Christ.

This role of Christ, *bestowing* meaning on the human undertaking is symbolically and efficaciously found anew in the mass of the baptised. To the degree in which they collaborate in the progressive liberation of humanity from all alienation (the forces of nature, the sacred, sin, the power of money etc.) and to the degree in which they work at the spiritualization of nature and its humanization, Christians can proclaim its profound and new significance and make it perceptible: the building of a humanity that is the daughter of God.

V. 1 Corinthians
6:1-11
1st reading
2nd cycle
Tuesday

Paul is offended because the Christians of Corinth continue to settle their legal disputes before pagan tribunals and he tries to convince them to renounce this estrangement. The three arguments he uses seem to come from a Christian "tradition."

a) The vocation of Christians is to *judge* the world and the angels themselves. How then can they have recourse to the justice of this world (vv. 1-6)?

Clearly there is involved here an idea inherited from Judaism (Ac 9:2; 18:12-18; 2 Co 11:24) and adopted by the Judaeo-Christian communities where the imperial government would tolerate it. For the Jews as for Paul, the pagan judges can only be "unjust" since they judge in the name of a human justice and not as representatives of the justice of God (v. 1).

Undoubtedly the justice granted in the pagan tribunals had close affinity (at least because of the oaths) with idolatry, involvement in which was forbidden to the faithful of the one God. But Paul is not thinking simply of this involvement with the idolatrous sacred, for he places himself there and then on an eschatological plane, already seeing in the Church the Kingdom that is coming. For the members of the Kingdom will judge the world (Ws 3:8; Dn 7:22; and for the Twelve: Mt 19:28; Rv 20:4) and even the angels (v. 3). This idea goes beyond all that Judaism, for whom God alone would judge the angels, hoped for (Is 24:21; 2 P 2:4; Jg 6). How could the future judges of the world allow themselves to be judged by men and their tutelary angels?

In conclusion Paul wants the "wisest" from within the community (this was in fact a role that Judaism reserved for them) to be set up as a tribunal for judging the litigations of the brethren (vv. 5-6).

b) The second argument is more striking (vv. 7-8). Why would difficulties arise between Christians? Are not mutual *pardon* and patience sufficient to regulate these problems? (cf. Mt 5:38-42; Col 3:13; 1 P 2:19; Rm 12:17-21)?

c) Finally Paul recalls that the Christian can no longer be unjust (to be understood in the moral sense this time), a drunkard or depraved (vv. 9-11). Rather, *justice* must prevail among Christians who ought to avoid resorting to lawsuits. These are only evidence that conversion has not yet done its work. The expression "do not deceive yourselves" (v. 9) is common in a diatribe where the positions easily hardened and oppositions established themselves without nuance.

Paul ventured the use of a diatribe style because he was convinced that the Church already constituted the Kingdom and that the judgment of God is for tomorrow. Since then, however, the Church has become more conscious of the distance that separates it from the Kingdom; it has gradually emancipated itself from the ideas of Judaism, and involvement with the world through secular jurisdiction has deprived it of the final illusion which it was still able to foster by considering itself the Kingdom.

How then understand this passage and especially Paul's first argument? First of all it is necessary to guard against concluding that the Kingdom of God is the work of God, whereas the secular city is the work of man. Such a lesson cannot be drawn from one text of the New Testament where the essential message consists precisely in revealing that neither God nor man act alone. The coming of Christ has put an end to the distances; Christ belongs to God and to men, and the Christian, in his turn, is at the crossroads of two worlds. To believe in the Kingdom of God, without collaborating in the building of the secular and thus of its tribunals, would involve an aberration.

Let us not go on believing any longer that the Kingdom is only for promoting the values of repentance and conversion (vv. 8-10) and that the secular city has no other motivation but enjoyment and the search for success. In fact the building of the city entails a conversion which often goes further than simply changing one's moral attitude.

Finally it would be wrong to believe that the Kingdom is reserved for the future, for the moment of judgment (v. 2). It is already at work in the involvement of the Christian in a world where he is continually finding fulfillment through success and failure, progress and regression.

VI. Luke 6:12-19   In drawing up the list of the "Twelve" the
Gospel   synoptics have undoubtedly made use of a
Tuesday   range of information among which was a complete list of the apostles and in particular some accounts about the vocation of five of them (Lk 5:1-11,27). But since they did not possess details about the vocation of the seven others, they inserted the list of the Twelve in a sort of ceremonial of general investiture.

a) Luke presents the ceremony of investiture in terms of a whole night of *prayer* (v. 12) which is a way of indicating the solemnity of the moment. It also makes clear that Jesus was not a simple rabbi who recruits disciples (which he could well be in Luke 5:1-11), but someone who is conscious of playing a role in the world in the name of God and who knows for sure that he will be unable to fulfill it except in union with his Father.

b) This consciousness of his role explains and justifies the choice of the *Twelve*. In an ancient tradition which Luke does not use, Jesus promised them that they would sit at his sides at the judgment (Dn 7:22) which will establish the definitive people (Mt 19:27-28). Just before Pentecost the Eleven were still preoccupied with completing the number Twelve, as if they feared the imminence of the judgment (Ac 1:16-26). Later events and the frustration of that hope will convince them only of their missionary vocation.

At the moment when Christ institutes (the term has a juridical and official sound) the Twelve, he still envisages his own mission in the context of the prerogatives granted by the Ancient of Days to the Son of Man (Dn 7:22). The number Twelve had for them a symbolic value: they are the living stones (cf. the stones of Gilgal: Jos 4:1-6) of the new sanctuary, the patriarchs of the new people and the judges to whom the discernment of the citizen of the future Kingdom will be confided.

Scripture is fond of the number twelve because it recalls for the Jews the initiative of God in their election. The Hebrews were originally scattered in tribes that were distinct from each other and the organization of worship centers in the amphictyony was necessary because they were used to living as twelve in the service of God. This living together of the tribes, up until then independent, took time to form (Jg 5:2-11) and it became a reality only through faith in the promise made by Yahweh to the twelve patriarchs (Jos 24; Gn 49; etc.). It was not the people who had chosen God, but God who first associated himself with Israel. Twelve therefore calls to mind the national conscience of the people, founded on the transcendent liberty of God.

By choosing this symbolic number of companions to share in the founding of the new people, Christ seems to insure the transcendence of God's initiative. To believe in the apostolic Church comes to granting absolute priority to the election or reconciliation with God (cf. 2 Co 5:14-21).

c) Luke alone mentions the title *apostle* which Jesus gives to the Twelve (v. 13). This title seems to have been given them by the original community when they came to realize that they could spread the foundations of the new people only in becoming missionaries of the gospel throughout the world. By ascribing to Jesus this mandate and this title, Luke gives proof of apostolic concern, for he demonstrates the unity of the message of those who are at once the witnesses to the public life of Jesus and the missionaries of his resurrection.

The various accounts of the apostolic vocation are presented in the gospels as three successive stages in the progress and venture of the vocation. The first account (e.g. Mk 1:16-20 or Jn 1:35-51) reveals a teacher of doctrine, a rabbi who recruits disciples ("come follow me"), engages in deep personal relationships with them and depends on the bonds of brotherhood, friendship and neighborliness to form his group of disciples. Jesus is still only a teacher and they follow him because he speaks with authority.

A second layer of accounts, among which is the gospel for today, places the vocation on another level. Jesus became conscious that he was the Son of Man, charged with reestablishing the chosen people and its twelve tribes. He chose and "established" with authority the twelve persons who will help him in this still very "nationalistic" task.

The third stage is realized only after the death and resurrection, when Jesus appears as Savior of the world and of humanity and only the twelve, under pressures like St. Paul, will discover for themselves a mission and powers of an apostolic and universal nature.

Thus every vocation develops gradually with the discovery of Jesus and his mystery. The initial motivations are not often the most decisive: it is only after long experience that they finally discover that the death and lordship of Jesus constitutes the only valuable motive for a call to the ministry.

VII. Colossians This passage is both a conclusion and a pre-
3:1-11 amble. It concludes the account which Paul
1st reading had just made about Christian liberty over
1st cycle against the alienating practices of paganism
Wednesday and heresy (Co 2:16-3:4) by showing that the
Christian who is dead with Christ is beyond the reach of human methods of salvation (v. 3). It serves as an introduction to the parenthetical portion of the letter by pointing out how life with Christ (vv. 1-4) demands a new behavior for the Christian in the world.

a) If the life of the Christian comes from below, that is to say from the world, it is automatically fettered by a thousand and one regulations of "religion." If it comes from on high, that is to say from the world where Christ lives at present, it is "given" to the Christian who no longer needs to be preoccupied with keeping it alive by earthly methods of salvation since it does not cease to be given from above, as by resurrection.

No compromise is possible: to acknowledge that life is a gift from God comes down to breaking with a world that wants to procure for itself its own life, by the subterfuge of frail and sinful means.

For this rupture with the earthly life is already accomplished for the Christian, since by his *baptism,* he is dead to the world like Christ.

b) Baptism is above all a *death* to sin. The passage from death to resurrection which established Christ the lord of the universe takes place at the moment of baptism (Col 2:12-13, 3:1-4), but is to be realized gradually in the course of the "earthly" life (v. 5).

This mortification does not involve the members of the body as such (the author rejects a purely ascetical piety, Col 2:23), but it does concern "that which is of the earth." It seems then that we must translate verse 5 as follows: "Mortify, your members (of Christ), that come from the earth." In fact, Paul just spoke at length about the death and resurrection of the Head of the Mystical Body (Col 1:8; 24; 2:10, 17, 19): he presently asks the members of this body to die also to the powers of the world incarnate in sin, especially in the most serious faults such as immorality and cupidity which constitutes the principal matter for the judgment of God (vv. 5-6; cf. Ep. 5:3-6).

Because of baptism the Colossians have put aside their old conduct (vv. 9-10): consequently they must now live by putting aside also their faults against charity (vv. 8-9).

c) By imposing such a "privation," baptism permits the believer to understand the sudden transformation in his existence. To the old man which he was in sin, succeeds a new man (v. 10; cf. 1 Co 1:30; 6:11) who actually rediscovers the power to be truly the image of God, thanks to the recreation achieved by Christ (Ep 2:15) and to the deepening knowledge of God which opens him to the indwelling of the Spirit.

This state of the new man is not however acquired once for all; the words "regenerate," "to form anew" and "to grow" remind the Christian that he must now continually place his reactions to Christ and to his brothers in a new light, by abandoning every-thing that is divisive and by rejecting racial, religious, cultural or social opposition.

Man seeks the absolute. The experience of life causes him to feel this basic aspiration: only an absolute can supply him with the confidence and assurance he needs. And the religious history of humanity teaches us that, throughout his history, man has devised techniques and methods to stabilize his life in an absolute manner: for the pagan this is the "elements of the world," for the Jew it is the law.

But the Christian is not only in search of the absolute; he believes in the presence of a person in his life: the Spirit of Christ. For that reason his existence no longer depends on just any absolute, for which he might be able to establish a medium of access; it depends on a person who gives him life at every moment.

The authentic experience of faith is an invitation to discover that we no longer live by ourselves, but that Christ is our life. To say yes to Christ is to live with a life which is indeed ours but which is lived at every moment as received from a person. It is this, to live as resurrected: to have the experience that the life which is in us, comes to us endlessly "from above." For us to want to be basically autonomous would be to root ourselves in things "below," it would be to accept death.

VIII. 1 Corin-   This entire chapter is devoted to the states of
    thians   Christian life. Paul speaks in turn about the
    7:25-31   situation of spouses who live together (1 Co
    1st reading   7:3-5, 10) and asks what continence represents
    2nd cycle   for them; spouses who live apart (v. 11), those
    Wednesday who live together but are divided by their
                   beliefs (v. 12-16). Then he speaks of celibate
Christians and, among these, of "virgins," young men and young girls not yet engaged (v. 25-35); then of fiances who dream of

their approaching common life (vv. 36-38) and finally of widows (vv. 39-40).

But in this simple and logical design Paul himself introduces disorder. Thus he speaks of continence (and of his very own) in the midst of his discourse to married people (vv. 6-7) and of marriage in the heart with discourses to people still available (vv. 27a, 28, 29b, 33). This confusion in the account undoubtedly reflects the tension which reigns in the community at Corinth, where they are both for continence (1 Co 7:1-5) and the most shameless sexual liberty (cf. 1 Co 5:1-13; 6:12-20).

Paul simultaneously maintains the indisolubility of marriage and the charism of continence and he shows how each derives from the Lord.

At times Paul gives the impression of scorning marriage; in reality he is only presenting the right of a citizen in the light of this new state, that of the celibate, in view of a state already known and considered up to now the only possibility: marriage.

The counsel in favor of continence which he lavishes on non-married persons (the "virgins" of v. 25 applies to boys as well as girls) rests on a basic motive: the "present time of distress" (v. 26) or the "trials in this life" (v. 28). The point here is not simply the turmoil of the present life, especially conjugal life: the word "*thlepsis*" is essentially eschatological and it must be understood in the context of the times. It does not have the same meaning as before Jesus Christ, where, from generation to generation, it moved towards its end. Today this end is practically attained since God is present in all and marriage is no longer a state as absolute as before for the spouses are shared, owned both by God who is present in them and by each other. Because God is now present with his eternity, time is becoming shorter and an institution like marriage, strongly based on the temporal is made relative by the appearance of the last days whereas the spouses are more "shared" than before Jesus Christ (vv. 33-34). No longer does marriage symbolize by itself the reign of God, for continence also has this "charism" (v. 27) and by that fact conjugal life becomes relative.

Since Jesus Christ each man lives with the presence of God in him and the Christian commits his entire life to it. But he can do so only in union with reality and other men. The marriage state, if it loses its exclusive role of perpetuating the human race from generation to generation, remains the place *par excellence* where the presence of God lives through interpersonal relations. But this presence is implicit; it will only be explicit in the Kingdom where God will be all in all. One can not always live implicitly! That is why married people must at times be alone before God; that is why the Church has a place for "widows" for whom the charism consists precisely in trying to live more explicitly. This relation between the implicit and the explicit is fundamental; the Christian lives the presence of Christ in an implicit way in his life in the world and he offers there the spiritual sacrifice foreseen by Romans 12:1-2. But this worship in the world must be based on the explicit worship rendered by Christ and this reference of the implicit to the explicit takes place in eucharistic worship. The life of the Church is thus divided between profane worship and eucharistic worship, between implicit and explicit worship, between marriage and celibacy: neither function is any longer exclusive, but complementary, the second seeking to live in the explicit what the first lives in the implicit. The two states are then as necessary, one to the other, as life is to rite and rite is to life.

IX. Luke 6:20-26   The beatitudes have very likely been con-
Gospel   ceived by Christ as short maxims of prophetic
Wednesday   quality announcing the arrival of the Kingdom
foreseen by Isaiah who made the poor, the afflicted and the starved the beneficiaries of the salvation granted by God (Is 58:6-10; 61:1-3; 49:8-13, etc.). They signified that the times had arrived when the privileges of the Kingdom would be

named, not in the light of merits and particular conditions, but simply because God decided to save them.

a) In the redaction of Luke, the prophetic quality is toned down: one no longer perceives as such the original eschatological significance onto which the evangelist has superimposed a sapiential teaching promising to the poor compensation in the hereafter. He interprets the original beatitudes in the light of the teachings of Christ on poverty and the use of riches, in order to make a defense of it for the social class in which he is recruiting his first converts (Ac 4:34-5:11).

The preoccupations of Matthew are of another order. Solicitous for a moral deepening of the gospel, he interprets the beatitudes in terms of the *new justice* and the spirit of the Sermon on the Mount. That is why he suppresses the present-future antithesis introduced by Luke. In fact the Kingdom is already there for the one who knows how to seize it by a life consistent with its justice. The two evangelists have thus blurred the prophetic character (God comes to save) of the words of Christ in favor of moral (Mt) or socio-eschatological (Luke) values.

b) Since then the *poor* who, in the first redaction, were the beneficiaries of the salvation of God (Is 61:1-3), become under Luke's pen the actual poor. In the same way, the persecuted, victims of circumstances in which the Jews saw the omen of new times, appeared to him as the privileged ones of the future Kingdom. Matthew himself demands that the persecuted be so for justice sake and not simply because they were chosen in a random roundup. He also introduces a correction of the same type to the beatitude about the hungry. Isaiah saw in them the privileges of the future Kingdom (Is 49:6-13); Luke still considers them as those actually hungry for bread (see also the parable about the rich man and Lazarus). In Matthew they become those hungry for justice.

c) The antithesis *blessing-curse* preserved in Luke's version is shocking. It reinstates a literary form frequently found in the Old

Testament (cf. e.g. Jr 17:3-10, then Dt 11:26-32; 27-28; 30:15-20, etc.).

The beatitudes are not promises to the poor because they are poor and the maledictions do not concern the rich because they are rich. In fact, Jesus praises first those who live in two worlds at the same time: the present and the eschatological and he threatens those who live only in one world, the comfortable life that inevitably enslaves.

Satisfied with his possessions the rich man does not search the depth of his being because nothing calls him to that. But let a reversal in fortune occur, as we know can happen, and the rich are carried away with the world, at times externally expressing their fear and despair, their hate and their rancor.

The poor man possesses only his solitude. But he accepts it with that courage that leads him to the depth of his being where he perceives another world. Solitary in this life, he is rich because he participates in that life in which he now shares victories and union. He is the revealer of that beyond which is achieved with difficulty, through fortune and misfortune, success and failure, victory and betrayals.

**X. Colossians
3:12-17**
1st reading
1st cycle
Thursday

In contrast to false idols who capture the attention of men, there is now the person of the Lord, for his victory over death makes him the only one capable of bearing humanity to its fulfillment and the world to its success.

This primacy of Christ, the basic theme of this letter to the Colossians, has repercussions on the moral plane: thus, opposed to the effort and asceticism acceptable in the worship of idols or in the search for material wealth (Col 2:16-23), is, with an absolute priority, the asceticism which liberates by the knowledge of the lordship of Christ over the world (Col 3:1-4).

a) Christians are called to live in such a way that they are a sign of the lordship of Christ over humanity. St. Paul moreover calls them saints or the chosen (vv. 12-15). But the idea of *holiness* also contains that of separation. In the Old Testament, God was the Saint because he had nothing in common with men and the people of Israel was holy in its turn to the extent that it was different from other nations (Is 4:3; Dt 7:6). In Jesus Christ the holiness of God is revealed as communication and his transcendence is manifested in his immanence. Consequently, the holiness of the Christian is not superiority or contempt, it is communication and sharing. St. Paul characterizes it in terms which the Old Testament reserved for God's behavior towards man: the "goodness" and the "kindness" proper to the Father (Pss 24/25: 6-7; 39/40:11; 50/51:1; 68/69:17; 20/21:3; 30/31:20; 64/65:12; 118/119:65-68; etc.) the "pardon" and the "peace" proper to Christ (v. 15.)

b) The lordship of Christ is also manifest in the elements of *liturgical celebrations* (vv. 16-17): the proclamation and the exposition of the Word of God, the singing of psalms and hymns, the act of thanksgiving (vv. 15b and 17). But liturgy cannot be divorced from life and so Paul is concerned with the implication of the Word, songs and act of thanksgiving in the hearts and attitudes of daily life as well as for its implications for the liturgy itself.

"Put on sentiments of kindness . . . ," "Pardon as God pardons. . . ." These counsels would seem to indicate that the virtues of kindness and pardon are typically divine and therefore a theological and supernatural motive is needed in order to pardon and love one's brother. This amounts to saying that we can love a poor man only because God loves him, that we can encounter an atheist only with the patience of God himeslf, as if the Christian was unable to love the poor man and the atheist on his own.

Such an idea would disqualify the pardon and love wasted by those who do not seek in Jesus Christ the motivation for their brotherhood.

In fact the originality of Paul consists in showing Christians that there is a means of pardoning and loving in the name of God whereas, up to now (and even now) man imagined that violence, punishment and power were the only means of revealing an avenging and all powerful God.

Revelation did not invent new virtues: kindness and pardon, power and violence are innate to human nature; but it has revealed that God is present in the exercise of kindness and pardon by a presence which brings these attitudes to perfection. It has given man the power to go to the very depth of love. It has shown that these attitudes are the signs by which God saves the world.

Still, God can be understood only where gratuitousness and goodness are manifest. For the goodness of God is not a metaphysical value seizable in "itself"; it is accessible to man only through faith and through the actual practice of gratuitousness.

XI. 1 Corinthians
8:1b-7, 11-13
1st reading
2nd cycle
Thursday

In the Greek world, meat was immolated in the temples; a part was burned in sacrifice, another part was used to feed the sacred ministers and the final portion was given to the butchershop to be sold. Judaism strictly forbade its members to eat such meat and the meeting which followed the Council of Jerusalem and which dealt with the question of commensality between Christians who come from Judaism and those who come from the Gentiles, imposed the same attitude on the Christians of Jerusalem (Ac 15:20, 29; 21:25). But this last decree does not seem to have caused any real repercussions. At Corinth, in any case, it was ignored since the community was divided on the question (vv. 1-3; cf. Rm 14-15) and because Paul does not appeal to it in their situation. His discussion of it is particularly verbose for he arrives at his conclusion only in 1 Co 10:31-11:1.

a) In this particular case, the *weak* about whom Paul speaks (vv. 7-13) are undoubtedly the Judeao-Christians who fear staining themselves by contact with meat offered to idols and who react like James at the Jerusalem assembly. This behavior by

Christians of Jewish origin involves two tendencies: that of the strong who do not make allowances for anyone and defend their liberty at every cost (vv. 4-6) and that of Paul who expressly tries to join charity and liberty (vv. 1-3) by preferring abstinence from this meat rather than scandalize one who is weak (v. 11).

Neither good nor bad on the religious plane (v. 8) this inclination of the strong nevertheless scandalizes the weak (vv. 11-12).

Neither good nor bad, the tendency of the weak is simply fragile in this sense that if their conscience is sound, it is insufficiently enlightened by faith; but the ostentatious example of the strong will hardly help them in complying with it.

b) The *conscience* referred to in this passage is essentially religious: it is the attitude of the man who holds God as witness to his actions. It is weak because it involves an insufficient idea of God whom it believes to be desirous of formalism and mere observance.

The conscience of the strong, like that of the weak, is in general expressed in religious convictions which vary, either in favor of liberty or in favor of compliance. At no time is this puralism to be presupposed; on the contrary, the conscience of each, his profound religious conviction, must continue in a climate of great mutual charity.

XII. Luke
6:27-38
Gospel
Thursday

In this passage Luke takes up the basic issue of a parallel text in Matthew (Mt 5:43-48) where the "new justice" proclaimed by Jesus is characterized in six antitheses.

Luke does not make use of these antitheses. Thus it seems clear that the process is proper to Matthew who seems to present more primitive sayings than Luke does. Luke in fact replaces the diatribe against the publicans and pagans (Mt 5:46-47) with another against sinners (Lk 6:33-34), in order not to offend his readers. We find the Jewish theme of perfection in Matthew 5:48 considered as the accomplishment of all the perfections of the law and practiced moreover as carefully by God himself. The evangelist is content to go beyond this formal perfection by announcing the perfection of the gratuitous gift, equal to that which the Father in heaven sends to men (Mt 5:17, 20; 19:21). Luke goes further in disregarding the ideal of perfection God, of his perfection or of his mercy (Mt 5:48; Luke 6:36).

He utilizes a system of triads on a level with ideas (vv. 27-29) such as in these examples (vv. 32-34). In the conclusion he returns to the antithetic process ("on the contrary . . .": v. 35), but the antithesis bears less on the justice of Judaism and the justice of Christ than on an interested and gratuitous love.

For all that, the lesson is obviously the same both in Matthew and in Luke: love must transcend the natural communities in which it is expressed spontaneously or in the name of sociological and psychological laws and extend to the dimensions of all humanity, enemies and adversaries included. But this passage from limited love to a universal love can only be done in imitation of God, of his perfection or of his mercy (Mt 5:48; Luke 6:36).

There is not only question here of a quantitative enlarging of love. The modification is qualitative and is situated on the level of faith: the disciple of Christ loves all men because he seeks to be a sign of the love of God for the world.

XIII. 1 Timothy Today the liturgy begins the pastoral letters
1:1-2, 12-14 of St. Paul. Although addressed to his com-
1st reading panions Timothy and Titus, these letters go
1st cycle beyond the bounds of purely personal bonds
Friday and constitute a sort of ecclesiastical instruction in view of the problems of structure which
Christian communities experienced around the years 65–67. The danger came especially from syncretism and heretical gnosis. Paul presents a plan for solid refutation and reinforces the hierarchical powers so that the leaders of community can exercise their re-

sponsibility in this area. But the reading for today is concerned simply with the destination of the letter (vv. 1-2) as well as a short thanksgiving by Paul for the vocation he received.

a) Custom dictated that the introduction of private letters be very short. Paul departs from these conventions in order to give public value to his letters, even when they are directed to one person. Thus it is that he qualifies Timothy by a five word paraphrase, thus conferring on his introduction a solemnity uncommon until then in private correspondence. What is more, by retracing only the religious qualities of his correspondent, the apostle parts company with the practices of propriety which require formulas of salutation to conform with stereotypes.

He modifies also the very content of the salutation, speaking about peace and mercy where only a wish for "joy" in general was expected.

b) By giving thanks for his *vocation,* Paul underscores its origin in the mercy of God (v. 13). But he does not deny that Christ Jesus judged him "faithful" (v. 12) to be called to his service.

XIV. 1 Corin-
thians
9:16-19,
22-27
1st reading
2nd cycle
Friday

To the problems raised by the Corinthians, Paul offers tactful and flexible solutions. Thus, concerning marriage and continence (Co 7), the apostle affirms the superiority of the second but in such a way that married people will not feel uneasy (cf. e.g. 1 Co 7:28). It is permissible to eat meat offered to idols (1 Co 8) but abstinence from such is demanded if there is the risk of scandalizing those who considered them contaminated (cf. 1 Co 8:13). He adopts the same attitude concerning charisms (1 Co 14:39-40), though he sets up general principles (1 Co 14:1-5, etc.). He had already given proof in Romans 14:1-21 of that flexibility and of that opportunism created by the love of one and all.

This attitude, favorable to both the Jews and the Gentiles (vv. 20-21 are not included in this reading), brought much opposition. It was moreover to be feared that from then on they might be led to use the gospel in an opportunist and subjective manner. The apostle is also led to define the content of his vocation and mission.

a) From the very start Paul stresses that his vocation is a *charge*. He did not choose it, for he is at the service of a master who charges him with a task. He is in a controlled service (Jr 20:9) and can have no other attitude but fidelity to his command and disinterestedness where personal rights and benefits are concerned (vv. 16-18) and that irrespective of the philosophies and options to which he may feel personal allegiance.

The opportunism that he sometimes manifests cannot then be attributed to a search for personal notoriety or a defense of acquired rights. But then?

b) Paul explains himself in v. 19: The apostolic responsibility is a replica of the mission of the *Suffering Servant* (cf. Is 53:11: the theme of the servant and the multitude). Elsewhere the apostle frequently compared his ministry in Corinth to the mission of the Servant of God (2 Co 6:1-2 and Is 49:8; 2 Co 4:6 and Is 49:6-9; Rm 14:11 and Is 49:18; Rm 15:20-22 and Is 52:15). The flexibility which he shows is not then just an indication of personal discretion but is the very sign of his service for the Lord who charges him with serving all men by adapting himself to what is good in them so they can become toothing stones for the reign of God.

Because of his knowledge of God and of Christ, Paul places himself at a more profound level of reality than the casuist does. The solutions he offers seem at times opportunist, but only because the questions presented to him are very often superficial. The apostle possesses a knowledge of the main issue which permits him to see problems in a relative manner, but also to perceive in each of them what can lead to the essential issue.

Christ himself often acted in the same way by not satisfying people who wanted him to settle their debates (Lk 12:13). At first sight it would seem that Jesus is acting cunningly by disregarding embarrassing questions. But has he not revealed that his knowledge of God placed him at a level where human and religious problems lose their attractiveness and their absoluteness?

XV. Luke   The commentary for this gospel is supplied in
6:39-42   conjunction with that for Luke 6:43-49, on
Gospel   Saturday, p. 52.
Friday

XVI. 1 Timothy   Before charging Timothy with his responsibili-
1:15-17   ties (1 Tm 1:18-19) in face of the dangers
1st reading   which menace the Christian communities (1
1st cycle   Tm 1:3-7), Paul briefly recalls the message of
Saturday   salvation in Jesus Christ and he proposes himself as an example because he is one of the
first beneficiaries of this salvation.

a) Paul resorts once more to a *personal* apology (vv. 12-17). For whereas heretics develop clever intellectual theories about salvation, he prefers to announce that he, sinner that he is, has been saved by the goodness of God (v. 16). Thus he indicates that a minister of the gospel ought to have a personal experience of the grace which he proclaims, otherwise his message will be pure gnosis and theorizing.

The cry of Paul, accepting himself as the "greatest of sinners," expresses the memory of his life as a persecutor and the power of God which converted him.

b) To express his thought, Paul returns to a hymn already

classic in the first communities and from which we can reconstruct a portion:

> Christ Jesus has come into the world
>> to save sinners
> Christ shows the fullness of patience
>> as an example to those who believe in him
>> as the life eternal.

The themes of the hymn: the coming of Jesus into the world
(Jn 1:2; 6:14; 11:17), his saving mission (Jn 3:17; 12:47) and
eternal life (Jn 3:15-16; 6:40-47; 20:31) are all of Johannine
origin.

There is every reason to believe that a part of v. 16 is also an
excerpt from the main hymn which Paul considers a "word"
worthy of faith (v. 14).

By referring to this song Paul goes beyond his personal case to
the contemplation of the broad lines of the plan of *salvation*
willed by God: the patience and love of God and eternal life for
believers.

c) This contemplation inspires the apostle to formulate an act
of thanksgiving (v. 17) in which he attributes to God a series of
titles rather unusual in the New Testament. Some are probably borrowed from ancient Jewish liturgical formulas (King, for example,
which is found in daily prayer), but others convey a metaphysical
flavor rather striking in the Scriptures: "incorruptible," "invisible,"
"unique."

There is nothing philosophical there however. In fact the eternity of God (king of "ages") envisaged by St. Paul is not only that
which a philosophy can conceive of as without beginning or end,
but that which governs events and molds them into a history of
salvation. In the same way, when the apostle speaks of the "invisible" God, he does not intend to contradict the longing of Scripture
to "see God" (1 Co 13:12; 1 Jn 3:2) with a philosophical definition.
He simply wishes to affirm that God reveals himself where a hu-

man religion or a simple philosophy would not expect him. God does not appear in wisdom, but in folly; he is not visible in power but in poverty; he, the incorruptible one, manifests himself in flesh that is the prey of evil and of sin.

XVII. 1 Corin- Since the first letter to the Corinthians was
thians written in 55 or 57, this passage on the Eucha-
10:14-22a rist constitutes the oldest known Christian text,
1st reading even older than the synoptic accounts of the
2nd cycle institution.
Saturday A complete eucharistic doctrine already well
formed is presented here.

a) The first remark concerns eucharistic *realism*. Verse 16 makes a direct allusion to communion with the physical body of the Lord and verse 17 has the communion of Christians among themselves depend on their common union in the body of Christ. This realistic conception of the eucharistic body of Christ is in the continuation of 1 Corinthians 6:12-20 where Paul does not hesitate to compare the union realized in the Eucharist to the sexual union. Such a concrete encounter with Christ on the level of the Eucharist forbids the Christian all prostitution (1 Co 6:12-20), all contact with demons, all compromise with idolatrous worship (1 Co 10:14-21).

b) A second characteristic of the Eucharist is its *sacrificial* aspect (cf. 1 Co 11:26). It is in fact concerned with forbidding Christians any participation at meals where meat immolated to idols is eaten. Now, for the Christian, to be seated "at the table of God," is to agree to share his meal; it is to enter into the greatest intimacy with him. Why, then, sit at this "table of God" (an expression designating the altar of sacrifice in the Old Testament: Ml 1:7, 12) unless it is to eat the body of the immolated victim: the body of Christ?

XVIII. Luke
6:43-49
Gospel
Saturday

This passage forms part of a sort of moral catechism (vv. 39-49) put together especially for converts from paganism. It utilizes certain sayings of Jesus and groups them around certain key-words (measure, in verse 38, eye in verses 39, 41-42; tree in verses 43-44; mouth in verses 45-46; house, in the final verses). This unified mass therefore groups the essential themes of Christian morality for the use of Gentiles who are unaware of the law of Moses.

a) Verses 43-44 constitute one of the most important parts of the passage. We find them as such in St. Matthew (7:16-18 and 12:33-35) who applies them to false prophets, although Luke reserves them for the disciples themselves. A moral life is verified by its *fruits* (cf. Jm 3:12; Lk 13:6-9; 23:27-31; Is 5:1-7; Ez 19:10-14). The idea comes from the wisdom literature where the just man is often compared to a tree which gives fruit full of flavor while the other trees become sterile (Pss 1; 91/92:13-14; Si 24:12-27). The just man bears good fruit because he is irrigated by the divine waters; his fruit will be particularly abundant in the eschatological era (Ez 47:1-12). Actually, the Christian, a branch from the tree of life who is Jesus (Jn 15:1-8) produces fruits of the Spirit (Ga 5:5-12; 6:7-16) whereas Judaism becomes a sterile tree (Mt 3:8-10; 21:18-19).

b) The fruit theme directs the choice and the distribution of other maxims of Jesus which have a place in this moral catechism. It calls to mind in fact the themes of *effectiveness* and practicing what one hears. Thus verse 45 shows how good words presuppose a wellspring of goodness, and evil deeds a cesspool. This remark introduces another consideration about pious words uttered without meaning (v. 46) or hypocritically. But since it does not correspond to the basic perspective of the passage, Luke leaves it forthwith in order to return to the theme of effectiveness and practicing what one hears (vv. 47-48), because of the parable of the house.

c) The image of the house built on rock is easy to understand: the hurried contractor is content to build his house on the soil or the sand which covers the rock without digging down to it. This image recalls that of the seed that penetrates into the earth or, on the other hand, remains on the surface and dies (Lk 8:5-8). The gospel is a reminder therefore that there is no possibility of *efficacy* in the realm of faith unless we place the Word at the depth of our life. The theme seemingly has its origin in the wisdom milieu (cf. the allusion to the "wise" and to the "foolish" in the version by Mt 7:24-27). Luke however disregarded this source which was little known to his hearers, but he has presented its lesson: Christians are invited to deepen their faith rather than be content with a sociological faith or with insufficient motives.

TWENTY-FOURTH WEEK

I. 1 Timothy
2:1-8
1st reading
1st cycle
Monday

Paul is here concerned with the organization of the liturgy and the Christian community. He requires that Timothy make the decisions demanded by his pastoral charges and the powers he has received (1 Tm 1:18).

a) The first steps to be taken concern *universal prayer* (v.1), which the apostle designates by four names; petitions, prayers, intercessions and thanksgiving. It is quite possible that he has in mind the Aramaic terms used to describe the "eighteen prayers," a formula then much in use in Israel. He would then be inviting Christians to use a prayer of this kind in their assemblies.

But in contrast to the corresponding Jewish prayer the prayer which the apostle suggests would be clearly universal: it includes all men (v.1), especially kings and governors (all Gentiles at the time) and is concerned with the maintenance of peace (v. 2). The prayer seems to be specifically for men (v.8) and is to be pronounced, with hands lifted up to heaven, by people who live in peace with one another (cf. Mt 5:23-25; 6:14).

The Gentiles directed their prayer to the emperor himself who was divinized and considered a savior, when Christians pray to God for him they put him in his proper place, dependent upon the unique God.

b) Paul establishes the universal prayer on firm doctrinal bases. There are three reasons, as Paul sees it, for the Christian obligation to pray for the needs of all the world.

The first is the *unicity* of God and his will for universal salvation (vv.4-5a). If God is one, then all the problems of humanity are his concern, and if he is the only Creator, then he wills the salvation of all men and the Christian who prays in these terms is cooperating with that salvific will.

c) The second motive is the universal *mediation* of Christ (vv. 5b-6) which Paul associates with his humanity, or more precisely his absolute fidelity to the human condition. What Christ accomplished as the Messiah of his people is heavy with meaning for all mankind: he offered himself as a ransom "for all" (v.6) not "in place" of men, but "for" his brothers (cf. Heb 4).

d) The third reason is the universal *mission* with which Paul is invested (v.7). Because he is "doctor of the nations," he feels he has the right to "demand" (v. 8) that Christians join in his ministry by the intensity and universality of their prayer.

The basic criteria of Christian prayer are that it be representative of humanity before God and exhibit solidarity with the whole human race. Christ was the first to fulfill these criteria when he offered himself for the multitude in the sacrifice of the cross, still made present in the eucharistic prayer of the Church. The ministers of our eucharistic prayer then must have a genuine interest in the problems of humanity and search out means of associating all members of the assembly with them.

II. 1 Corinthians The Corinthians celebrated the Eucharist in
11:17-26, 33 the context of an agape feast which very often
1st reading became a source of division within the com-
2nd cycle munity because the well-to-do would gather at
Monday separate tables of their own and exclude the
poor from their feasting (vv.18-22). With a view
to putting an end to such abuses, Paul reminds them of the institution by the Lord (vv.23-26) and he points out the close link between the Eucharist and the Church, between the sacramental body and the mystical body (vv.27-29; cf. 1 Co 10:16-17).

a) The account of the institution as he gives it is reasonably close to the version in St. Mark (Mk 14:22-25), but the Pauline text is already somewhat hellenized and bears the marks of liturgical usage (perhaps the rite of Antioch). The repetition of the command is noteworthy: "Do this in remembrance of me" (vv.24-25). In the Pauline version there is question of a symbolic action (do this) which is to be a memorial of the Lord. But when we turn to a version closer to the Aramaic, the meaning of Christ's command would seem to be: "During your thanksgiving in the course of the repast, when you commemorate God's marvels in the old covenant, from now on add a commemoration of my work". By giving a more hellenistic emphasis to the memorial and by repeating the command twice, Paul is insisting on the realism of the commemoration of Christ's death and it would be hard to find clearer evidence than in verse 27 that Paul believes in the real presence of the Lord's body and blood in the Church's eucharistic rite.

b) On the other hand, while it is true that verse 29 can be taken as an affirmation of the real presence, nevertheless its immediate meaning, especially when we remember the general teaching of this letter about the *body* (cf. 1 Co 12:12-26), points to the fact that the unworthy celebration of the Eucharist constitutes contempt for the mystical Body of Christ which is the assembly (cf. further 1 Co 11:22 where the contempt extends to the Church of God). Paul is in fact concerned with the ultimate meaning of the liturgical assembly. It is the sign of all humanity's assembly in the Kingdom and in Christ's Body. An assembly where there are exclusive tables does not provide such a sign; it becomes a counter-sign.

The celebration of the Feast of Corpus Christi then is not exclusively concerned with the sacramental species. The species are central to the eucharistic celebration, so that the assembly will be enabled to "make commemoration" of Christ's death, which he encountered in perfect submission to the creaturely condition. And the members of the assembly are expected to affirm their determination, in imitation of Christ, and by his grace, to choose also the way of obedience and love. They are expected, in a word, to "form one body" with him.

III. Luke 7:1-10 The cure of the centurion's son is recounted by
    Gospel Matthew (28:5-13), Luke and John (4:46-54).
    Monday The first two evangelists agree in regarding the
miracle as a sign preceding the mission to the
Gentiles, a theme that is not found in John. All three however
are at one in stressing the point that the miracle was wrought at
a distance.

a) Whereas John speaks of a royal official (who could have been
a Jew), Matthew and Luke (v. 2) mention a Roman centurion,
unquestionably a Gentile.

Luke refers to the prohibitions for Jews about entering the
house of a Gentile (v. 6: cf. Ac 11:3) and he underscores the clear
sympathy of the centurion towards the Jewish nation (v. 5; cf. Ac
10:22). Matthew does not do this. Consequently Luke is much
more concerned than Matthew or John with stressing the insur-
mountable barriers that divided the Jews from the Gentiles. His
customary restraint is in evidence and he refuses to reproduce the
violent anti-Jewish diatribe related in Matthew 8:11-12.

Curiously enough Luke's account of the miracle resembles that
of the cure of the Syro-Phoenician woman (which Luke does not
relate): the same interceding for a dear child (cf. Mt. 15:22), the
same miracle performed at a distance (Mt 15:28), the same phrase
"in a bad state" (Mt 15:22), other people interceding (Mt 15:23),
the same admiration by Jesus at the faith of the person concerned
(Mt 15:28).

These parallels between the gospel and the accounts of the
conversion of Cornelius and of the miracle of the Syro-Phoenician
woman make the intention of Luke clear: to prepare for and to
justify the mission to the Gentiles which as yet the Judaeo-Christian
community was not ready to accept.

b) Out of respect for the Jewish tabu about entering the house
of a Gentile, Jesus performed his miracle at a distance, by means
of the *Word* only. Throughout his whole career as thaumaturge

there are only two such miracles (Lk 7:1-10 and Mt 15:22-28). Ordinarily he heals by simple physical contact and in silence, as if his body possessed a special lifegiving power that he was not always able to control (Mk 5:30; 6:5). Usually he subdues it by "touching" the sick (Mt 8:3, 15; 9:25, 29; Lk 14:4) or by "placing" his hands on them (Mk 6:5; 7:32; 8:23-25; Lk 4:40; 13:13). But this physical gesture of itself is not sufficient to indicate full responsibility for the action. Some miracle narratives make a point of showing how the healing gesture of Jesus is accompanied by a word (Mt 8:3; Mk 5:41) which gives it its fullest expression.

In healing the centurion's son Jesus is content with responding to the eulogy about the efficacy of the Word as spoken by the centurion (vv. 7-9). By asking Christ to confine himself to just his Word for this healing, he is probably making an allusion to Psalm 106/107:20 where God "sends his word to heal." Thus he is implicitly recognizing the fact that Jesus comes from God and that he has the very word of God which is powerful and efficatious (Ps 32/33:6-9).

It is worth remembering that the rite of communion is accompanied by an affirmation of faith on the part of the faithful in the words of the centurion: "But say only the word. . . ." Christian liturgy is so emancipated from ritual and magic as to depend upon the "Word alone." It was this that sustained Jesus throughout his life and it is this point which the communion rite brings out by its summons to faith and by putting the Christian in explicit relation with Christ.

Today's world asks if there is still a Word of the Lord. If we resort to it only after human words have failed we obviously risk hearing nothing. For the Lord's word is not distinct from our own decisions, rather it gives these their ultimate dimension. After many hesitations man places himself there where his actions are given their deepest significance. This voice heals selfishness, bestows courage, but never dispenses with anxiety or decisions. Only men who have never perceived a beyond for their life, as for example the Pharisee, walled up in his legalism or the pagan riveted to the flesh, are unable to hear it. Happy are the modern centurions whose heart and ears are listening!

IV. 1 Timothy
3:1-13
1st reading
1st cycle
Tuesday

After having given some directives to his disciple to help him maintain sound doctrine, Paul specifies some criteria for the designation of people who would exercise the desired authority over the faithful in order to confirm them in the faith.

a) It is rather astonishing to see that the qualities demanded of a good *leader of a community* are above all moral qualities, rather common in fact and without a specifically Christian character.

It seems that there is no need for a leader to be extraordinarily gifted or holy: it is enough to be balanced, moderate and having good sense, of easy and agreeable manner.

At the beginning of his apostolic life, St. Paul does not seem to have prized very much the charism of government which he usually placed very low in the hierarchy of functions (1 Co 12:28; 14:1; Rm 12:6-8; Ep 4:11). He gives it some importance here: "You can depend on this . . ." (v. 1) and affirms that the charism of government is a "good thing."

b) It would be useless to try to prove from this passage the existence of the episcopacy during St. Paul's time. The evolution of the hierarchy in the primitive Church must have extended over several years and been different from community to community.

The term *episkopos* which was used to designate the leader of the community, is rather vague. It conjures up the idea of an eminent and highly accepted dignity (which explains the apostle's concern for the good reputation of the episkopos). This function is never confused with specifically apostolic personnel, which indicates why it is a charism proper to the local Church: the episkopos is stationary.

Paul often uses it for the leader of a family group (vv. 4 and 15). As such he administers the community goods, judges and arbitrates conflicts, decides and directs the life of the community, welcomes strangers.

The authority of the episkopos is likewise written into the cultural domain. One can conclude this from the fact that this passage on the qualities of the community's leader comes after a series of liturgical prescriptions (1 Tm 2) which Paul mentions among his prerogatives, the "presidency" which presupposes leadership at prayer and finally what the term episkopos designates in pagan language, the guardian and manager of the temple.

Paul does not ask the bishop to be a "doctor" in the specified sense of the word (v. 2). No doubt the two functions of pastor and doctor are not yet as united as they will be later and elsewhere (cf. He 13:7, 17). The apostle hopes that the episkopos is capable of teaching. This ability will become in the letter to Titus (1:9) a real doctoral function.

Finally the function of the episkopos tends to become the bishop's function. This was far from clear in Acts 20:28 and in previous texts of the New Testament where the words episkopos and elders are still interchangeable. It is no longer the case in 1 Timothy 3, where the function of the episkopos is clearly enough defined (v. 1): no doubt the episkopos is one of the elders (presbyters) assuming a more important and extended function. But we cannot claim that this is the monarchical episcopacy which is encountered in the second century.

V. 1 Corinthians 12:12-14, 27-31a
1st reading
2nd cycle
Tuesday

Here Paul completes his statement on the diversity of the body's functions which he uses to show that the local churches include the same diversified functions which must be reciprocally structured and mutually respected.

a) The Pauline conception of the Church's functions indicates a few original traits. First of all the apostle seems particularly anxious to give importance to the charisms or functions of the Word. As in 1 Corinthians 12:8-10; 27; 30; Rm 12:6-8 or Ephesians 4:11, the three main functions of the Church are approximately that of the apostles who bring to the world the missionary word, that of the prophets who proclaim God's word in the liturgy and that of teachers who catechise.

These charisms of the Word precede in importance the extraordinary gifts: exorcism, healing and glossalalia (this one so cherished by the Corinthians), and the functions of charitable organizations (compassion and help) and liturgical functions (presidency) for the community. This is not one of the lesser aspects of Pauline thought to decree the inferiority of the liturgist compared to the missionary, of rite compared to the Word (cf. 1 Co 1:10-17).

b) Paul does not distinguish between fixed *functions* and extraordinary charisms, probably to convince the benefactors of the extraordinary gifts that they are an integral part of Christ's body. One and the same Spirit inspires the institutional hierarchy as well as the charisms. Separated or opposed, these two modes of action by the Spirit would end up amputating Christ's Body.

So many problems would be solved, so many tensions appeased in the Church if everyone were more aware of the common source of all the gifts and all the functions.

VI. Luke 7:11-17   St. Luke alone recounts the resurrection of the
    Gospel   son of the widow of Naim and he does so no
    Tuesday   doubt for a set purpose. A few verses further on
                 he gives us Jesus' reply to the Baptist: "The
blind recover their sight . . . the deaf hear . . . dead men are raised to life" (v. 22).

Up to this point there has been no instance of raising to life.

He had to relate a miracle of this kind to justify the reality of verse 22.

a) Moreover, the evangelist takes the opportunity which this account of a resurrection affords him to mention a woman, an outcast of society. He wants to indicate Jesus' anxiety to *reassemble* all humanity, men and women, children and adults, rich and poor, Jews and Gentiles.

b) Luke then introduced the account of the resurrection at Naim to justify verse 22. In fact the Jews awaited a messianic era when all human nature, suffering, sinful, humiliated would be fully restored. They based themselves on Isaiah 61:1 and 35:5-6: a Messiah would come to heal human suffering and weakness. In the same context Judaism foresaw at the end of time and the inauguration of the messianic era, a general resurrection of the sons of Israel who had died before this era. They cited Isaiah 26:19 for this: "your dead shall live, their corpses shall rise." Probably the prophet in using these words, thought only of the people's restoration (like Ez 37). But it is certain that at least one Jewish group anticipated a genuine corporal resurrection when the messianic age arrives (2 M 7:9-36; Dn 12:2-3).

c) The Jews awaited the return of Elias to preside over the inauguration of these times. They believed that they would find in the Messiah the *spirit of Elias* which ancient traditions had already discovered in Elisha (compare 2 K 4:25-38 and 1 K 17:17-24). The gospel writers certainly wanted to respond to this longing by relating the reanimation of a child which has some traits in common with that of Elias (compare 1 K 17:23 and Lk 7:16). But what a difference there was between Elias, Elisha and Christ. Whereas the prophets worked their miracles in secret, Christ does so before the crowds. Whereas the prophets used procedures that still had traces of traditional magic, Christ is content to speak and command.

The Jewish hopes are fulfilled by Christ, but certainly this falls far short of the ultimate possibilities of his message. He reanimates a child, but it is a sort of "recovery" (v. 15). Soon another type of resurrection is to be revealed to men; it will involve more than a mere "recovery" of a dead body; it will cause it to enter into a royal way of life that transcends all human categories.

VII. 1 Timothy   These three verses constitute the turning point
     3:14-16   in the letter to Timothy. The behavior of the
   1st reading   ministers of truth in the Church (v. 14), the
   1st cycle   house of God and pillar of truth (v. 15) has been
  Wednesday up to this point the constant concern of the
apostle who reproduces a strophe from a litur-
gical hymn used in the primitive community to explain the mystery
of the incarnate and glorified Jesus Christ (v. 16).

a) The *Christian community in the world* is first of all the "house of God" or the "family of God." The conviction of the first Christians about being the new temple and constituting the new priesthood is thus confirmed. Cut off from the temple liturgy by persecution (Ac 8:1) or remoteness, they discovered that they themselves were the temple "in spirit and in truth" (Jn 4:23; cf. 1 Co 3:16; He 12:22-24) and formed a real priesthood capable of offering the spiritual sacrifice of the new covenant (1 P 2:4-9; Rm 12:1). They discovered this in their daily life, during their fraternal and eucharistic reunions at their "homes" (Ac 2:46).

In this assembly of men who belong to God, the source of their life, is vested the role of pillar and support of truth. These images convey an idea of power and stability (cf. Mt 16:18; Ep 2:20): the Church, built on the foundation of truth, that is to say, the revelation of God in Jesus Christ, is itself the foundation for all humanity.

The Church is the pillar of truth by its teaching and sacramentality which extends the revelation of God in Jesus Christ. The

Christian community is, by its behavior, its witness and the involvement of its members, the truth of God in Jesus who continues in the world. It is still charged with revealing to man the "mystery of godliness" that was hidden until now (v. 16).

The nature of the Church is thus twofold: it is the house of God where the spiritual liturgy is carried out and the pillar of truth because of its mission to reveal Christ in the world.

b) But what is this truth that the Church must bring to the world? It is the "mystery"—which means for St. Paul God's consideration of man, the basis for religion—of "godliness" that remained hidden until its revelation in Jesus Christ (cf. Ep 5:32; 1 Co 2:7).

This mystery is the person of Jesus Christ (Col 1:27). The primordial object of revelation and of faith is not then God in himself, but *Jesus Christ as man-God*. Verse 16 of the hymn referred to by St. Paul says it clearly: he who is at one and the same time in the flesh and in the Spirit, in the world and in glory. This strophe is a kind of anemnesis of Christ's life, "manifested" in the flesh (his birth: cf. Tt 2:11), justified in the Spirit (his resurrection: cf. Ac 2:24-36), seen by the angels (cf. 1 P 1:12; Ep 3:10, unless one translates: seen by those "sent": the apostles: cf. 1 Jn 1:1; Jn 20:20-27), proclaimed and believed by the world (the object of the mission) and finally taken into glory.

The Church must then live and proclaim the "mystery" of the man-God. At a time when technologies and philosophies cause man to forget this earthly condition or to promote it inordinately, the Christian community proclaims Jesus of Nazareth, having entered freely into his condition as son of God without ceasing to belong to creation. The yes of Jesus to his earthly condition coincides with the final yes of the son of God.

The Eucharist which engenders the members of the true humanity, accomplishes its role among men by reassembling them in the familial unity of the Father, this "house of the living God."

VIII. 1 Corinthi- This passage can be considered a hymn in three
ans 12:31- strophes. The first asserts the dependence of
13:13 charisms on charity (vv. 12:31-13:3); the second
1st reading personalizes this attitude (vv. 13:4-13:7 or 8a);
2nd cycle the third (vv. 13:8 to 13:13) sets up a sort of
Wednesday antithesis between it and the other virtues;
those that endure and those that pass.

This hymn to charity, the binding force in this letter to the
Corinthians, is its source of unity. Paul treats very diverse subjects
here: celibacy and marriage, collections for the poor, the use of
charisms etc. He affirms that the answer to all these questions is not
equal to charity. Charity is worth more than all other charismatic
graces (vv. 1-2, 8-9). Charity is worth more than offerings (v. 3)
and charity is better still than subtleties about celibacy and marriage.

a) The canticle on the superiority of charity over charisms takes
a form that is common in classical and Jewish literature (Ws 7:22-
30, from which Paul takes several verses) which exalts several
virtues. Paul first describes the charisms which the Corinthians
esteemed so highly (1 Co 12): the gifts of tongues, prophecy, the
management of affairs, even suicide by burning which was then
considered the height of courage and devotion. But all this is
nothing, for charity is on another level. The apostle uses the word
"charity" ten times and each time he uses it without an article or
an object. He thus personalizes this virtue, but more important, he makes of it an absolute that nothing can determine or limit.

b) Verses 4-8a personalizes charity. It is patient, with that
patience that endures injury and does not brood over it (Mt 5:10-
11, 21-24). It is kind. It is not envious (a passion often indulged in
by the Jews with regard to other religions, Ac 5:17; 17:5). It does
not boast (1 Co 4:6, 18-19). It is never insolent (1 Co 11:4-6; 5:1-6;
11:21-22). It is disinterested (in the sense that it considers the
weak, 1 Co 8). Finally, it never fails (v. 8a); constantly tested, but

constantly overcoming evil. It is here that Paul shows most clearly his concern for praising charity in the manner which was used by the philosophers in praising the other virtues. The constructions "is not . . . ," "is not . . . ," "all things," "all things," are characteristic of the Stoic manner of writing.

c) The third stanza compares the knowledge we have on earth to that which we will have after death. Saint Paul does not mean to deprecate the theological organism in operation. Rather he states precisely that faith, hope and charity, all three, *remain*, but charity is the greatest. An exact translation of verse 13 is important. Paul does not say that faith and hope will disappear and only charity remain. His intention is rather to exalt the organic union of the three theological virtues, even though he allows charity to be supreme. It may seem that to affirm that faith and hope will remain together with charity, contradicts his statement elsewhere that faith and hope will cease (2 Co 5:7; Rm 8:24); but faith and hope must be understood here in the biblical sense as human attitudes of response to the divine Word. Under the new Alliance the Word has become Christ and it reveals love to us. But faith remains total cooperation with God and self-surrender to him. Why should this self-surrender and this cooperation, namely faith and hope, cease when the full vision in heaven is attained? Both faith and hope will indeed lose their present obscurity, a provisional condition belonging to the period of trial in which we live. Now and then (cf. Rm 8:24; 2 Co 5:7) St. Paul may have placed his main emphasis on the transitory nature of these circumstances. But in his mind this transitoriness does not affect the essential equipment of a child of God, given to us in order that we may always advance lovingly on the way to God, faithful, trusting in his goodness.

Faith, hope and love are then, after all, different aspects of one new and complex spiritual organism, to be sure, but still one.

From this passage we discern the manner in which Paul challenges all human definitions of love, here understood as the most spiritual and the most heroic. For him, love is not necessarily present where one widens the network of interpersonal relations.

The fact that the apostle sings about a love so different from human behavior, yet still human, indicates that our conduct is no longer related to a list of virtues or any legal obligation, but to the presence of Christ in us.

IX. Luke 7:31-35   In Luke as in Matthew this parable of the
Gospel   children playing in the square comes imme-
Wednesday   diately after the account about John the Baptist
                 (Lk 7:24-30; Mt 11:7-15). Perhaps it derives
from a popular proverb which Jesus expanded in reply to attacks which were made upon him (cf. v. 34, a quotation from Dt 21:20).

a) John and Jesus are the last messengers of God before the catastrophe. But their preaching interests no one; they encounter only *indifference*. The people, instead of being converted, criticize these preachers, either by opposing them or by simply ignoring them. This indifference will be to their own detriment.

b) However, the *signs* of the Kingdom are sufficiently clear for those who really want to decipher them: the penitent asceticism of John (v. 33; cf. Mt 3:7-10) or the messianic meal which Jesus shared with his own (v. 34; Is 25:6). By claiming the title "Son of Man" (v. 34), Christ affirms that the coming of the definitive Kingdom is perfectly discernible in these happenings.

The comparison which Jesus makes between himself and John the Baptist does not involve an attitude of preference for the other. The life-style of each, in its own way, announces eschatological times and it is precisely this inference that the crowds do not want to grasp.

c) The conclusion of the speech makes an allusion to *little ones* who are "children of the Wisdom of God" in comparison to the wise and the Scribes. The little ones are able to decipher the signs of the times and to read in them the coming of the Kingdom whereas the mighty and the wise (cf. Lk 10:21-22) run the risk of by-passing this event.

This gospel draws attention to the meaning of history and to the conditions necessary if one is going to be able to discern its essential stages. Will Christians, then, be on the side of the "Children of Wisdom" or on that of the "Children playing in the square"? Will they be able to read the signs of the time that are today the big questions of hunger, peace and revolution, so that the Church can be the sign of salvation among men, and the Eucharist, sign of the Kingdom being prepared in the heart of the Church?

X. 1 Timothy
4:12-16
1st reading
1st cycle
Thursday

The task of young Timothy is pretty weighty. It is mainly concerned with resisting the false doctrines of the heretics. But Paul not only asks his young disciple to specialize in theology in order to reply with facility to those false doctrines (v. 11); he reminds him that the moral effort is also valuable and necessary (v. 12).

Timothy seems too young and inexperienced to take over the government of a community founded by Paul, the prestigious sexagenarian. Therefore the disciple will not be able to rest his authority on age or experience. But he possesses other means of success, the first of which is the evidence of his good conduct (v. 12). Thus Paul insists once again on the importance of morality in the realm of faith.

Then, he possesses the charism of teaching (v. 13) that includes three liturgical functions or nearly liturgical: the reading of the inspired texts and their commentaries, the exhortation that orientates events towards their eschatological meaning, and teaching as such that organizes the deposit of beliefs.

But the principal advantage for Timothy is the ordination he has received (v. 14). It is first of all a gift, the free initiative of God as well as the decision of the entire presbyterate that imposed hands on him; finally it is an action of the community, because it happened within the context of liturgy.

XI. 1 Corinthi- Some supposed "wise men" from Corinth ques-
ans 15:1-11 tion, it seems, certain aspects of the final resur-
1st reading rection and even the resurrection of the body
2nd cycle itself (cf. 1 Co 15:29-34). In answer to them,
Thursday Paul can only refer them to the basic apostolic
kerygma.

In fact, the text seems to have been translated from the Aramaic and everything leads to the conclusion that it was composed by the primitive community at Jerusalem where it was considered a resume of the apostolic kerygma. Several years after the first letter to the Corinthians, St. Luke will still draw up various apostolic speeches (Ac 2:22-36; 3:15-26; 4:8-12; 5:30-32; 10:39-43; 13:27-41) in the form proposed by this ancient tradition: announcement of the death of Christ (here: v. 3b), reflection on the Scriptures (here: v. 3b), resurrection (here: v. 4b), enthronement (here the verse is absent), scriptural proofs (here: v. 4b), witnesses of the resurrection (here: v. 5-8), a call to conversion (here, too, the verse is absent).

a) Paul affirms that his kerygma is a *tradition* (vv. 1-3, 11). Actual exegetical studies confirm this: it is probably to the community at Jerusalem that the apostle owes the form of his kerygma. In every way, his message has nothing in common with wisdom or human gnosis, but with a tradition (1 Th 2:13; 4:1; 2 Th 2:15; 1 Co 11:23) that goes back to the very person of Christ (who passed on what he received from his Father: Mt 11:27). From the beginning the Church prepared a formula for the profession of faith which is somewhat expressed in verses 3b-4. Paul lists, without any change, the three elements contained in the traditional kerygma: death-burial-resurrection. But he takes some liberties even with these proofs. He makes certain allusions but lists only one in reference to the theme of the third day (v. 4; cf. Hos 6:2; Jn 2:1). His readers are less knowledgeable about the Scriptures than the members of the community at Jerusalem. On the other hand the proof through personal testimony could assume in their eyes a special interest; that is why Paul exposes it in detail (vv. 5-8). He reproduces an ancient list of witnesses who had benefited from these appearances: Peter, the Twelve and the faithful of Jerusalem, passing over in silence the later testimony of the women and the disciples of Emmaus (vv. 5-6). This list, one sees, is very hierarchical: one senses there the mentality of the Judaeo-Christian community at Jerusalem which made little reference to the appearances to the women and the disciples. The mention of James, brother of the Lord (v. 7), was no doubt added later, but at Jerusalem, and Paul in his turn mentions the opposition he experienced on the way to Damascus (v. 8; Ac 9:17).

b) The faith handed on to Paul is essentially based on the paschal event. Certainly it is less concerned about the historical event and its material proofs than its doctrinal repercussions which appear especially in the contrast of the verbs: "is dead" (in the aorist) and "resurrected" (in the perfect, the past tense that extends into the present). This construction is found seven times in 1 Corinthians 15. The resurrection of Christ thus introduces an unheard of religious regime that concerns us directly: it involves, in fact, a new style of life (Rm 6:1-6), sign of our own resurrection (1 Co 15:20; 2 Co 4:14).

Thus, faith is founded on three events: the death, the burial and the resurrection which are not only ancient events but which in the strict sense are written into our new life: because we too will die to sin and we will rise.

The faith of Christians in Christ's resurrection is sometimes shaken. They would like to have an objective representation that would reveal its reasonableness. Too many elements in the traditional formulation seem to them linked to a mode of perceiving religious realities which, though valuable in itself, is little adapted to the legitimate needs of modern man.

This desire is admissible so long as it does not confuse faith and wisdom and respects the "traditional" aspect (beyond experience and rationality) of faith in the resurrection.

If the Christian believes in the paschal event, it is because he sees in it both Jesus of Nazareth assuming fully the mystery of human contingency (death), yet realizing at the same time the fundamental longing of each man for the absolute, by his active response to the prevenient initiative of God (resurrection). Because the death on the cross was not only the death of a condemned man, but that of the God-man who did not cease living his dependence as Son of the Father, even in his fidelity to the human condition. It is here that is realized the most perfect encounter there can be between God and man; the most complete adjustment of the human response to the divine intervention. The Eucharist is the memorial of the paschal event because it renews at the same time the Father's intervention for his children and their response, the best possible to that initiative.

XII. Luke   This reading which presents the anointing of
   7:36-50   Christ by the sinful woman and the parable of
   Gospel   the two debtors, present a problem which the
   Thursday   exegetes still do not agree on.

The pre-evangelical tradition spoke of an anointing at Bethany, in the house of Simon the Pharisee (Mt 26: 6-13; Mk 14:3-9), by an unnamed woman. Christ justifies this expense, knowing that Judaism attached more importance to the care of the dead than to alms for the poor.

John incorporated this story into his gospel at a time when it was already charged with new elements (Jn 12:1-8). He gives a name to the woman: Mary, sister of Martha and Lazarus; he stresses that the anointing was made on the feet and not the head, as indicated by Matthew and Mark and that Mary wiped them with her hair. Finally, although he includes the discussion of the expense of this anointing, he stresses that this oil was actually meant for the burial of Christ. But since Jesus had to rise, does not concern for his burial become senseless? Thus, offered by Mary before the Lord's death, this perfumed oil becomes the expression of her certitude, confirmed by the resurrection of Lazarus, that Christ could not die (Jn 11:25).

Luke's version (7:36-50) has some original elements. He mentions a host named Simon (Lk 8:40; Mt 26:6); the anointing is done; contrary to Matthew's version, on the feet and wiped away with hair (Lk 7:38; Jn 12:3). Luke does not refer to an anointing at Bethany before the passion, conscious no doubt of the repetition it would involve. He does not mention the discussion about the opportuneness of the anointing (Mt 26:10-12; Jn 12:5-8), probably because it presupposes an acquaintance with Jewish scale of values in reference to "good works," the knowledge of which would be lacking to his Greek readers. He prefers to replace it by a parable that reflects his main interest, forgiveness.

Whether or not the evangelist relates the same event, it is in any case evident that we must distinguish in the account of St. Luke the history (vv. 36-39, 43-50) of the parable that is added there (vv. 40-43).

a) The *meal* scenes in St. Luke constitute a true literary genre proper to the third gospel and subject to very precise laws (cf. 7:36-50; 5:27-32; Lk 14). Luke no doubt considered the reference to the meal as an opportunity to present, more or less artificially, some unpublished parables. He attaches them moreover rather skillfully to one or another incident that happened during a meal (sometimes the place at table, in this case, Jesus' omission of the ritual ablutions). However, there is no reason for attributing any theological value to the meal at the home of the Pharisee; for Luke, it is only a form which he borrows perhaps from Mark 14:3-9 and in which he introduces themes taken from the oral tradition (the sinful woman, vv. 37-38; the parable of the two debtors, vv. 40-43) or from the written tradition (Mk 14, the anointing, v. 37). But he adds to it redactional elements proper to the symposiac genre (vv. 44-46) and personal commentaries (remission of sins, vv. 41-42 and 47-50).

b) The basic lesson of this account is the pardoning of *sins* by Christ. The context (Lk 7:34; 8:1-4) makes direct allusion to the promiscuity of Christ with sinners. The scandal which the Pharisees witnessed (v. 39) derives from the prohibition in Deuteronomy 23:19 about accepting gifts from a prostitute for sacred use: if Christ were a man of God, he would then refuse the gift of this woman. Imprisoned by such legalism, like the hardened Pharisees of Mark 2:23-3:5, the host does not seek for the reason why Christ dispensed himself from this prohibition. In the face of this "hardening" Jesus establishes personal contact with the sinful woman; his love and his pardon dispenses him from the rules of purity and discrimination decreed by the Deuteronomist. This meeting of person with person where the gift of God (the remission of sins) is united to the love of man (gratitude of the woman) is so privileged that it substitutes for the traditional means of justification: ablutions and various other rites (v. 48).

c) The parable of the two debtors (vv. 40-43) is conceived with considerable finesse. To the Pharisees, anxious about a religion of obligation and duty, it suggests the example of a creditor who forgives the debt of his debtors and debtors manifesting sentiments of love and gratitude: traits so unprecedented in contemporary life.

Certainly, the parable can be misunderstood when it speaks of degrees of love and when it establishes a kind of higher-bid atmosphere between the two debtors: love and gratitude can not be translated into numbers! But this quantitative aspect is due to the polemical context in which the parable is placed.

We will not then make allowances for this context: the essential interest of the parable is to cause those involved to pass from a quantitative notion of religion to a religion of encounter where a merciful God rejoins man and his loving fidelity.

This gospel can be understood only when we find in it the person of the God-man, the ideal place for the encounter between God and man. It is because Christ has succeeded in this encounter that he dares to approach the worst human situations and propose to sinners to realize for themselves the conditions required for the encounter: an openness to the gift (or to the pardon) of God, a loving "yes" to the initiative of God.

To bring together the conditions for such an encounter and to accomplish it in the Eucharist, automatically dispenses one from the false encounters proposed by rites and external ablutions and liberates from excommunication and ostracism expressed in a too abstract legalism.

The sinful woman in the gospel is a real sinner and Luke is in no way tempted to excuse her. In the same way the just in the gospel are really just, careful guardians of a law entirely valid. The opposition between the just and the sinner is then total. But it is precisely this opposition that Luke wants to eliminate by appealing to a kind of unique event that justifies both and which is anterior to both; the mystery of God's love in the person of Christ. Our concern here is not why the sinful woman was forgiven: it would involve joining her unduly to the clan of the just and imposing on her a kind of avowal of her error and an acknowledgement of the justice of the just. That would be the victory of one clan over the other. In fact, God has forgiven her even before she admitted her guilt, the pardon of God being independent of her sin as of the justice of the other. It was necessary that Jesus encounter his Father with an extraordinary intensity in order to act independently in reference to justice and sin. This quality of the person of Christ is at the very heart of the mystery of the Church: it alone in fact explains how just men and sinners could coexist as they do at the table of Simon.

XIII. 1 Timothy The comparison between true and false teach-
  6:2c-12 ers involves especially the disinterestedness of
  1st reading the first and the cupidity of the latter (1 Tm
  1st cycle 6:3-10).
  Friday

To the cupidity of heretics Paul contrasts the "great gain" to be had from piety (to be understood as doctrinal and moral fidelity to the Word) and from disinterestedness (v. 6). The apostle seems to be influenced here by pagan thought (piety indicating contentment with what one has and uses—all a gift from God) and not by Jewish thought (where piety implies receiving from God everything that is necessary to man).

In verse 7 Paul presents an argument in favor of this disinterestedness which he takes from the Old Testament (Jb 1:1) as well as from pagan wisdom. Love of money is the source of all evil (vv. 9-10) because money provides the opportunity to fulfill the most senseless desires. This entire passage is a Christian second reading of Jewish wisdom (Si 7:1-3; 11:25-28; 31:1-11).

The last verses encourage Timothy to keep himself unspotted by this cupidity by a total consecration of his energy to the promotion of the faith. He must do it for it is the object of his vocation and of his constant profession of faith (v. 12).

XIV. 1 Corin- **thians** **15:12-20** *1st reading* *2nd cycle* *Friday*	The Corinthians did not doubt the resurrection of Christ, but they refused to join the resurrection of the bodies to the paschal event (v. 12). Presumably we are here concerned with either disciples of the Sadducees, Jews who denied the resurrection (Mt 22:23), or individuals permeated with platonism who did not see the

necessity of recovering in the hereafter a body that could not but fetter the enjoyment of spiritual happiness.

Paul's reasoning takes place on two complementary planes. On the one hand if Christ is risen, we too are promised the same *resurrection* because we have the same nature he had (v. 20). On the other hand, Christ's resurrection cannot be understood except as that of man (vv. 13-18). If there is a link between the two resurrections, Paul does not utter a word because he puts himself on the plane of salvation and not on the philosophical plane. He affirms that if the dead would not rise, this would prove that Christ did not come to save humanity. Salvation involves in fact victory over bodily death.

Unconsciously the modern Christian could easily be brought to reason as the Corinthians. He would like to admit, in an apologetic way, Christ's resurrection as an extraordinary miracle that sanctions the mission and the teaching of Jesus, but he badly understands how this resurrection means his and that of all men!

He also has some difficulty in admitting that this buried and decomposed body could receive life back again, for the Christian willingly dissociates the soul from the body in the name of a dichotomy borrowed from Greek philosophy which he has inherited and which hardly credits the unity of the human person.

The opposition between the Corinthians and St. Paul on the subject of the resurrection derives to a large extent from two different anthropological concepts: Greek dualism that separates the soul from the body to the point of conferring to the first a quasi-autonomous existence, and the Jewish unitary concept where body and soul together constitute the human person.

XV. Luke 8:1-3   Luke alone mentions explicitly the group of
    Gospel   women who accompany Christ during his apos-
    Friday   tolic travels. Two themes seem to be at the
                     origin of this tradition.

a) The first theme concerns the removal of the interdict so often placed on *woman* by the Old Testament. Luke insists on the fact that a large part of the women who follow Christ are ancient demoniacs. This image still carries with it the scent of the past where woman was interdicted, the object of mysterious forms alienating her life and her functions (Lk 4:38-39; 13:16; Mk 5:25-34; 16:9; Mt 15:22), cursed when she was sterile and unhappy when she delivered in pain.

The attention Jesus gives to these women and the healing that he performs on them are the sign that with him woman attains a free status, because the humanity he proposes does not recognize any form of alienation.

b) But the evangelist indicates still another interest in the presence of women around Christ from the beginning of his public life. In fact, he gathered a rather large number of traditions which came from feminine circles and whose testimony seemed strange, especially with respect to the apparitions of the risen one (Lk 24:9-11). The fact that these women had accompanied Jesus since the beginning of his ministry, just like the Twelve (v. 1), conferred on them a title similar to that of the apostles, to announce the first Christian kerygma. Woman is then the equal of man, even in the *apostolic announcement* of the message.

XVI. 1 Timothy
6:13-16
1st reading
1st cycle
Saturday

In contrast to the heresiarchs (1 Tm 4:1-5), Paul outlines for the use of Timothy the portrait of the ideal pastor. This section is divided into three parts.

The pastor can exercise his function only in a continual struggle that he has to engage in courageously (vv. 11-12) if he wants to remain faithful to his baptismal commitment, to the two divine witnesses that observe him and to the solemn commandment of the Church (vv. 13-14). He will do so even more courageously since the light of God will not be long in appearing, hiding the shadows that tarnish the actual Church and justifying the efforts that are undertaken there (vv. 15-16).

a) The theme of *fight* is one of the most important in Pauline morality (cf. 1 Tm 1:18; 4:10; 2 Tm 4:7; 1 Co 9:25; Col 1:29). It is a fight for the faith: that is, it involves fighting against enemies, but because the choice that one makes of this virtue automatically involves the exercise of fidelity and constancy, a fight against one's self for the individual palm and concern for the faith of others and their salvation, if one is responsible for a community.

b) In this context, *baptism* appears as the moment when the call of God invites one (v. 12) to share his life, where there is expressed the profession of faith of the believer who gives himself (v. 12) in front of the united community and before the surety of his own testimony: God and his Christ, as the moment when the command-ment is formulated (v. 14), to know the ensemble of behavior that faith imposes upon the believer.

In fact, beneath the words of the call, of the profession of faith and of the commandment, there is hidden only one and the same reality: it involves preserving intact and without compromise, the teaching and the Spirit of the Lord until the day of his mani-festation.

c) Paul sings in the form of a doxology about this future *mani-festation* of the Lord, borrowing his vocabulary from the cere-monial of the divinization of emperors and from the Jewish prayers of the synagogue.

But in order to stress the distance that separates the emperor from God, he designates the latter by substantives (King, Lord, vv. 15) and the former by paraphrases ("those who reign, those who exercise the sovereignty"), as if their power was only momen-tary in relation to the immortality of God (v. 16).

XVII. **1 Corin-** Paul tries to explain for his readers the manner
thians of the final resurrection. The Jewish milieu to
15:35-37, which he belongs is in fact very divided on this
42-49 subject. The Pharisees imposed this dogma at
1st reading the time of the Seleucid persecution as the
2nd cycle normal stage in the coming of the Kingdom
Saturday (2 M 7:11, 23; 12:44); the Sadducees adhered
to the biblical traditions that hardly envisaged
more than a very meager survival; others, still influenced by Hel-lenism, believe only in the universality of a soul finally liberated from the body (cf. the book of Wisdom).

Christ takes sides with the pharisaic context and the primitive Christian community draws its faith in the resurrection of bodies from the paschal event itself. The letter of Paul to the Thessalonians reflects the thought of the Pharisees and the Judaeo-Christian communities (1 Th 4:14-17; 2 Th 1:10; 2:14). For the apostle the bodies recently deposited in the tombs will be reanimated: he believes then in an authentic bodily life before and after death.

But this doctrine of the resurrection of bodies is too simplistic for the Greek world (Ac 17:32). Paul sees himself opposed by a series of objections, especially on the part of the Corinthians, to whom he replies in this chapter 15.

a) Paul presents his first argument by way of an analogy between the body and seed (vv. 37-38). In order to live and bear fruit both must die and disappear in the earth. Only then does the power of God intervene and give them life.

The second argument concerns the quality of the body (vv. 39-44) that we will gain again: the same or another? It is still by drawing an analogy with nature that the apostle explains the differences between the actual and corruptible body and the future, glorious body.

Paul then proposes a more philosophical argument (v. 44). On earth the body is animated by the vital principle of the "psyche," the living soul, which remains a natural principle. But the Spirit, the pneuma, already at work in man, tends to animate him progressively to make him a son of God. On earth this animation is still mysterious: it influences the spiritual faculties, the will, faith, love, but does not seem to have any apparent influence on the body, still destined for death. For Paul, man, after the *resurrection of the body*, will enjoy a body totally animated by the Spirit.

b) The apostle distinguishes humanity before Christ (the first man, v. 45) and humanity after Christ (the last man). The soul is the vital principle of the first man *(psyche, nephesh)*, but it cannot lead him to bodily resurrection. The vital principle of the last man is the Spirit, who allows him to spiritualize his body and attain resurrection. It is a free gift (the meaning of "heavenly" in verses 47-48), in this sense that this is not demanded by nature and it does not reduce itself to a natural principle.

In fact, this "spiritualization" of the body, started in this life and

achieved in the *resurrection* and incorruptibility, does not necessarily produce, in the mind of St. Paul, immaterialization. The
Spirit of God is certainly beyond matter, it is light and holiness, but
the apostle does not define it on the philosophical plane (which
would involve the notion of immateriality), but on the religious
plane. The Spirit is participation in the divine; it animates the man
who does not rely on his own means of flesh and blood (v. 50), but
opens himself to God's action in him.

XVIII. Luke   The parable of the sower contains two parts:
    8:4-15   the story itself (vv. 5-8), which goes back to
    Gospel   Jesus Christ, and its explanation (vv. 9-15),
    Saturday   supplied by the primitive community. The
                    proof for this is that the "Word" is here desig-
nated in an absolute manner, in conformity with the usage of the
primitive Church, and that the different manifestations of the
Word are precisely those that Paul complacently accepts (cf. 1 Th
1:6; 2:13; Ac 17:11; 2 Co 11:4, the word received; Ac 6:7; 12:24;
19:20; Col 1:6, the word that grows).

Other indications are discernible in the vocabulary: "to sow"
for "to announce"; "roots" (v. 13) for "inner strength" (Col 2:7; Ep
3:17); "to bear fruit" (v. 15, cf. Rm 7:4-6; Col 1:6-10), "perseverance" (v. 15), typically Lucan images. Finally, the Gospel of
Thomas which, although apocryphal, sometimes repeats traditions very close to Christ, but reports only the account without the
interpretation.

The commentary on the gospel for this day must then distinguish
between the "account" and the eschatological aspect of its "interpretation," far more moralistic.

a) The account is integrated into a succession of parallel parables, unified around the theme of sowing. They draw attention to
the slowness of the growth of the Kingdom of God, to the painful,
indeed frail, growth of this kingdom, until the day it is fulfilled
(this latter is in no way compromised).

Jewish *eschatology* expected a sudden and glorious manifestation of the Kingdom of God. Jesus rejects this: the law of trial is the condition for success; it involves patience and being willing to allow God to act.

b) The explanation of the parable of the sower (Lk 8:11-15) already involves a particular interpretation, made by the first community. There is no longer a direct concern with the problem of the extension of the kingdom but rather with the *diffusion of the Word.*

Certainly, the Word implies the reign and is the proclamation of the reign (Ac 12:24); but his explanation of verses 11-15 does not at all reduce the interpretation to the conditions of the apostolic preaching. The Lord's story looks at things from the point of view of the seed which grows despite difficulties; this point of view envisages the psychological conditions of the welcome received for the preaching. Let us add that Luke has taken a further step in the interpretation of the parable than Matthew and Mark did. For these latter the explanation is completed by a definition of the good earth: that which yields a hundred percent, sixty percent or thirty percent (Mk 4:20). Luke does not accept the eschatological definition of the "good earth," but adopts another, more moralistic one and connects it with "perseverance" (v. 15). Furthermore, while Mark and Matthew name those who lose the fruit of the Word: "When some pressure or persecution overtakes them" (eschatological vocabulary, cf. Mk 4:17), Luke speaks of the trial, of the "temptation" (v. 13). He thus again blurs the eschatological aspect supplied by the other evangelists; for him, it is in the trials of daily life and not only in the cataclysm at the end of time that the "good earth" reveals its perseverance, its fidelity and assures the development of the reign of God. St. Luke, who benefited from a longer experience of the Church's life, knew the unfortunate results of a naive eschatology, where Christians dispensed themselves from all moral effort in the expectation of an immediate eschatological catastrophe. He also reacts against the Quietist mentality; modifying a very eschatological vocabulary, he substitutes it with a more demanding one: the Kingdom of God does not come like a *Deus ex machina,* but in the humble reality of everyday life and in putting up with one's daily burdens.

Luke moreover considers this "trial" (v. 13) as the replica of the temptation in the desert (same word as in Ex 17:7; Dt 4:34; 6:16; 17:19; Ps 94/95:8-9): everything that can verify the faith and fidelity of a Christian, reproduces the very "temptations" of Christ (Lk 4:13; 22:28).

Faced with ideologies that proposed and still propose the salvation of man by man, Jewish thought elaborated an eschatology clearly affirming that the salvation of man would come from heaven as fast as lightning, as free as the very love of God. Isaiah 55:8-11 is a witness to that hope of Israel in the effectiveness of the intervention of the unique God and in the direction already taken by human history towards its eschatological fulfillment.

Nevertheless, Christian faith does not share entirely these views. At an equal distance between these ideologies that save man by man and those which save him by God, Christ offers to humanity a salvation, the initiative of which goes back to God but which cannot be realized except with the collaboration of man, called upon to become God's partner. The Lord's intervention in the parable of the sower is to show that salvation remains a divine undertaking and that as such it will certainly be achieved, but also that this salvation will only be accomplished progressively because God has to consider the weak and limited means which his human partners possess. The Incarnation teaches an unheard of lesson: God's power is manifested in the weakness of man and especially in his death and in his apparent failure!

Jesus is the first to manifest this divine power in the weakness of a human conscience which puts everything to work in order to contribute actively to the design of the Father.

The Church, in its turn, cannot grow unless it continually dies in order to bear fruit. By giving, quite fittingly, priority to weak means, it displays a very vulnerable love, because it is continually confronted both by the atheistic world and by the masses of Christians who do not want to question themselves for they are content with a superficial religiosity.

TWENTY-FIFTH WEEK

I. Ezra 1:1-6 Probably it was a single compiler who edited
1st reading the books of Chronicles, Ezra and Nehemiah.
1st cycle The final verses of the second book of Chroni-
Monday cles are identical to those found in the first
verses of the book of Ezra. To a certain extent
the author avoids speaking about the exile which for him was
an unfortunate interlude that came to an end with the edict of
Cyrus (558).

However, the exile did influence the perspective of the author
for he considers the chosen people as having passed from a dy-
nastic regime to an absolute *theocracy:* henceforth God remains
personally in Sion to govern his people (v. 3). The house of David
seems no longer to have a role to play in the realization of this
theocracy. This affirmation is especially remarkable since in his
preceding work the author constantly linked the reign of Yahweh
with davidic institutions (1 Chr 17:10-14; 28:4-7; 2 Chr 13:4-8)
even to the point of forgetting the Sinai covenant. But it is rather
obvious that although David and Solomon served the theocracy,
their successors did not. From then on the Chronicler transfers to
the people of the future the theocratic perspectives reserved until
then for the davidic dynasty. The temple is no longer as in the
past the work of David and Solomon, but the fruit of the will of
God himself, expressed through the decrees of a Gentile king.

The temple foreseen by the Chronicler is thus freed of the dy-
nastic structures, but still other destructions and purifications are
needed before the lordship of God over the world and over
humanity finds in the man-God its true sign.

II. Proverbs
3:27-34
1st reading
2nd cycle
Monday

This passage is part of the introduction to the book of Proverbs (the 5th century before Christ). This indicates that it is relatively late and that the doctrine, in this case charity towards others, is the fruit of a secular reflection on the law.

The author formulates the precept about *love of neighbor* in a negative way, as if the virtue consists solely in "not doing," as if it were not a reality to be enhanced by action and involvement. However, he does not stick to a mere analysis of human behavior but refers to the intention that animates it.

By introducing the idea of love into the Jewish moral system, the author plants there a revolutionary ferment. In fact the morality of authority, so characteristic of the Jewish milieu, becomes through love, a morality of risk, for love is creative.

What is more, the morality of the law becomes through love a morality of grace. The law can only confront man, but as soon as morality no longer consists in the experience of that which is "ordered," but of that which is "given," the law has lost its exclusive authority.

III. Luke 8:16-18
Gospel
Monday

The parable of the lamp is probably found in its original form in Mark 4:21-25 (cf. his interrogative style, characteristic of a source close to the oral tradition). By adapting it, Luke did not deform it; it is the same and in a sense it is purer, for unlike Mark, he did not overload it with the parable about the measure (Mk 4:24).

a) Originally the parable of the lamp was, so it seems, a simple proverb used to stress the necessity of *becoming active*. No one who has grasped the truth can keep it quiet; every aspect of his life must be influenced by it. Luke reinforces this interpretation in his ending for verse 16, which is his own.

b) However, during the course of its transmission this proverb on *effectiveness* became an allegory on the ministry of Jesus. Verse 17 verifies this: "There is nothing hidden" designates, in fact (less clearly however than in Mk 4:22-23), the *teaching of Jesus*, temporarily hidden and not understood by the crowd until the day he is manifested to the consternation of those who have not understood (v. 18).

c) Finally, the second half of the last verse confers an eschatological interpretation on the lamp. It describes the eschatological *manifestation* of the light announced in verse 17. Those who will have known the secrets of the Kingdom will enjoy its fullness ("To the man who has, more will be given"), just as those who have heard the Word will bear fruit (Lk 8:15, a verse which immediately precedes our passage). In contrast, those who have barely understood the secrets will find themselves relieved of the little they have received, like the various types of ground described in Lk 8:11-15 which lose not only their fruit but even the seed they have received.

The idea then is perfectly clear at the conclusion of the parable about the sower: the word of Christ is a seed or a lamp; it is made to produce fruit or light. As long as the Word of God is proclaimed in the rule of faith, it is like a lamp under the bed: one sees only a slight brightness; it is even necessary to resign oneself to it with confidence and fidelity so that it truly gives light. But the kingdom is growing; the lamp will one day pass to the lampstand and will glorify those who in secret and mystery have put their trust in its rays.

Let us simply reflect on the parable of the lamp and the themes of *effectiveness* and *yield*. They are from those Scriptures which are never very concerned with seeking out the mythical and ontological principles of reality but rather are concerned more with practicality and effectiveness. When it says that God is true, it does not claim to reach his essence, it simply analyzes and measures his fidelity in man's history. There is in Scripture a pragmatism that shares somewhat the modern mentality where thought is less concerned with "essences" than with the functioning of society and the effectiveness of the activities in which we are involved.

There is certainly a danger of absolutizing pragmatism, but it is essential that the Christian derive from the gospel a mentality that permits him to place himself in the world as being ready to "witness the truth."

IV. Ezra 6:7-8, The Persian kings who had just laid the foun-
12b, 14-20 dations for their empire by the conquest of
1st reading Babylon, were conscious of the centrifugal
1st cycle forces of their vast territory. They were tolerant
Tuesday of special customs and especially local religious
practices. The Jews carefully preserved the official text authorizing the reconstruction of a national forum around the temple (Ezr 1:2-4) and above all an administrative note (Ezr 6:2-5) specifying financial aid granted by Cyrus for the reconstruction of the sanctuary.

The construction of the new temple of Jerusalem was completed the first of April, 515. Immediately thereupon the rites for the new *Passover* were celebrated (Ezr 6:21-22). But the liturgy was modified and the Levites reserved for themselves the right to sacrifice the Pasch (v. 20), excluding the laity (Dt 16:2; Ex 12:6). What is more, by inaugurating the temple within the context of a Passover feast, the Jews gave it priority over the ancient feast of Tabernacles. Now, the feast of Passover stresses less than that of Tabernacles, man's affinity to nature: it is more concerned with his history and with the manner in which he adapts himself to it. Whereas the feast of Tabernacles celebrates the fruit and grain harvest, Passover celebrates the liberation of man, the progress of the people from the Exodus to the return from exile.

In time Christians will also suppress the feast of Tabernacles from the calendar in preference for the more humane feast that is their liberation in Jesus Christ and the liberation of the world in the Church.

V. Proverbs This passage belongs to the most ancient part
21:1-6, 10-13 of the collection of Proverbs. Many exegetes
1st reading believe that most of these maxims were
2nd cycle grouped together in the time of Solomon. The
Tuesday connections between them are either nonexist-
ent or artificial. Here, however, the first group
of proverbs (vv. 1-6) have a common theme, the *knowledge* which
God has of things and human intentions in contrast to the superficial knowledge of man, especially when wickedness obscures his
vision.

The maxims which follow (vv. 10-13) describe this *wickedness*
and put the just man on guard against it.

VI. Luke 8:19-21 Luke probably separated this passage from its
Gospel original context (still obvious in Mk 3:31-35)
Tuesday in order to use it as the conclusion to Jesus'
parables on sowing and the lamp (Lk 8:4-18).
Thus he gives this reading a special meaning.

a) This incident between Jesus and his family is placed immediately after the parables of the Sower and the Lamp, both of
which are geared towards the elaboration of a doctrine of the
Word. It is also in some way a parable. Just as there is already
good ground or a lamp on the lampstand, so those who hear the
Word and practice it are the *family* of Jesus in the sense that they
share his life and can count on his support in all circumstances, as
was then the custom in families.

b) Because the Son of God became flesh, he faced the inevitable
generation gap and transgressed the rules of the family milieu.
This rupture was neither revolt nor opposition, but the necessary
and painful road towards personal autonomy where we encounter
the only absolute there is: the Father in heaven.

Now, religious systems and civil law tend to make the family absolute by consecrating the bonds which are created in it. In this respect Christ sows a seed for contention: the family is not unconditional; it is not the exclusive goal in life.

VII. Ezra 9:5-9   After the exile, despite the universalist influ-
1st reading   ence of the books of Ruth and Jonah and the
1st cycle   texts of the law authorizing marriage with
Wednesday   strangers (Gn 41:45; Nb 12), the trend towards
strict observance will be used to forbid a union with pagan women, both to preserve Jewish blood (Ezr 9:2) and so that man can be presented before God in purity (Ezr 9:1, 11).

Ezra was in favor of this doctrine and he views marriages contracted with strangers as the cause of all the evils that continued to plague the Jews when they returned to Palestine. In the context of evening prayer he directs a penitential prayer to God containing just as many exhortations to the people as supplications to God and largely inspired by deuteronomic ideas and vocabulary.

The consciousness of sin is the first sentiment which the author of this *penitential* prayer presents to God. Man cannot encounter God except in humility (vv. 6-7), for what power could his pride have before the transcendence of God, when sin annihilates all his efforts.

But this sentiment of prostration gives place to an act of thanksgiving, for God manifests his goodness and pardon towards sinners by allowing a remnant to remain which he permits to reestablish the temple (vv. 8-9). The principle aim of the penitential prayer is not the expression of the sinfulness of the one praying. Such an attitude would turn man in on himself and would be, all things considered, only a psychological matter. The object of prayer is God himself, and through it God is continually present to man despite his sin, forever pardoning and reconciling the sinner to himself in fidelity to his plan of love.

VIII. Proverbs
30:5-9
1st reading
2nd cycle
Wednesday

This extract belongs to a group of proverbs which were joined rather late to the collection of Solomon and ascribed to a certain Agur, probably a fictitious name. However its Arabic origin is a witness to the importance of this strange wisdom in the culture of the Hebrew people after the exile.

a) The first two verses describe the word of God and its purity and ask that the faithful man not interpret it according to his own insights. Perhaps the author has in mind the growth of rabbinical schools which are beginning to modify their manner of *teaching*. The rabbis in fact are not concerned, like the prophets, with being faithful interpreters of the thought of God; they seek rather to defend their own ideas, more like casuistry and philosophy than the will of God.

b) The second part of the reading (vv. 7-9) deals with the idea of the *just milieu* that is proper to the wise man of Israel; neither too rich or too poor, for the two extremes make communication with God difficult. This is the ideal of the middle class, the intellectual bourgeoisie who count the risks and, in order to reach it, repress suffering, passion and desires, such elements as are quite indispensable for participation in the paschal mystery.

IX. Luke 9:1-6
Gospel
Wednesday

This is Luke's version of the discourse on the mission of the Twelve to the Jews. In two verses Luke defines its objective: to proclaim the Good News of the Kingdom, to heal and to cast out demons (vv. 1-2). The coming of the Kingdom thus appears as interrelated with the victory over evil (cf. Mk 16:17-20).

Luke interprets rather liberally the discourse about the mission. For example, he omits certain directives of Christ (cf. Mt 10:5-6) in order to preserve only the elements that shed light on the mission of the Church.

The description of how the one sent should live reflects in fact the experience of the primitive Church, especially its ideal of poverty. Although Matthew 10:10 considered the need for justifying the commands on poverty, Luke provides no justification: in his eyes poverty has value in itself since it is indispensable to the Kingdom that comes (Lk 6:20; 14:25-33; 16:19-31; 18:18-30).

The practices of the early Church likewise appear in the array of instructions about the problem of lodging for the missionary (v. 4; cf. Ac 9:43; 16:15; 17:7; 18:3; 13:51).

In rereading the discourse about the mission in view of the primitive missionary experience, Luke accomplishes one important step towards the definition of the apostle's role. The actual formulation does not yet appear in this account, but the idea is already present.

"Disciples" of a rabbi who speaks with authority, the "Twelve" were all convinced that they would be judges of the eschatological people (cf Mt 19:28). However, after the resurrection they understood that they ought to be, above all, witnesses of the death and resurrection of Jesus. Still, that is not enough for defining the idea of an apostle: the Twelve did not have a monopoly on it, neither as disciples of Christ nor as witnesses of his resurrection. It seems that it is in the school of Paul that Luke discovered this idea, based above all on the command of Jesus (theme of the one "sent," in vv. 1-2) and on its universal extension (whence no allusions here to the territorial restrictions supplied by Mt 10:5-6).

Putting aside the role of Peter, the Twelve went to work at founding the Judaeo-Christian community and, somewhat paradoxically, it is Paul, one who did not belong to the group, who especially takes the apostolic function upon himself. But without the efforts and help of those first sent to witness, there would be no Church. For its faith and that of its members is connected with their faith in the Good News they proclaimed.

X. Haggai 1:1-8 Cyrus has just authorized the return of the
1st reading Jews to Palestine and the reconstruction of their
1st cycle temple (537; cf. Ezr 1:2-4; 6:3-5). Once back in
Thursday Sion, the exiles are eager to rebuild it though
not losing sight of their need to insure their
sustenance, however precarious, because of the poverty of the
land (v. 6).

It is within this context that the prophet Haggai speaks during a
four month period in 520. His message is directed to the temple
and to its cult. He often refers to the prophecy of Ezechiel and
shares the views of Third-Isaiah and of the prophet Zechariah,
his contemporaries.

Once back in the country the Israelites begin to construct comfortable homes (v. 4) and to work the land. But they are anxious
about their failure (v. 6). Haggai then invites them to reconstruct
the temple in order to receive abundance in return (cf. Hg 2:15-19).
The prophet thus became the instigator of the cultural theocracy,
the direction the nation will take in the years ahead. Material
blessings are closely bound to the temple cult and we can already
foresee that the priests will not hesitate to regulate the conduct of
the faithful in order to assure more visibly than ever the bond between the temple and life.

Haggai's perspective is interesting. The prophet has an intuition
about the profound unity between life and ritual, and he devotes
himself to this in the manner of his predecessors. But he sees this
unity apart from ritual and in the direction of life, as if the first
must give meaning to the second. The modern technical era seems,
on the contrary, to give life an autonomous meaning with respect
to ritual: the layman is united directly to God in his life, where
he learns to read his presence and his action, and he no longer
experiences the same need for ritual as his ancestors.

The relationship between ritual and life is basically changed in
comparison to that which Haggai knew, but the need for their

relevance remains. Any life, even religious, which cannot be expressed ritually will not last long, not only because it would lack expression on the psychological plane but also because it would sever itself from the source of all holiness: the temple of the perfect priesthood where Jesus offered once for all the oblation which makes all life sacrificial and liturgical.

XI. Ecclesiastes   In contrast to Job, "Qoheleth" is a man upon
1:2-11   whom happiness and fortune seem to have
1st reading   smiled. But the meaning of existence disquiets
2nd cycle   him just as much as it does Job, for if the latter
Thursday   revolts against the senselessness of suffering,
Qoheleth sees only vanity in a happiness which
leaves one unsatisfied. He belongs to a world in which the idea of
the beyond is practically unknown: the solution he seeks must then,
in his mind, be found "under the sun" and it is in the light of this
that the meaning of life must be sought.

According to Qoheleth, if we settle only for the light of the sun
to see the value of life, we need to conclude that there is nothing
that is worth the pain of having lived. If man has only man to shed
light on what he is and if the world has only the world, so to speak,
then there is nothing but *vanity* (v. 2). And the cause is to be
found in the cyclic character of life (vv. 4-9): all is repeated
indefinitely in a sad monotony and if man thinks he has discovered
something new, it is only because his memory is faulty (vv. 10-11).
Even the four elements (vv. 4-7) undergo a perpetual beginning
anew; but they remain, whereas man changes without knowing
the joy of enduring (v. 3).

Ecclesiastes does not have that sense of history which would
permit him to share the optimism of Psalm 103/104 or of Job 38-40
about the world. His wisdom is not yet enlightened by meditation

on the history of salvation which no longer carries a cyclic character, but it hastens the experience of liberty for man and for God. He does not hope enough in his own times regardless how new the gifts of God are. And because he does not know the meaning of history, he likewise does not know the meaning of man. He cannot imagine him freed from constraint and alienation and capable of collaborating in the construction of God's time. He is the spokesman for those who, not having before their eyes the fullness of revelation, despair of the world and of life or who wait for the day their true significance is revealed.

Even in his pessimism Qoheleth is the witness beforehand of a sort of "Christianity without God." Conscious of the anguish and the absurd, he does not want to resort to God who would dispel absurdity, but by alienation. It is only at the heart of man's vanity that a response to his anguish can be found. But in order to formulate this response, a man will have to bear this vanity even to death. Qoheleth, like modern existentialism, awaits the man Jesus and his death.

By celebrating in the Eucharist the memorial of an event that is past yet always new, "until he comes again," the Christian shows the liberty which the Lord brings to humanity in spite of the determinism of a universe which would not take its meaning from a beyond.

XII. Luke 9:7-9   This gospel reading relates Herod's opinion of
Gospel   Jesus. In Matthew and in Mark it serves as an
Thursday   introduction to the account of the martyrdom
of John the Baptist. But Luke, in contrast,
places the episode after the mission of the apostles, thereby showing that Jesus is truly the awaited prophet.

Herod deals with the news circulating among the people about the personality of Jesus. He sets aside the possibility of a reincarnation of the Baptist (v. 9), but he believes in a reappearance of one of the great *prophets:* Elijah or some other (vv. 7-8; cf. Luke 9:18-19; 7:16; 9:17).

We can easily understand the popular belief. Prophecy was extinct for a long time in Israel and they were waiting for God to break this silence at long last by sending a new Moses (Dt 18:15) or a new Elijah (Ml 3:23). The return of a prophet belonged then to the eschatological hope which he fulfills. But if they are in doubt about the identity of this envoy, they knew that he would come to announce the final secrets of God and to urge penance, to restore the chosen people to its integrity and to conquer its enemies.

Jesus takes up his task as the prophets of Israel did. He passes on the word of God by causing the divine aspect of events to appear—concretely the healings which he performs—but above all he places his own person at the heart of the proclamation of the Word. Luke understood this and he is the only one of the evangelists who stresses the welcome Jesus gave to the crowds (Lk 9:11). These were to sense the radical unity between his Word, the Kingdom that he announces, and his person. His share of personal compromise will become greater and greater throughout his ministry: true prophets in fact experience the word of God in a singular manner and many have pushed this experience of God even to the point of death (Mt 23:37-38). Jesus, too, knows that his prophetic role is going to lead to his death (Lk 13:33, a text that is proper to Luke and which goes to prove that he was sensitive to the prophetic aspect of Jesus).

Thus the title, prophet, given to Jesus gathers together a good part of his earthly witness: his preaching, his miracles, his exhortations to penance and his references to the end of time, his fidelity to the message even to death.

The Eucharist prolongs the prophetic activity of Jesus, not only because the gospel is proclaimed there but because the Kingdom that comes is displayed and the memory of the fidelity of the prophet of the truth to which he was the witness, is accomplished there.

XIII. Haggai   This oracle, probably the third pronounced by
    2:1b-10   Haggai, is in reality the continuation of Haggai
    1st reading   2:15-19 which was spoken on the 24th day of
    1st cycle   the sixth month in order to announce that the
    Friday   continuation of the building of the temple
    would lead to material prosperity. The opti-
mism of the prophet is explained no doubt by the festal atmosphere
of this day. One month later, the final day in the octave for the
feast of Tabernacles (Lv 23:36; 39:43; Nb 29:32-34; Jn 7:37), Haggai will announce not only material happiness but the approaching
messianic era.

This *messianic era* is no longer centered, as it was for the ancient
authors on the davidic dynasty but on the temple and its worship.
Haggai transfers to these the blessings so long awaited from the
hands of the royal Messiah: the closeness and presence of God (v.
4b; Is 11:1-5; 7:14; Jr 30:11), the outpouring of the Spirit of God
(v. 5b; cf. Ez 36:27; 37:14; 39:29; Jl 3:1-2), the assurance of peace
(v. 9; cf. Is 9:5-6; Mi 5:4), the ascent of the nations to Sion (v. 7;
cf. Is 44:5; 45:14-24; 60:3-9).

The messianic era is the image of salvation. But there is the
danger of giving the wrong idea by stressing the supernatural and
eschatological aspect. In fact, salvation remains supernatural from
the very moment it becomes ours and it is ours without ceasing to
be supernatural. In other words, salvation, to be supernatural, need
not come entirely from a source external to ourselves; and to be
ours, it need not be completely immanent.

It would be so if salvation were "something" before which
man had simply to place himself, a gift from God which man had
only to receive, an order which God causes to prevail. Salvation is
an encounter between God and man where each accomplishes the
entire journey; it is a covenant in which the common action which
consecrates it is entirely the work of each cooperator.

This rule is especially true for the sacraments which are the visible signs of the messianic era, but which are only fully operative when both the grace of God and the faith of man are present.

XIV. Ecclesi- It is impossible to date this work (2nd or 3rd
astes 3:1-11 century before Jesus Christ). Its author, like-
1st reading wise, is unknown. It is a book full of melan-
2nd cycle choly.
Friday   The author seems to have submitted already
              before the time to the secularization which we
experience and to have really tried to live the terrestrial realities without reference to any explanation external to itself. But apparently even human history loses its "meaning."

The poem used today takes up the theme of Ecclesiastes 1:4-11, about the rhythm of the world. The author enumerates eighteen contrasting actions which give rhythm to the life of man according to a law, sometimes of necessity, sometimes by chance. Man knows only that for a given action the contrary will succeed and that he is not the master of the time in which this reversal of a situation occurs and that he does not control this alternation which punctuates *time*.

Thus man cannot always act in the same manner; he is led to contradict himself continually, always beginning over again. Things have their time: this time once completed, they disappear and give place to others. Others, by their very nature, are called according to a rhythm and an inescapable periodicity.

This alternation is deceptive because it makes all continuity in the effort impossible; it is however a source of happiness since it allows itself to be liberated from past actions and to forget what has not been pleasing (vv. 9-10).

Yes, times passes, but this endless disappearance of time is not only death, it also involves birth. Man parts company at every moment and painfully with the present, but this is not necessarily simply negative. On the contrary, it reveals that the insertion of man into time removes in him a spiritual need of his deepest self. Certainly he is subject to the universal mobility and each of these actions is borne away by the flux of history, but the fact that he feels this extreme mobility as sorrow proves that he is made for an eternal and immutable possession of himself and of things.

This does not imply that this stable possession can be attained by avoiding the flow of time. On the contrary, it is by living it as a continual death and by consenting to this latter that the fluctuation of time becomes the terrain of the myserious accomplishment of a new and permanent time at the very heart of the decomposition of the present time.

Thus in final analysis time has a meaning which does not come to it from outside or from an alienating beyond, but from itself: by offering to each his temporary condition, he proposes to him at the same time an assent to death which is conversion and participation in the paschal mystery.

XV. Luke
9:18-22
Gospel
Friday

Peter's confession (vv. 18-21), the prophecy of the passion (v. 22) and the teaching about the conditions for becoming a disciple of Jesus (vv. 23-26) were not originally recounted together. Peter's confession, of which we have the primitive version in Matthew (16:13-20), was originally the introduction to the discourse call "ecclesiastical" (Mt 18; cf. in both passages Peter's predominant role and the identical phrases, etc.). The prophecy of the passion on the other hand, and the list of conditions for discipleship, must have originally belonged to the passion narrative, of which they would have formed the prologue. The first portion then is of apocalyptic genre, and ecclesiological in purpose. The second is prophetic, and concerned with the passion.

Before the final redaction of the synoptics, these two differing traditions had been conjoined, for literary and theological reasons, to the point that Mark 8:27-31 makes them the central axis of the gospel. His first part which is centered on the Messiah, ends with the first; and his second part, centered on the suffering Servant, begins with the second.

The Lucan version of the traditions is the least satisfactory, unfortunately. Luke is at this stage eager to broach the most important part of his gospel, the journey to Jerusalem (Lk 9:51-18:14). Consequently he makes chapter 9 a sort of hasty appendix, dividing his first part from the account of the great journey. It contains some important elements which he could not avoid mentioning, but his treatment of them is sometimes cursory. Thus he says nothing about Peter's vocation (Mt 16:17-19), or about Jesus' response to Peter's lack of faith (Mt 16:22-23). He omits all geographical precisions. These would tend to distract attention at the point where he is about to give us the journey to Jerusalem.

a) From the very start Jesus wishes to have from the Twelve an affirmation of his *Messiahship*. They do so affirm it through the mouth of Peter, having first discarded other possible hypotheses. However, according to current notions, their idea of Messiahship remains ambiguous, with some suggestion of a restoration of the Kingdom by violence and a judgment of the nations. Accordingly Jesus imposes silence on them, suggesting that there can be no true Messiahship without death and resurrection.

At a particular point in his ministry Jesus became aware of what Messiahship would really mean for him, and he conveyed this knowledge to his followers. It is noteworthy that the insight came to him during prayer (v. 18). In his anxiety to respond as perfectly as possible to God's will he did not wish his Messiahship to have any political or vengeful overtones (cf. Mt 8:4-10). It would be all gentleness and pardon. The choice was not an easy one to make, or to sustain. It engendered opposition of every kind and soon he became aware that it would lead him to his death (v. 22). The agony of the decision can be imagined. The messianic call must be answered: it must be pursued with inadequate means in an atmosphere of gentleness, and there was always the realization that death must intervene before it could be realized. Surely the meaning must be that God's design was accomplishment on the other side of death. God would not abandon him to death. So Jesus begins to proclaim his ressurrection (v. 22).

b) Each time that he is about to make an important decision or embark on a new stage of his ministry, Luke shows us Christ in prayer (cf. Lk 3:21; 6:12; 9:29; 11:1; 22:31-39). Indeed he is the only one to tell us (v. 18) of Christ's prayer before he secures a profession of faith from his followers and tells them of his passion. As in the other Lucan instances, the suggestion is that Jesus is praying about a mission, the dimensions of which he can see only in vague outline. But why does Jesus pray? To give his apostles an example? This would be ludicrous on his part, to pray knowing full well in advance the unfolding of events. This is simply a very weak explanation supplied by theologians who fruitlessly maintain that Jesus had an exact knowledge of the future.

Jesus prays because he does not know the future as with all men. His human will was incapable of itself of accomplishing his mission: consequently he asks for God's help and he seeks insight. As in the case of every man, the future was dark for Jesus.

The prayer of Jesus is then real: it shows us that he faces the mystery of death that is on the horizon of his ministry in the darkness of his consciousness and human knowledge.

If the prayer of Jesus proves the reality of his humanity, it is not the least sign of his divinity. This prayer is in fact impossible to man, for it is not a discourse that has God as an object. It has God as its subject, who knows the depth in us which we must reach to pray, but which we can attain only with the help of his Spirit (Rm 8:26-27). That Jesus could reach in his prayer the depth of his person where his messianic vocation begins is an indication that he draws upon the Spirit of his Father.

**XVI. Zechariah
2:5-9,
10-11a**
*1st reading
1st cycle
Saturday*

The prophet began his ministry just as Haggai was finishing his (520-218; cf. Zc 1:1; 7:1). Only the first eight chapters of his book can be attributed to him; the others (9-14) are by one or several later prophets. Zechariah does not possess the originality of his predecessors and his "visions" are simply anthologies of the most significant passages found in Ezechiel and Isaiah.

Thus the third vision of Zechariah is identical with that of Ezechiel (Ez 41:13). This flashback is willful. The prophets invite the surveyors to measure fully the site of the future temple and the outline of the new ramparts: the future city must one day be the gathering place for all nations. Thus, they do not hesitate to do things in a big way (v. 4; Jr 31:27-29; Is 49:19-20; 54:2-3), and in constructing the ramparts they do not lose sight of the fact that Yahweh himself is the real protector of Jerusalem (v. 5; Is 36-37). After this vision the prophet presents a song of acclamation that is inspired by past poems of a *universal* nature: the call to joy (v. 14) comes from Zephaniah (Zp 3:14), the proclamation of a universal covenant (v. 15) is an extract from Second Isaiah (Is 45:22).

The universalism of Zechariah is noble, for it is affirmed at a moment when the Jewish ghetto is being formed and when fidelity to Yahweh is synonymous with xenophobia. Sometimes the prophet is not very personal and he even professes a universalism more narrow than that of Second Isaiah (Is 44:5; 45:14-24; 51:4-5). Thus the wall of fire with which God protects Jerusalem is the replica of the column of fire which separates the Hebrew from the Egyptians in the desert (Ex 14:19-20).

By associating the reconstruction of the temple with the promises about universality, Zechariah lays the groundwork for the notion of worship as missionary sign which will be fully realized only in Jesus Christ (Mt 21:12-17; Ac 11:19-20). The worshiping community gives glory to God to the extent that it shows to the world the call which God addresses to all men (Rm 15:15-16).

XVII. Ecclesi- Qoheleth's final words of advice are directed to
astes young people. They are based on a dictum
11:9-12:8 which encourages the young to enjoy them-
1st reading selves (v. 9) and are expressed in sensitive and
2nd cycle poetic terms.
Saturday

        a) The exhortation of Qoheleth is partly op-
timistic. *Youth* must be made the most of, lived as a gift knowing
the while that it is fleeting (v. 10). Aging is present, watching
us (v. 1).

b) The author describes *aging* at one time as twilight, at another
as winter (vv. 2-5a). But he is troubled at seeing old age immobilize
a life whereas nature does not cease to live and to renew itself (v.
5b). Four images symbolize death (v. 6) and the conclusion is
quickly drawn: man is definitely merely dust (v. 7), his body returns to the earth (Gn 2:7; 3:19) and his breath to God (Jb 12:10;
Ws 15:16). All is decidedly vanity.

Qoheleth judiciously stresses the emptiness of human life and
the meaning of old age, while revering and encouraging the vitality
of youth which must be lived as a gift.

The actual bond between generations must be clarified in the
light of this attitude. Is it really trusting youth to induce it to model
itself as quickly as possible after preestablished structures? Is it
placing confidence in youth to propose to it a society without
vision, where responsibilities and the important positions are outside its reach?

How can the young discover God if the only area in which he is
present to them, their life and their youth, is forbidden territory?

XVIII. Luke For the second time Jesus reveals the immi-
9:44b-45 nence of his Passion. In St. Luke the words he
Gospel uses differ rather obviously from those which
Saturday the other synoptics attribute to him, and not
only with reference to this second announce-

ment of the Passion (Mt 17:22-23; Mk 9:30-31) but also in the
other two. The variation involves a rather important element:
Jesus announces that he is going to be delivered over to the tribunal, but he speaks neither of his death (nevertheless it is a practical
conclusion to the foregoing), nor of his resurrection. It is then only
a step (to take the step too quickly involves risk) to affirming that
he has in reality expressed his conviction about the brutal end to
his mission and that it is the primitive community which added to
this declaration the certainty of his immediate resurrection.

The essential declaration of Christ concerns the union in his
person of the two images, *Son of Man*, an image of transcendence
(Dn 7:13), and *Servant* "delivered up" (Is 53:8). The Son of Man
has a heavenly origin (which does not however necessarily presuppose his divinity), but an earthly mission, one concerned with
the history of human kingdoms. Jesus reveals that this earthly mission fades with the death of the Servant.

But this confrontation between the role of the Son of Man and
the Servant automatically inspires in the consciousness of Jesus
the hope of resurrection. The Son of Man is too bound up with
the Parousia for his existence to end with the death of the Servant.
Certainly he must assume his function with limitations and suffering, but this mission will be fulfilled in eschatological glory. Christ
himself has then announced his resurrection and has become certain of it by simple meditation on his vocation as Son of Man and
as Servant.

But the apostles do not understand this association between two
titles that for them are contradictory (v. 45). Why must the Son of
Man suffer to attain the Kingdom?

TWENTY-SIXTH WEEK

I. Zechariah
8:1-8
1st reading
1st cycle
Monday

Chapter 8 of Zechariah gathers together some oracles which have as their common theme the messianic salvation (vv. 2-8).

These poems are probably more original than the preceding visions. The prophet permits his sensitivity and his emotion to come through (v. 3), but he does not fail to refer to the preceding anthology (v. 4 and Is 65; v. 3 and Is 60:14; 62:4, 12; v. 8 and Jr 31:31).

The prophet's love for *Jerusalem* shines through each of the oracles. We could say that here Zechariah shares the ardent jealousy of God (v. 1). He is in every way convinced that God is present in the heart of the city as he was in the column of fire and in the tent in the desert (Ex 24:9-11; Nb 12:4-6; Ex 25:8-9; 40:34-35, etc.). This divine presence is a gauge of stability: the old shall see their small children (vv. 4-5). He will bring marvels into being, but what action is really surprising in the sight of Yahweh (v. 6)? In every case God will bring the exiles back and will seal a definitive covenant (v. 8). He will accomplish all this out of "jealousy": his love for Jerusalem is such that no obstacle could destroy it, no failure on the part of the people compromise his work.

II. Job 1:6-22
1st reading
2nd cycle
Monday

Since the book of Job probably dates from the 4th century, it is contemporary with Plato. It's main concern is a religious crisis. The Jew at that time no longer meekly submits himself to the law; he probes events and scrutinizes rules, taking a position inspired by the skepticism and by the individualism of the Greeks. He questions providence and the value of human life, the meaning of suffering and of retribution.

103

Job is the name of a person from Syrophoenician folklore in whom Ezechiel (14:12-20) sees a type of the just man of prehistoric times. Numerous legends circulated very likely about him and the redactor from the 4th century probably rewrote one of them for the prologue of his work.

a) The first scene unfolds in heaven. God is presented as a *potentate* living ostentatiously, surrounded by a court of servants and of "angels" (the sons of Elohim: v. 6). Among these last is Satan who disparages humanity before the monarch (v. 7). He has nothing to reproach Job with, but in his eyes he is just only because he enjoys the prosperity which God grants him. And Satan challenges Yahweh: he does not believe in the justice of man, he does not believe in morality without obligation or sanction. By taking up the challenge God truly acts like a despot for whom neither possessions or persons count (v. 12).

b) The second scene takes place on earth where various *curses* fall upon Job who loses successively his lands, his cattle and his children. But he stands up to the trial. He mourns and celebrates the rites (v. 20) without showing any revolt. Satan has lost the first round.

III. Luke 9:46-50 The two episodes united in this passage have
Gospel   nothing in common except the use of the
Monday   "name" of Jesus (vv. 48-49). This characteristic
                  blending of the first oral traditions of the gospels is not however absolutely artificial, for it is the replica of the mission of the Twelve (Lk 9:1-6). Jesus had then given to the apostles the power to head (which amounts to healing in his name) and makes some observations on the kind of welcome and the audience which they would encounter. He reveals here that the welcoming of the lowly and the poor is a welcome "in his name" and that every healing is an action "in his name." The semitic

redactional process of inclusion is then at the origin of this combination of texts.

a) To heal or to cast out demons *in the name* of Jesus is a power granted to the apostles by Christ (Lk 10:17; Mk 16:17; Mt 7:22-23; Ac 3:6; 16:18, 19; Jm 5:14). Jesus himself possesses the power to heal and has no need to turn to an outside authority (Mk 11:28). It is not the same with his apostles who have this power at their disposal only by a sort of delegation of the powers of Jesus and by a profession of faith (Ac 3:16) in his person and in his name.

They can then cast out demons and prolong the messianic action of Christ only by recourse to his authority and by expressing their faith in it, through the accomplishment of healing. This is the reason why Jesus does not fear those who secretly use his name to exorcise (vv. 49-50): they can do it only by faith in his salvific power.

b) The *welcome* of the child "in the name of Jesus" (v. 48) sets a new direction. The name of Jesus also possesses a power of assembling and of relationship. It is in his name that an assembly of Christians gather to deliberate (1 Co 5:3-5). In all these cases the name of Jesus designates more exactly his lordship, that power acquired after the resurrection, which he used to organize his Church, also utilizing it when necessary to advance his reign in beings such as a child or a humble apostle.

IV. Zechariah 8:20-23
1st reading
1st cycle
Tuesday

Zechariah is open to universalism. The heavenly Jerusalem which he celebrates and the construction of which he sings is not a ghetto; it opens its doors widely to the Gentiles.

The meaning of the return from exile appears to Zechariah as essentially missionary. This is not simply the return of exiles to their country. They have in fact displayed in the Gentile country an attitude such that it brings these Gentiles to accompany them to Palestine in order to discover the secret of their faith and to rally there (cf. Zc 2:15). There is nothing political in this *universalism* that is inherited from Third-Isaiah (Is 60:4-13) and essentially motivated by faith (cf. the profession of faith in verse 23b).

V. Job 3:1-3,   Job is not the first to curse the day of his birth.
   11-17, 20-23   In fact, Jeremiah has left an interesting exam-
   1st reading   ple of this type of literature (Jr 20:14-18). With
   2nd cycle   Jeremiah however the emphasis is personal and
   Tuesday   dramatic; with Job the drama disappears be-
         neath the style and the myth, beneath the
vehemence and the violence.

Job does not formulate any curse against God, but he curses his work in words that are pathetic. He even curses the day of his birth, that is to say, the position of the stars which bring him his misfortune (v. 1): he holds in execration the night of his conception (vv. 3 and 7) and the day which saw him born (vv. 3 and 4). He also regrets that he was born alive (vv. 11-12, 16, this last is probably misplaced; cf. Ps 57/58:9-10). Stillborn, he, the lowly, the unfortunate one, would have joined the powerful and the rich in sheol (vv. 13-15).

These last verses are the most important. Job asks the why of suffering (vv. 20-23), the important question for man. There remains for the unfortunate simply to ask God the reason for his misfortune.

To curse is to affirm the devilish character of life; it is to define evil as the converse of good. But to question is to ask whether evil exhausts the meaning of life. The simple fact that one "why" slips into the core of the curse, with indignation and revolt before evil, suffices to prove that existence is not reduced to evil. In fact, why these questions unless man is capable of proving the contradiction between fact and law? Why can man ask the why of evil unless it is because he can become engrossed in it and retreat from it? And in the name of what, save a dynamism written in him and from which God alone had the secret?

VI. Luke 9:51-56 This passage begins a long section, exclusively
Gospel Lucan, that concludes only with Luke 18:14. It
Tuesday contains of course a number of items that we
find in other synoptics, but the third evangelist
modifies them much more arbitrarily than he does in other chapters. He adds special comments and in general manipulates everything to illustrate the particular theme that is so characteristic of him: such as the one (or several) journey of Christ and his followers towards Jerusalem. Indeed, when we consider style, the rarity of geographical and chronological data, the Aramaic vocabulary, and the repetition of certain times that have already appeared in the earlier section, this section seems almost like an independent gospel within a gospel.

a) The first verse is a very solemn introduction to the great theme of Jesus' journeys to Jerusalem. There is emphasis on the Johannine themes: the fulfillment of time (cf. Jn 13:1), the "taking up" from the world (John will speak of "glorification": Jn 7:39; 12:16, 22; 13:31-32; cf. Jn 12:32) and Jesus' determination to follow his destiny to the end ("resolutely": cf. Jn 18:4; 19:11). Thus, in this verse which foreshadows clearly the mystery of Christ's death, we have the key to the whole passage. The evangelist immediately goes on to consider the conditions necessary in order to be Christ's *disciple*, not only just now, in the journey to Jerusalem, but also in the accomplishment of his destiny.

b) The first condition is *patience* in the face of failure. James and John thought they should have fire from heaven to deal with the hostile Samaritans (cf. 2 K 1:10-12). Jesus, however, consistent with his teaching in the parables of the darnel and the dragnet (cf. Mt 13:24-35 and 47-48), recommends his disciples to allow the necessary time for conversion and development (vv. 54-56).

VII. Nehemiah
2:1-8
1st reading
1st cycle
Wednesday

Nearly a century has elapsed since the edict of Cyrus authorizing the return of the Jews to Palestine (538). But the people were constantly on guard against invasions from neighboring people and against the hostilities of the Hebrews who had stayed on. On the other hand certain exiles were so well adapted to the Babylonian culture that they had no desire to return to the land of their origin. Nehemiah is one of those Jews who exercised a very special post in the court of Artaxerxes. The time has now arrived for the elite to rejoin their countrymen and to help them establish their structures.

Like Moses in Egypt, Nehemiah was formed in the political and juridical usage of the court of Artaxerxes. Now, the Hebrews who returned to Palestine did not come to organize themselves independently, especially since their traditions speak only of a utopian monarchy. Nehemiah, then, discovers his vocation: he cannot preserve his *competence* for himself alone or for the benefit of pagans; he must give the best he has for his people. Thus, he will go on a temporary mission to Palestine, as a specialist delegated for a time to a country in view of development and in order to provide counsel.

VIII. Job 9:1-12,
14-16
1st reading
2nd cycle
Wednesday

The three friends of Job come to mourn with him over his trial. One can speak about the problem of evil with someone who suffers: one never adequately answers the why of evil. However, it is to this end that Bildad devotes himself (Jb 8:1-22). First he recalls that God is just and that the trial born by Job can only be punishment for sin, his own or that of one of his children.

But Job's retort is violent: he does not admit suffering for sin and he enters an action against God. We can regret in this respect that the liturgical excerpt from this discourse is more concerned with the poetry of God's grandeur than with the actual indictment of Job against God (v. 14-35).

a) The divine power is described with clear detail. God removes the mountains (v. 5) where they claim the most important divinities were sheltered. He commands the stars (vv. 7-9) to maintain their omnipotence over the heavenly forces and the angelic beings. He holds in his hands the foundations of the earth and shakes them as he wills (v. 6). This terrible God adds still to his power by remaining invisible and ever elusive (vv. 10-11).

b) However, this list of divine power is not an end in itself. It shows above all how ridiculous and pretentious it is for Job to institute *proceedings* against God. How can man argue with such a God (vv. 1-4)? Even if he is right, how can he demonstrate it (v. 15)? This last observation is especially strong. But in that time an oriental would consider a judge as thoroughly unjust: he sees things from above in order to occupy the anxieties of his servants (vv. 16-24).

His friends counsel him to turn to God: Job rejects such a solution. Rather he would take the route of an indictment which God would have quickly crushed, that of a prayer which he would not even understand (Jb 9:25-31).

If the problem of evil has to find a solution in the omnipotence of God, it would be necessary then to deny that God is love and consequently we do not see what the Christian response would be. So long as man sticks to a notion of an all powerful God, he has no hope for a solution. He will find an explanation perhaps in the fact that he belongs to creation just as the mountains and the constellations of verses 4-13, but he will not understand the significance of suffering. Man has need of a God other than the all powerful in order to decipher the mystery and the meaning of suffering.

But how can Job—or any man in his situation—discover the meaning of suffering when God is silent (v. 11)? Certainly man often has the impression that God is silent because he closes his ears. But Job is innocent and indeed some beings are all ears. To these God no longer seems to speak.

Perhaps the silence of God is a form of his love and a manner of revealing himself? Could it not be an invitation to strip oneself of reason in order to place one's confidence in him who one day, perhaps when we are ripe for listening to him, will send among us his Word, crucified?

IX. Luke 9:57-62   Luke has just begun that part of his gospel
Gospel   which is most dear to him (Lk 9:51-56), that
Wednesday   which relates the (last?) journey of Christ to
                    Jerusalem. He immediately recalls the conditions necessary in order to follow Jesus. He has already spoken about patience (vv. 54-56): he now enunciates the other necessary qualities.

a) The second condition demanded of the disciples is *common life* with the master. As in all the rabbinic schools, this is manifested by the material services which the disciples perform for the rabbi (vv. 52-53; cf. Mt. 26:17-19). Christ being an itinerant master above all, common life with him will entail discomfort and poverty (vv. 57-58). The disciple may have to live in the open air, or content himself with whatever hospitality is offered, something that will train him to share the tragic destiny of the suffering Servant (Lk 14:27; 17:33).

b) A third characteristic of the disciple must be his *missionary involvement*, to which everything else is subordinated (vv. 59-60). The passage immediately following in this gospel (Lk 10:1-11) will stress this heavily, but it is already clear in verse 60. Here Christ demands from his disciples the severance of ties necessary for "proclaiming the Kingdom."

c) Finally the disciple must *renounce all human ties* (vv. 59-62). This follows the severity of Elias with his disciples (1 K 19:19-21). Several rabbis followed this tradition, and it was inherited by ancient monasticism (cf. again Lk 14:26). Following Christ then becomes really a state of life, of common life, which parallels a family life (vv. 59-62).

After the death of Christ, the recommendations tended to be interpreted rather more in the context of personal salvation than in that of service to the Kingdom of God (cf. Mk 10:17-26). The concept of disciple, which was originally confined to those persons who followed Jesus in his journeys through Palestine, was extended to the actual Christian state (Mt 10:42; 7:21-23).

There can be no doubt that St. Luke was influenced by this idea of the primitive community. Contrary to Mark and Matthew, he does not name the candidates called by Christ in order to address his message to each reader.

This means that even within the synoptic tradition the concept of following Christ has different meanings. In the gospel of John and in Paul's letters, the meaning will be completely different again. But there is always a common ground, and that is imitation of Jesus by communion in his life.

X. Nehemiah 8:1-4a, 5-6, 7b-12 *1st reading* *1st cycle* *Thursday*	A description of the importance of the feast of Tabernacles in 444 (?). The people are called to an assembly during the course of which the law will be read and interpreted, and the covenant with God sealed anew in order to give birth to Judaism proper.

a) The *feast of Tabernacles* was the most popular of the Jewish feasts, the end of the good season, culminating in grand rejoicing (v. 10). But the biblical writings spiritualized these manifestations and we can say that the assembly described in this excerpt constitutes the first fruits of this effort towards purification. Another effort will appear thereafter in the priestly milieu of the same century (cf. Lv 23:26-43).

b) The effort towards purification consists in transforming the feast of Tabernacles into an *assembly* of renewal of the Covenant, such as Deuteronomy 31:9-13 already prescribed it, and for which the ritual (proclamation of the law, the *Amen* acclamation by the people, etc.) literally applies the prescriptions of Deuteronomy 27:9-26 (v. 6). The Word has a special place there: it convokes the people; for seven days the Scriptures were read, translated and interpreted. The organizers attended to the understanding (v. 8) and to the adherence of the faithful (v. 6). The Word is thus constituative of the assembly, as it will be in Christianity (1 Co 12: 27-28). It convoked the first assembly in the desert (Ex 19-24) and will continually reassemble the faithful up to the moment when it will be made flesh in order to unify all men.

XI. Job 19:21-27   This passage has always been considered by
1st reading   tradition as one of the most important witnesses
2nd cycle   of the eschatology of the Old Testament. But
Thursday   later versions made modifications in it such as
can still be found, throughout the Hebrew text, the Syriac, the Greek or the Latin which has the greater possibility of being close to the thought of the author himself.

a) The basic meaning is however rather clear. Plunged into trial, Job reacts against the injustice. He dreams about a judgment where Yahweh would confound his detractors and would recognize his innocence. He would even be disposed to begin *proceedings* against God himself (Jb 9:1, 14-16; 13:18).

But the difficult trial and the horizon does not clear up. The suggested proceeding will not take place and Job is at the gates of death without having won his case (Jb 19:20). He wishes that his words were at least written in stone (vv. 23-24) so that one day, after his death, the proceeding can be unfolded, his pleading heard and his memory restored.

But he goes still further. Death, so dreaded, will perhaps be for him the occasion for standing before God, either under the form of a shadow or a scepter ("without my flesh" verse 26 and not "from my flesh"), and he knows that he will find a "vindicator" in the divine court of the angels (v. 25; cf. Jb 1).

In fact, Job will not institute proceedings: in time he will understand that the significance of suffering cannot be discovered on the juridical plane, but on the ontological. What is man that he should complain about his weakness and what is God that man should dispute him (Jb 40:8)?

b) The reading of Job 19:1-27 cannot support faith in a resurrection of the body. But it is a precious testimony for the will of man searching even in death for a beyond to death. It is also a precious avowal of man placing his cause in a *defender (goël:* Nb 35:19) who one day will be the Redeemer himself, defending so well his client that he will raise him up at the price of his own life.

Job's reflection thus becomes more precise as the discourses mount. At present he believes in the existence of a salvation in which he has confidence. Beyond death, a defender will arise to aid him. The salvation he awaits is not then earthly; every method of assuring here below a future without suffering escapes his preoccupation. Even individual holiness is unable to create a world without evil.

But, for the Christian, salvation is no longer purely celestial and it cannot be realized without taking account of reality and temporal responsibilities. Salvation is in the beyond, but it appears as such in the measure in which it is incarnate in the here and now of daily life: we are saved only in being savior. There is the complete difference separating Job from Christ.

XII. Luke **10:1-12** *Gospel* *Thursday*	Two different versions of the mission discourse have been preserved by the evangelists: the brief version in Mark 6:8-11 and Luke 9:3-5 which is directly concerned with the mission of the Twelve and the longer version, Luke 10:

2-16 which is concerned with the seventy (or seventy-two) disciples. Frequently, Luke stresses the particular traditions he inherited from the disciples' circle, where Matthew and Mark keep strictly to those traditions that emanated from the Twelve. Matthew 10:5-16 takes account of the two versions to which he has added outside material. It is sufficient to compare the longer and the shorter version on the one hand and the version of Matthew 10 and that of Luke 10 on the other to grasp the originality of the passage for that day.

a) It was perhaps the sight of a *harvest* field that provided the occasion for the discourse (v. 2; Mt 9:37-38; Jn 4:35-38). He transforms harvester of wheat into harvesters of men just as he has already done with fishermen. However, the harvest theme had in Scripture an important eschatological dimension (Am 9:13-15; Ps 125/126:5-6; Jl 4:13; Jr 5:17; Mt 13:28-39; Rv 14:15-16). It also contributes a particular dimension to the disciples' mission. This becomes the involvement here and now of humanity in the Kingdom that is coming. The mission is a prelude of the judgment of God because every divine Word has its function in judgment, in discernment of hearts. Consequently it is not surprising that the mission is destined sometimes to encounter persecution (v. 3).

b) Where Matthew's version gives a distinct apocalyptic flavor to this note of persecution (Mt 10:16-20), Luke prefers to confine himself to the practical counsels which Jesus gives the disciples. Buoyed up by messianic hope the object of which is close at hand, the disciple must no longer attach value to the means employed by the present world. Because the Kingdom is at hand he is dispensed from any occupation with terrestrial security. His poverty has a prophetic meaning (v. 4; cf. Lk 6:20).

Verse 7b however ("for the laborer is worth his wage") gives a more sociological and institutional emphasis to the missionary's poverty, in contradistinction to the eschatological. It is because this poverty announces the advent of the Kingdom, and because Christians realize this fact, that they will give God's minister the material assistance necessary to maintain him in his calling.

c) The second counsel given concerns relationship with hosts (vv. 5-9). The disciples must always be careful to preserve their role as *pilgrims*, nomads who never rest, but continually journey towards the Kingdom (1 P 2:11; Heb 11:8-14), grateful for any hospitality received.

Poverty defines the ontological condition of the believer in the Church, the condition of adopted child of the Father. But like every spiritual principle, it must become visible in both the individual and collective life. This does not happen automatically: each Christian is responsible. In the evangelization of the world, the sign of poverty must be held out to men. But to be legible it must bear the context of the life of those men at whom it is aimed.

The Church must bear witness to poverty on a two-fold level: each Christian in his individual life and the Church community in its institutions and various methods of apostolic action.

As to the first, Christians, anxious about evangelization do not hide their anxiety. Often having abundant possessions, they present the ambiguity of the material wealth which they have at their disposal. Wealth engenders security and nourishes the instinct of power. Does fidelity to the gospel imply the voluntary renouncement of wealth? Not everyone has that vocation; but everyone must ask himself how he can escape from slavery, how he can use his wealth (material or other) in the spirit of universal service. Poverty that defines the condition of the believer in the Church demands of him concrete behavior in the matter of wealth. An urgent and grave commandment, since on the whole the material situation of the Christian is nowadays clearly superior to that of most men. In fact, the Church urgently calls for voluntary evangelical poverty. Its prophetic warning invites each one to review his life-style.

As to the second, the exegencies are not less demanding. For institutions above all attract attention. Although a bishop lives poorly in a luxurious episcopal palace, the wealth of the latter will be criticized. It is important then that ecclesial institutions as such (the style of liturgical celebration, methods of the apostolate, etc.) and Christian institutions avoid appearing as instruments of prestige or power. This demands constant review of all institutional machinery which the ecclesial community has at its disposal.

One is not poor simply by deciding to be so. Only the sacramental initiative can establish this poverty in man, because it is above all the accepting the stages of salvation history and God's intervention in the world. It is in this sense that the Eucharist is the assembly of the poor in Christ.

XIII. Baruch
1:15-22
1st reading
1st cycle
Friday

The beginning of the great penitential prayer of the exiles (Ba 1:15-3:18). The original Hebrew or Aramaic has been greatly reworked with the Septuagint version.

The beginning of this prayer is marked with the doctrine of *reward* (Dt 28:15-68; Lv 26:14-39). Misfortune befalls the people because they have sinned, and just as all generations are jointly liable to sin and punishment, so as the misfortune is taken away, recognition in the name of past generations for incurred responsibilities is called for.

An avowal of these faults is then for the people a manner of beginning anew the history of salvation.

The penitential prayer and the avowal of faults no longer have the importance in the New Testament which they had in the Old. The context of reward in which they were written, especially in Baruch, is clearly surpassed by Christ. God, in fact, forgives independently of the avowal and in spite of faults: there is the whole difference between the avowal of the Hebrews and that of Christians. The penitential step is not at first a sort of recovery of innocence or a recognition of violation of law and of justice; there is no Christian avowal and no true contrition except where one confesses God and his unfailing mercy. The avowal is not a sort of restoration of a justice momentarily lost and easily recovered with the help of God. It is no longer a move towards reconciliation with God, as if we had to extend our hand to him. The Father forgives indiscriminately the just and the sinner, he reconciles men even before they make the least move. The Christian avowal exists outside all justice. That is why, if it is an anthentic move of conversion, it is especially a celebration of the gratuity to which God invites all men.

XIV. Job 38:1, 12-21; 40:3-5
1st reading
2nd cycle
Friday

The response of Yahweh to Job on the origin of evil. The liturgical excerpt for this day is taken from the discourse by God.

God brings the understanding of Job to its proper dimensions: how could he pierce the *mystery* of evil when he is unable to discover the mystery of things and of nature?

Man must accept the fact that there are, in the knowledge and in the mastery of things, areas of total mystery. But this attitude is not a spontaneous one. By reducing all things to their usefulness, man evidently does not perceive their mystery. Thus a text like this from Job fittingly enough reminds modern man that things do not exist only in view of the satisfaction of needs.

In fact, man belongs simultaneously to two distinct worlds: that of coherence where things are perceivable, and that of uncertitude and anguish, where things do not have an immediate sense. It is only by the acceptance of this double existence that the search for the Being and the knowledge of mystery are correctly shown. At this moment, knowledge becomes culture and intelligence can be strengthened by faith.

XV. Luke 10:13-16
Gospel
Friday

This gospel is a combination of two rather heterogeneous passages. The first relates the curse of the cities by the lake (vv. 13-15) which Luke probably took from its original context; the second defines the authority which those sent by Christ possess (v. 16).

The *curse of the cities* is a theme that is dear to the prophets of the Old Testament. There is, it seems, two reasons for this: on one hand, their constant care to lead Israel back to the nomadic spirituality of the desert which allowed the Covenant with God (Heb 11:8-9; Ps 38/39:13), and on the other hand, their opposition to pagan overtones in the city. Improper pretensions to the hegemony (Rv 18:16; Is 13:21; 47:7-10; Jr 50-51), idolatry and immorality are their sins. So the prophets pour out continually their invectives against Sodom, Gomorrah, Babylon, Tyre and Sidon.

But a day comes when the prophets no longer direct their words against the Gentile cities, but against Jerusalem itself (Is 3:9; Am 4:11; Jr 23:14; Ez 16:48-53; Dt 23:37). They themselves, who never doubted the survival of Israel, announced the fall of their city which in their eyes had, like the pagan cities, an improper confidence in itself, relying on wealth and power and the inhabitants of which gave themselves over to debauchery (Rv 17-18).

The curse with which Christ strikes at the cities of the lake shore is written in this strain of protest.

Man is not made to live alone: he grows only through relationships; the familial and clan type of relationship found in primitive society, the personal and selective type, found in urban society. But the Bible continually recalls that God alone has the secret of the inevitable communion between men. Furthermore, Jesus himself restates, just after the curse of the cities, that the unity of men will be made around the hearing of his Word (v. 16). Nevertheless, one who hears God must not isolate himself from the modern city. Why accuse them of every evil? Israel cursed the cities in order to stress their relativity. But it is evident that the Word pertains where men multiply their effort for communion, building around them the city of God which will accomplish the history in which God will be all in all (Rv 21).

XVI. Baruch
    4:5-12,
    27-29
    1st reading
    1st cycle
    Saturday

An excerpt from a prophetic text composed no doubt in the 2nd century before Jesus Christ in the communities of the Diaspora in order to revive their hope of returning to Jerusalem (Ba 4:5-5:9).

The Jews, dispersed in the Gentile world, turn with nostalgia towards Jerusalem, taking seriously the prophecies of their return to the city (Is 60:1-5). This hope, however, takes on very strong nuances, especially in the successive curses of all the Gentile cities where they sojourned (vv. 31-35). These invectives encourage them to resist the temptation of collaboration with these cities and any attraction to paganism.

In this atmosphere of tension and polemics, Baruch cannot have the peaceful and serene tone of Third-Isaiah: the return to Sion is in his eyes the occasion for revenge on the Gentiles. In this respect, he rejects those ideas which are already present in the general assembly of Jews and of Gentiles in Jerusalem (Zc 14:14-20; Is 56; etc.).

As long as Israel believed itself a kingdom among others, he was not able to envisage the definitive assembly of people except after a bloody confrontation, a persecution and a final victory. It is only in refusing to be added to the societies of the earth that the Church can envisage a universal assembly beyond the confrontations of nationalism. But history teaches us that the Church suffers sometimes from persecutions and encounters oppositions which she would have been able to avoid by adhering to the announcement of a Kingdom which is not of this world.

Does this mean that the Christian must not become involved in the present world? By dint of waiting for salvation and the eschatological assembly and the apocalyptic initiative of God, the dispersed disassociate themselves from the present age, and with their insertion into the world and with the sign that they would be able to give to the world. But Jesus revealed to his disciples the importance of the present moment in the eschatological preparation, and he transformed the remote expectation to a vigilance at every moment. Thus the Christian is a citizen with a two-fold allegiance: his "heavenly" citizenship does not jeopardize his earthly citizenship.

XVII. Job
42:1-3, 5-6,
12-17
1st reading
2nd cycle
Saturday

Job directs his last discourse to God and he declares the intellectual indigence of man in the face of his fathomless designs.

Job reflected at length, he debated with his friends, he penetrated the designs of God and discovered the grandeur of the divine thought (the meaning of the "vision" in verse 5). He adopts anew the attitude of *resignation* which characterized him at the beginning of his misfortune (Jb 2:8), convinced that divine wisdom is elusive but that it gives suffering a certain meaning.

The cross is the revelation of that which Job awaited. God no longer explains evil as before; he comes only to share it and to make suffering a mediation between him and the believer.

There is no question of consenting to suffering as if existence was nonsense: evil can never arouse anything but indignation and rejection. The participation of the Christian in the mystery of the cross is in no way anesthetizing; it reveals to him that God gives to suffering, by sharing it, a meaning the secret of which rests only in his love. Henceforth one can no longer surrender in the face of it. It is because they have read this meaning in their suffering that certain individuals figure among the prophets of humanity and the greatest advocates of the ideal and the absolute.

But such an attitude is possible for the Christian only in the certitude that God has given a meaning to suffering by communicating in it with man.

XVIII. Luke   The mission of the seventy-two disciples is at
     10:17-24   times balanced by failure (cf. Lk 10:10), but
     Gospel   was more often crowned with success (v. 17).
     Saturday   The cursing of the hostile villages (Lk 10:10-15)
         is the recompense for the others (vv. 18-20).

a) The disciples return from the mission knowing that they have freed men from moral and physical evil (v. 17) by the use they made of the messianic power (the name) of Jesus.

The latter explains for them that such a victory is the sign of defeat for the cosmic forces that dominated man up until now (v. 18). Satan and his troups were, in fact, considered to live in the air whence they imposed on creatures a lot of insanity. The arrival of Jesus abolished that state of slavery and allowed man to have access to liberty. Such is the message of this gospel reading.

b) Verse 20, however, expresses the difference in the joy of Christ and in that of the disciples. It is not liberation that counts, but the end to which it leads: the participation of man in the Kingdom of God (represented here in a rather "Jewish" manner, under the appearance of an inscription in the registers for *citizenship* in heaven).

The Church has the duty of revealing to man that he truly escapes fate and that he holds his life in his own hands. It fulfills this role when its members denounce the bondage of man to economic and political powers and collaborate in the building of a truly humane universe. It fulfills this role when its members liberate their brethren from the grasp of atavism and practices of legalism and illusory sacralizations.

But it is not enough to denounce these alienations; it is necessary to heal the wounds. To make "Satan descend from heaven," is to make the cities more humane, is to fight against all sorts of segregation, is to suppress the rationale behind oppression; it is to reform political structures when they clearly show that they are unable to solve the problems of modern society (housing, teaching, etc.); it is to fight against mental illness, old age and loneliness; it is to reject the pressures which draw men to vice and injustice.

TWENTY-SEVENTH WEEK

I. Jonah 1:1-
2:1, 11
1st reading
1st cycle
Monday

There is nothing historical in this account which dates from the 5th century before Christ. Recounted in an ostentatious manner, it declares to Israel that the love of God extends to all men (Gentile sailors, the fish, the King of Ninevah, etc.) and that the only human being who causes him anxiety is a Jew.

Jonah, placed in a Gentile milieu, has the opportunity to verify the prophecies of Third-Isaiah and to be a "light to the nations," but he refuses to bear witness and to announce the Word to people whom he considers unclean. Besides the case of Jonah, the isolation of the Jew in a Gentile country is also placed on review. It is seen as an excellent opportunity for missionary activity, but *exclusiveness* inhibits the scattered members of the people, paralyzing all missionary work.

Silence and discretion are the real criteria for missionary activity: it is not by noisy announcement of the truth but by the insertion of the Christian search into the depth of the human search that the Kingdom is announced. The mission is paschal; it is not exempt from living the death which it witnesses.

II. Galatians
1:6-12
1st reading
2nd cycle
Monday

The Council of Jerusalem has just taken place where Paul received the greenlight for his mission to the Gentiles. However, the council did not put an end to the controversies: the Judaizers even urge converted Gentiles to comply with the practices of the law in order to be joined to Christ. Paul is at Ephesus around 57 when he learns about these misguided manuevers.

The apostle immediately tackles the problem (v. 6): the betrayers of his trust intend to harm this message. His riposte is clear, and if he speaks of his person (vv. 7, 9), it is not so much for show but to respond to the attacks of his adversaries who seek to discredit the gospel by discrediting the evangelizer.

a) *Gospel* is a typically Pauline expression (the word occurs sixty-one times in the epistles of Saint Paul) and, what is more, the precise expression: "the gospel of Christ" (v. 7). In the synoptic gospels the preaching of Jesus is concerned exclusively with the "Kingdom of God": it is essentially theocentric and eschatological. But in St. Paul it centers on Christ himself: God is always at work, but more like the author of the apocalyptic revelations which permit the apostle to construct his gospel (1 Co 2:10; 2 Co 12:1; Ga 1:16; 2 Th 1:17) with Christ as its object.

In other words, Paul sees God at work in his gospel, and because of this the call of God (v. 6) and his grace (here: the gift of faith) are offered to men. To abandon the gospel is then to lose both the faith and the call. The apostle thus sees Christ as the object of his gospel. But we must understand this object well: it does not involve simply content ("the preaching of Christ"), but an active presence (cf. Rm 1:16; 1 Co 1:18; 2 Co 5:20). That is why turning away from the gospel of Paul is tantamount to attacking Christ himself (v. 7).

b) As the instrument of this gospel sent by God through Christ, Paul presents himself as his *servant* (v. 10). He has "received" it as a tradition (1 Co 11:23-25; 15:1) and he has "taught" it as a trust (v. 12; terms used in the Jewish wisdom schools). But above all he has been entrusted with a mission by "apocalypse" or "revelation" (v. 12; cf. Ep 3:1-2; Col 11:3-4) which has Jesus Christ as its object. Paul does not then receive from Christ or from the other apostles a tradition or a teaching. Rather, he receives a revelation for which God alone has the initiative and the content of which does not deal with the earthly life of Jesus nor with the many regulations of Christian faith (this, Paul "will receive" from the primitive community) but with what God alone can reveal: on the one hand, the mystery of the death and resurrection of Christ on which God places the salvation of the world (Ga 1:1-5), and on the other, the particular call of Paul to announce this mystery to the Gentiles (v. 6). To attack this last part of the content of his gospel, as the Judaizers do, amounts to questioning its apocalyptic character.

III. Luke   Today's gospel includes three distinct sections:
    10:25-37   a) The blessing promised to the apostles who
    Gospel   saw and heard the things which past kings and
    Monday   prophets would have greatly desired to see and
hear and who are privileged to witness the fulfillment of God's plan.

b) A discussion on the greatest commandment which Luke introduces here but which more likely occurred during Christ's entry into Jerusalem. That is, in fact, where the other synoptic writers place it (Mt 22:34-40).

c) The parable of the Good Samaritan which is proper to Saint Luke.

The discussion on the greatest commandment disrupts the unity of the account. In fact, to the question of the Scribe "who is my neighbor?," Christ replies by a parable which tells *how* one should love the other. Thus there seems to be no direct relation between the discussion and what follows. Luke must have recorded the parable in this place as a kind of moral conclusion to the discussion. On the other hand, if we omit the discussion, the account of the Good Samaritan takes its place as a parable of the Kingdom like that of the Good Shepherd and of the Seed.

a) Certain words used in it indicate that an exclusively moral interpretation would be erroneous. For example, in verse 33, the Good Samaritan is said to be "touched with compassion." In Greek this word is used only to denote either God's mercy or Christ's (Mt 9:36; 14:4; Lk 7:13; 15:20). The Samaritan thus experienced a divine emotion; he is the image of God, the *revelation of God's love for man*. The "return" of the Samaritan (v. 35) also has definite implications. It would be meaningless if the parable was only a story with a moralistic or edifying conclusion. Does it rather refer to the return of Christ at the end of time? We have an indication inasmuch as the word occurs only once in the New Testament with this precise meaning (Lk 14:15).

In structure this parable bears a curious resemblance to the parable of the Good Shepherd and to that of the son of the master of the vineyard (Jn 10; Lk 20:9-18). Just as the Good Shepherd comes to save his sheep after robbers had stripped them, beaten them and put them to death (Jn 10:10), and as the son of the master of the vineyard arrives after the prophets have been sent in vain, so the Good Shepherd comes on the scene after the priests and Levites who neither desired nor were able to save wounded mankind. The Samaritan reveals God's love to men; he takes care of men with the sacraments of oil and wine and entrusts them to the inn of the Church. This explains the introductory section of today's gospel: the apostles are blessed because they assist at last at the manifestation of the love of God and because they, in their turn, are going to reveal it more effectively than the Jewish priests and Levites.

b) The parable was probably meant to express the *history of salvation* in the manner of the great parables of the Kingdom. Christ comes in the figure of a Samaritan, that is, a despised man (Jn 8:48), as the son of the master of the vineyard, in order to reveal the love of God in a situation where pagan and Jewish attempts at salvation had failed. The idea of the Good Shepherd may have come to Christ from 2 Chronicles 28:15, in which Samaritans are shown behaving charitably to Jews in a sequence of activity strikingly like those in Luke's account: Jericho is mentioned; those who have escaped from a massacre are cared for; the weak are mounted on donkeys and they are "sheltered."

c) The reason why Luke introduced the discussion on the great commandment was probably because he wanted to show that *charity* has now acquired a wider scope since Christ. Now it is no longer enough to love our neighbor as we love ourselves; we have to love him as God loves him. This is the intention of the discourse after the Supper when a new commandment was given; to love others as we have been loved (Jn 13:34). Charity is not now a moral obligation; it is a reflection of God's own love, the sign that the last days have come when God's mercy takes the place of Jewish legalistic methods for the attainment of salvation. By altering the position of the discussion on the greatest commandment and making it lead up to the parable of the Good Shepherd, Luke adds a development to the doctrine on charity (note the distance that separates the account of Luke and that of Mt 22:34-40 and Mk 12:28-31) and prepares for the specifically Christian idea in the gospel of John.

Love is then the fulfillment of history. Faced with paganism which establishes religious procedures for escaping time and the event, and confronted with the Jewish eschatology which leads towards a new heaven and a new earth, the exclusive fruits of Yahweh's intervention, Christ has been the first to push the confrontation with the event to its conclusion. In this respect he is the first to appraise history fully. But the crucible in which this is worked out bears a name: the love of Christ, obedient to death where he reveals his filial love for the Father and the universal brotherhood which he inaugurates.

By his baptism the Christian receives the ability needed to reveal in the very history of mankind, the love which makes it a history of salvation. He is, then, glad to see what the prophets would have wished to see (v. 23)! The Good Samaritan shows us how to fully value the history of the last times: he recognizes the essentials where he exists by being radically available to an unseen encounter with his brother. No obstacle to this encounter, not even the fact that the wounded one is an enemy! Real love does not show partiality to anyone; it involves the total gift of self.

In a world which pretends to know the meaning of history and which challenges the event itself, the Christian still adopts the only attitude which does not alienate man. The reforms of political structures, the settlement of peace, social justice will only be stages towards a centralized universe, unless a world of free men emerges from them, free men recognizing each other in the mystery of their otherness. For the Christian is especially equipped to propose a human promotion by his encounter with the other in the experience of diversity in brotherhood.

IV. Jonah 3:1-10
1st reading
1st cycle
Tuesday

The book of Jonah appears for no apparent reason in that part of the Bible which is reserved for the prophets. Certainly there was a prophet by this name (2 K 14:25) and it is perhaps of him that the author of the book is referring. But we are dealing with a story or a romanticized life which contains very late language (5th century?). In any case, the author wants to be read and he does not hesitate to employ easy procedures, even grotesque. However, he gives an important message: this is the first time in the Old Testament that an envoy from God goes to Gentiles and converts them, even though it was despite himself.

The decrees directed by God against the Gentile nations can then be questioned because of their *conversion:* this seems to be the basic message of the parable. This was a new teaching, for the Jews thought until then that the curses pronounced by the prophets on the nations were inescapable and that only the decrees against the Jews could be reevaluated. Jonah however does not admit this way of looking at things; he protests against the pardon granted to Nineveh (Jon 4).

The author seems to point to another teaching and to put to shame the Jews for their slowness in being converted (cf. Jr 7:25-26; 25:4; 26:5), whereas Nineveh was converted from the very start.

Jonah was not a missionary. In his eyes his expedition to the Ninevites is punitive and no evidence shows in him the least departure as regards Jewish exclusiveness. The conversion of Nineveh seems then the unexpected result of his preaching; the conclusion surpasses the promise.

Had Jonah been a missionary, the call to conversion that he proclaimed should have concerned him from the start. One does not invite a people to stop making itself the center of history except by giving the sign that he himself has been displaced and by supplying as the center a witness of what it means for him. The true call to conversion must be retained at the heart of the people's spiritual vitality and not alongside it; it must touch the soul and the heart if it is to lead to the stripping of self.

Are not Christians very often new Jonahs? If the call to conversion rests on the witness of one's own "decentering," a triumphant and powerful Church is unable to make it heard as it should be.

V. Galatians   Paul affirms that he owes his gospel to a revela-
  1:13-24   tion and not to the Christian community of
  1st reading   Jerusalem (vv. 11-12), from which however he
  2nd cycle   had borrowed quite a few formulas and tradi-
  Tuesday   tions (cf. 1 Co 15:1-3). But the actual content
                      of his message is of an "apocalyptic" (revela-
tional) order.

a) In order to strengthen this presentation of proofs, Paul recalls the events that had preceded and followed his "conversion" (vv. 13-14).

The basic idea revealed there is that Saul, the old persecuter, has not only begun a process of individual conversion; he becomes a disciple after having been an adversary. His conversion coincides with a more basic call that made of him the Apostle to the Nations (v. 16). Conversion, access to *apostleship* and openness of this to the nations are the essential characteristics of the event on the road to Damascus which therefore dispensed the apostle from any mandate from the Twelve.

It is not so much in content that the gospel of Paul differs from that of the Twelve but by its diffusion among the nations which in the eyes of the apostle was an integral part of his message.

b) If Paul makes contact with Jerusalem (v. 17 or Ga 2:1-2), it is not to verify the correctness of his gospel but to defend his stand about a gospel for the nations (and thus about access to Christ without the law or circumcision) (cf. Ga 2:6). In fact, the Twelve could in no way reject him on that issue for it is a gospel that comes from God himself; rather Paul lays great stress on his contact with Jerusalem in order to underscore the *unity of the mission*. He seeks agreement with the apostles at Jerusalem not because he has any hesitation about the content of his gospel but because he fears the least harm to the unity of the mission.

Unity and mission are inseparably united in the Church. The ecumenical problems, for example, were never correctly posed except in a context of Church-World encounter. Outside this context they lose themselves in a labyrinth of quibblings and institutions. But as missionary inspiration passes, unity is required as an exigency that does not suffer useless delay.

In fact, there is no real mission in the Church except in unity: consider the loss of momentum and the scandal caused by the rival preaching of the gospel to the Asiatic and African world. Still, one must admit that a certain type of unity, uniformity, kills the mission. If the Church rests on the Twelve Apostles, plus Paul the thirteenth, and not upon one alone, it is well to show that its mission depends on a variety of mentalities and cultures restored to unity in the crucible of collegiality. By going to Jerusalem, Paul did not seek unilateral and uniform instructions. He integrated his direction in collegiality so that there too, where he took original options, the other apostles would recognize the one gospel at work.

VI. Luke   Too often the anecdote recounted in this pas-
10:38-42   sage has been transformed into an allegory in
Gospel   which Martha would represent action and
Tuesday   Mary contemplation and which aimed at show-
                 ing the superiority of the second to the first.
In fact, we have here an anecdote gathered by St. Luke from
the circle of the disciples, especially the circle of women, who
preserved the original traditions.

a) The family of Lazarus is at the center of three important
gospel traditions (Lk 10:38-42; Jn 11:1-44; 12:1-8) where Mary
and Martha appear each time in specific roles. Faithful, no doubt,
to family customs of the time, Martha is preoccupied with the
domestic tasks while Mary welcomes guests. The three accounts
underline the smooth running of domestic roles which assure the
most amiable *hospitality* possible.

b) This anecdote will however appear with diverse interpretations. One interpretation of the account sees it as an expression of
eschatological expectations. Time presses too much for one to be
still preoccupied with material cares. Martha no doubt wanted to
honor her host by presenting him choice cooking but this intention
turns against her who must now solicit the help of her sister (v. 40).
The Lord then asks her to worry a little bit less about food ("one
thing only is required": v. 42; "indeed only one": v. 42a). Luke
attaches great importance to this teaching: it is not worth worrying
about worldly affairs while the kingdom is so close (Lk 12:22). One
can moreover wonder whether the evangelist has become a disciple
of St. Paul: a common vocabulary is found in Luke and 1 Corinthians 7:29-35 and an identical doctrine tends to prove that virginity (for Martha and Mary are both considered virgins) allows
one to await the Kingdom to come without being fettered by the
obligations of marriage.

c) If Luke shows a predilection for poverty, the sign of eschatological longing, he likewise attaches great value to *listening to the*

Word (Lk 11:27-28). Thus, in another place he compares the family of Christ, preoccupied with its sustenance (Lk 8:19; clarified by Mk 3:20) to those who prefer to hear his word and to practice it (Lk 8:20). This does not mean that Christ prefers contemplation over action but rather that attention to the realities of the Kingdom (often represented as a Word: cf. Lk 8:11-15) cannot allow itself to be distracted by too great a care for earthly realities. For Saint Luke, hearing the Word does not imply idle contemplation but always action (Lk 8:15).

VII. Jonah 4:1-11   When he finally reached Nineveh, Jonah tra-
1st reading   veled through it for three days, proclaiming
1st cycle   the imminence of the judgment of God (Jon 3).
Wednesday   But, contrary to his expectations, the city is
converted and the prophet who thought that he was charged with a mission of vengeance, suddenly found himself at the source of a movement of conversion that he did not want. Once again, God makes him ridiculous in his own eyes.

a) The author devotes the final chapter of his book to deriding the *exclusiveness* of his contemporaries. Perhaps he is making an allusion to the disillusionment that took hold of the people after the failure of the prophecies of Ezechiel against Tyre. The prophet had announced the destruction of the city (Ez 26-28), but the siege of the city, undertaken by Nabuchodnosor for thirteen years, was resolved by a resounding failure. Ezechiel then published a new oracle (Ez 29:17-21)), but the people remained under a cruel deception: God was not as intransigent towards the nations as they thought him to be.

b) The author softens this deception by describing the *universality* of the love of God. He even transposes to the universal plane the text of Exodus 34:6 which describes the particular love of God for his people (v. 2; cf. Ps 102/103:8; Ne 9:7; Jl 2:13).

The story of the gourd plant (vv. 6-10) is told in the same perspective: if God is truly the God of the universe, is it normal that he would care for only one individual or one people whereas hundreds of thousands of persons wait for life from him?

It is true that such an universalism was not unknown to Israel, but the account of Jonah is coincident with the reconstruction of the temple and consequently with a mentality which imagines the universalism as centered around Sion (as Is 2:2-5 already wanted it). The author reacts against such a conception and, like Is 19:18-25 and Malachi 1:11, he opens up the perspectives of decentralized universality: it is impossible to be a citizen of Nineveh and adorer of the true God.

Thus, the cult which the book of Jonah presents is no longer that of Jerusalem, but a cult in spirit and in truth, relieved of all special and formal attachments.

The book of Jonah has a big place in the New Testament, not only by reason of the allegorical theme of the "three days" in the sea (Mt 12:39-40), but especially because of the comparison it makes between the faith of the Ninevites and the incredulity of the Jews (Mt 12:41). Thus Jonah is the book of Good News for the nations and the proclamation of the love of God in their regard. True universalism is not centripetal.

VIII. Galatians To accept the chronology of Paul and to resolve
2:1-2, 7-14 at the same time certain difficulties raised by
1st reading the Council of Jerusalem (Ac 15), it seems we
2nd cycle can consider the development of events as
Wednesday follows.

The problem of the conversion of the Gentiles involved above all the question of knowing whether or not to impose on them the prescriptions of the law. It was to resolve this problem that Paul and Barnabas came together with Peter and the elders at Jerusalem (Acts 15:1-12). After they reached agreement about the liberty of the Gentiles as regards circumcision, Paul and Barnabas returned to Antioch. A little later, Peter in his turn left Jerusalem (Ac 12:17), probably for Antioch. There arose then a new controversy: if it is agreed that the converted Gentiles are to be considered disciples of Christ, without being bound by the law, they remain, nevertheless, unclean in the eyes of the law. Consequently, Christian Jews who continue to submit to the law, are not allowed to have their meals with Gentiles, even though Christian.

A dispute broke out in this matter between Paul and Peter, and Simon the Black was sent to Jerusalem for a ruling (Ac 13:1; 15:14). James, the brother of the Lord, who ruled the community at that time, called a council during which he made the decision to allow a common table for Christians of Jewish origin and Christians of Gentile origin (Ac 15:13-35). The episode recounted by Paul would then be situated between the two "councils" of Jerusalem and bear on a minor application of the decisions made during the first.

a) The "gospel" which Paul states (v. 2) does not involve the totality of his preaching, which is especially directed to the cross of Christ, but this particular aspect of the Good News, freedom from the law. It is this precise point that the apostle wants the "pillars" at Jerusalem to accept.

He won his case in its entirety. The leaders of the community completely admitted that the Gentiles were not bound to become Jews before entering the Church.

Paul then makes allusions to decisions taken during the "council" of Jerusalem (Ac 15:1-12) where he received recognition of his mission to the Gentiles and on their behalf, the authentication of a gospel freed of the law.

b) Paul then recounts the incident at Antioch (vv. 11-14), namely the *common* table among Christians, because he sees there a new argument in favor of the authenticity of his gospel and especially of that which concerns the salvation of the Gentiles. Coming from

Jerusalem where the problem of this common table did not exist, Peter, we understand, had no precise opinion about this subject. Paul, on the contrary, is well informed about this matter which represents the daily practice at Antioch. He then takes advantage of this in order to gain more support for his gospel and to save once more the unity of the Church, the necessary preliminary for his mission.

The distinction made in verses 7-9 between the gospel of the circumcised (confided to Peter) and the gospel of the uncircumcised (confided to Paul) was probably in the mind of the Council of Jerusalem simply a geographical division of the apostolate of the Church. But experience proves that anyone who allows himself to be limited, say for territorial reasons, will soon find himself limited on the missionary and theological level. Because he preaches only to the circumcised, Peter was inevitably influenced by their theology (Ga 2:11-14). It is only by leaving Jerusalem that he will save the universality of the mission (Ac 12:17).

IX. Luke 11:1-4
Gospel
Wednesday

Matthew (Mt 6:1-15) and Luke (Lk 11:1-13) each present a sort of catechism on prayer. But while Matthew addressed this message to the Jews who became Christians, conscious of the defects in Jewish prayer: the routineness and verbalism, Luke directs his to Gentiles who have to learn everything with respect to prayer and have to be encouraged in this time consuming enterprise.

Each of them makes the Our Father the center of his booklet on prayer, but each proposes the text in use in his respective communities, and it is difficult to know which version reproduced the exact prayer of the Lord. Matthew seems to supply a text very close to the Aramaic, at least in the parts which he had in common with Luke, but it is hard to believe that Luke would have suppressed the important parts of this prayer had he been aware of this. We ascertain, moreover, in the liturgical evolution a progressive growth in prayer texts which would allow us to affirm the later character of elements proper to Matthew. In fact, this explanation remains very hypothetical.

We will now comment on the Our Father, petition by petition.

The call to the Father presupposes a communication of life and the possibility of rejoining the attitude of fidelity shown by Jesus. *Abba,* from the original Aramaic, was probably maintained for a long time in the Greek version which would explain the differences between Matthew and Luke and the presence of this address in Romans 8:15 and Galatians 4:6.

After the call there are two wishes: the sanctification of the name and the coming of the Kingdom. A name designates the person: that God be known for what he is: holy and transcendent. And, moreover, this holiness is communicated to a Kingdom, this transcendence is made immanent (Ez 36:23) and the gratuitous gift of the Father is accomplished through the collaboration of man: may your kingdom come.

A third wish is added to the first two; it might be that it is not primitive, for Luke ignores it: "your will be done. . . ." This plan of God is the salvation of man by his sanctification and his entry into the heritage of the Kingdom (Ep 1:3-8). In this respect this third wish simply repeats in other words the context of the first two.

After these wishes there are some requests: bread, forgiveness and protection. It is impossible to know if Christ thought in terms of material bread for each day or the bread of eternal life. But why contrast one with the other? Is it not by distributing material bread to the hungry that Christ revealed the bread of life?

The request for protection bears on the "temptation" which, in the Aramaic context of the time, consists in the great trial of believers and the final assault by the Evil One, envisaged before the establishment of the Kingdom. The *Our Father* asks then for God's help in order not to apostatize (Mt 24:4-31; Lk 22:53; Jn 12:31).

In conclusion, the *Our Father* asks that the manifestation of God and his Kingdom, and the communication of his life to man be accomplished through bread, forgiveness and the protection granted to the faith of the disciples.

X. Malachi   This is the conclusion to the third and last dis-
3:13-20a   course in the book of Malachi (Ml 2:17-3:22).
1st reading   Written between the announcement of the re-
1st cycle   turn from exile and the period of reform
Thursday   organized by Ezra, this discourse is addressed
                   successively to unbelievers (Ml 2:17-3:5), to
the indifferent (Ml 3:6-12) and to the faithful (Ml 3:13-23). These last found, when they returned to Jerusalem, a very different situation and they are surprised that God does not recompense their fidelity more promptly. The temptation is great to collaborate, out of spite, with the surrounding Gentile world.

a) In order to give them confidence, the prophet announces to them the closeness of *judgment:* the oven for the impious (v. 19), but the "sun of justice" for the good (v. 20). This last expression seems to be borrowed from the Phoenician mythologies where one month of the year was consecrated to the cult of the sun (approximately our month of October). The use of this title is perhaps a veiled indication of a foreseen date for the salvation of the people.

b) Since Isaiah 10:16-17; 30:17; Zephaniah 1:18, 3:8; Amos 5:18, *fire* holds a great place in the prophetic descriptions of the Day of Yahweh. It is rather normal that the prophets see in this element the instrument of judgment, because God promised never again to use water to punish humanity (Gn 9:12-17). The New Testament will at times remain loyal to this idea (2 P 3:12), but it will spiritualize it by making fire the purifying element which introduces the last days (Ac 2:1-4; Mt 3:11). In every way, we are concerned with an image evoking above all the reality of the presence of God in the life of man.

XI. Galatians
3:1-5
1st reading
2nd cycle
Thursday

This passage unites the first part of the letter (a personal apology) to the second, more doctrinal (justification by faith). Captivated (v. 1) by preachers without scruples, the Galatians accepted without discernment theories which bound them to the legalistic practices of Judaism.

The role of the apostle is to lead the Galatians to read in their actual situation the presence of the *Spirit* of the Risen Christ (v. 2).

Now, it is not the law that procured this Spirit for the Galatians, since Paul did not announce it to them. They have then received it even before having accomplished one single work of the law: they have received it because they have adhered with faith to the apostolic message.

By evoking the spectacular manifestations of the Spirit in the Church (v. 5), Paul does not mean to reduce the Church to these phenomena. In his mind the Spirit of God exerts a much larger and more diversified action and if he mentions spectacular wonders, it is no doubt to show how God had taken the initiative in the access of the Galatians to the faith and how it is consequently ridiculous to return to a religion where man would have the initiative (v. 4).

XII. Luke
11:5-13
Gospel
Thursday

The beginning of Chapter 11 of Saint Luke constitutes a short treatise on prayer. The evangelist relates first his version of the Our Father (vv. 2-4), then the parable of the pestered friend (vv. 5-8), then, by way of conclusion, a series of remarks (vv. 9-13) on confidence in prayer. The whole is presented in great unity and in fact constitutes a commentary on the petition of the *Our Father:* "Give us this day our daily bread" (Lk 11:33; a theme that reappears in verses 5 and 11). Let us note in passing that Matthew comments on the *Our Father* by dwelling especially on the petition for pardon (Mt 6:14-15).

a) In telling this parable, Christ wanted to form a catechism on *confidence in prayer* (vv. 5-8). We could recover the original text by presenting verses 5-7 in an interrogative form. Jesus then holds his audience as a witness that it is unthinkable that a man would not rise in the night to welcome a friend in the name of hospitality (v. 6) or even to have peace (v. 8) and that regardless of the annoyance caused by this unusual rising (v. 7).

The conclusion is obvious: if that is unthinkable of a friend, *a fortiori*, it is of God. Our concern here is not, as we said, with the parable of the annoying friend but rather with that of the annoyed friend: the principal character is not the one who knocks on the door and asks for bread but the one who is inside the house. Verses 11-13 prolong perfectly the teaching of the parable: there still the audience is held as a witness of the unthinkable character of refusal. If the father of the family cannot really refuse the bread asked for, God can still less do so. Luke modifies moreover a part of the phrase by replacing "the good things" given by God to those who ask for them, with "spirit." The thought of the evangelist reflects undoubtedly the mentality of the first communities, sure to be living in the final days and anxious about sharing the blessings and the happiness promised by the prophets.

b) Luke has however transformed the first part of the phrase (v. 7) in such a way that the "Who among you . . ." does not designate any longer the annoyed friend but the annoyer. Luke thus makes the parable a doublet of the story of the corrupt judge (Lk 18:1-8). Suddenly, the attention passes from the annoyed friend to the annoying friend for whom *perseverence* is very necessary; but because he does not hesitate to insist and to continue knocking on the door, it will be opened for him.

Verses 9-10 which constitute the primitive commentary on the parable confirm this point of view: "ask for bread, we will end up by giving it to you." The beggar is obstinate, he does not allow himself to be put down when he is refused and he succeeds in opening the hands of his equals, as bad as they are. *A fortiori*, perseverance in prayer will cause the hands of God to open, God who is good!

Luke affirms the optimism of the Christian concept of prayer: not because the asking is obstinate but because God is good. However, an important element is lacking in this doctrine on prayer: the effectiveness of the latter is not only the fruit of an untiring eagerness, but results from the very meditation on Christ and from the presence of the Spirit in the heart of man. In this respect, the teaching of John 16:23-26, which can be thought of as inspired by the passage from St. Luke, goes much further and rightly places at the heart of Christian prayer the role of the unique intercession of the Lord.

XIII. Joel   Joel is probably a contemporary of Jeremiah
    1:13-15;   and of the first temple. His first oracles share
    2:1-2   the pessimistic idea of the Day of Yahweh such
    1st reading   as Zephaniah, Jeremiah etc., had elaborated it.
    1st cycle   We cannot however read them without think-
    Friday   ing of those which the prophet will publish at
    the end of his career and which are clearly
more optimistic and a source of hope.

The book of Joel has perhaps been used as a booklet for a ceremony of expiation. Verses 13-14 would be an address to priests; verse 15, although important, could be an interpolation; verses 16-18 would reproduce a chorus with many voices. Chapter 2:1-2 would be the beginning of an oracle which follow an exhortation (2:13b-14) and a new address to priests (2:15-17), a new oracle (2:19-20) and a popular hymn (2:21-23).

The prophet addresses in succession the chiefs (Jl 1:2-3), drunkards (Jl 1:15), farmers (Jl 1:11-12) for whom he predicted the destruction of the fruit and grain harvests (Jl 1:6-7, 8-10). He now asks the priests to organize a penitential ceremony to drive out the plague of grasshoppers.

No doubt the redactors of the book did not want to hold on to this simple anecdote and they added verse 15 to transform the plague of grasshoppers to a sign announcing the *Day of Yahweh*. In any case, Joel arrives at this theme (Jl 2:1-2). It is not impossible that the ceremony proposed by the prophet coincides with the feast of Atonement, at the vigil of the Feast of Tabernacles. The allusion to trumpets (v. 1) would refer to the sounding of the horn which announced the beginning of the great annual feast.

Now, this feast of Tabernacles was built in large part on the theme of death and life, of the old and the new creation. Joel probably borrows from this ritual the "darkness-light" theme (v. 2) just as Christ will do for the same feast (Jn 8:12; 9), by contrasting the old darkness to his own light.

The Day of Yahweh is like the Day of the New Year which the feast of Tabernacles celebrated: entry into a new era, much better than the old, more luminous and more fruitful (v. 2b).

XIV. Galatians 3:7-14
1st reading
2nd cycle
Friday

Despite the consecration granted by the Church to the theses of Paul on salvation by the cross and on the free access of Gentiles to justification without the law, some "false brethren" infiltrated the Christian communities to affirm there, in particular, that Gentile converts are not completely members of the descendants of Abraham unless they accept circumcision and its requirements.

Paul first of all puts forward a series of scriptural references (vv. 6-12) and then affirms the fact that humanity is saved by the cross (vv. 13-14).

a) The biblical references have been chosen with the deliberate intention of proving that the Pauline doctrine of *justification* by faith is rooted in the scriptures. The basic text, Genesis 15:6 (cf. Rom 4:3; Heb 9:8-10, 17-19), clearly establishes that Abraham is the father in the faith and thus the model of the new justification. Paul thus goes back to Abraham first of all to shatter the criticisms which the "false brethren" direct towards him and to destroy their very narrow idea of descent from Abraham, but also because he finds in the life of the patriarch an allusion to Gentiles (Gn 18:18; cf. v. 8), an ideal text in his mind for uniting Abraham, the faith and the Gentiles.

Now the idea of believers being blessed in Abraham (v. 9) soon gave birth in the mind of Paul of the idea of a curse (mentioned in Gn 12:3). He soon applies this antithesis blessing-curse to the antithesis faith-law: blessing is on the side of the faith and the Gentiles; curse on that of the law and the Judaizers (v. 10; Dt 27:26), for no one can fulfill the law and be justified by it.

Paul then brings forth a new quotation (Hb 2:4; v. 11) which the Jewish tradition had already compared with Genesis 15:6. The apostle finds there again the basic themes of his statements: faith, justice, life. This last word brings up a new quotation: Leviticus 18:5 (v. 12); Paul does not fully respect the literal meaning of this passage but his use of it is clear: the law cannot lead to life unless one observes the totality of its prescriptions which is patently impossible.

It is then that Paul turns his attention to the cross: he sees there Christ in death, under the curse (Dt 21:23; v. 13; cf. Ac 5:30; 10:39), also under the nonobservance of the law and thus under sin. The expression is particularly audacious, all the more since the apostle agrees with the argument of his detractors who could not admit that a Messiah could be cursed. But Paul introduced this idea of the curse of Christ only to present the idea of redemption.

b) He extracts this idea of *redemption* from his meditation on Isaiah 53; the Suffering Servant saves humanity to the extent that he takes upon himself its faults and its curses. But the word itself probably comes from a paschal context: the liberation of the Hebrews from Egypt (Dt 7:8-9; 9:26; 13:6; 15:15; 21:8; 24:28).

Thus cursed, Christ strikes the law and sin with death and in rising he offers liberty and redemption to believers (vv. 13, 14). Henceforth, Christian existence is freed of law and sin; it passes over to the blessings and the promises made to the faith of Abraham.

XV. Luke
11:15-26
Gospel
Friday

These verses are part of a larger section (Lk 11:14-32) which clearly lacks unity. It contains successively the healing of the dumb man (v. 14), referred to again in the beatitude about those who hear the Word (vv. 27-28), then the demand for an extraordinary sign (v. 16), referred to in the announcement of the sign of Jonah (vv. 29-32), then the discussion about the relationship between Christ and Satan (vv. 17-20) and the parable of the strong man (vv. 21-22), referred to in the description of the agressive return of the unclean spirit (vv. 24-26). At the heart of this series of insertions is the word of Christ (v. 23): "He who is not with me is against me."

a) The most ancient part of this passage is marked with the Jewish idea of the *two spirits*. The world is at the mercy of the spirit of evil and men follow the downhill path mapped out by it; but the last times will see the appearance of a new spirit, the spirit of goodness, which will reorientate man towards good. The Qumran documents have stressed the idea of these two antagonistic forces which set out to conquer the world. By casting out the demon, Christ shows that the spirit of good has appeared in the world; the two forces are involved in a merciless combat for man to place himself under the leadership of one of them. In Matthew's account the discussion turns at once upon the opposition between the Holy Spirit and Beelzebul and on the sin against the Spirit, a sin that consists in denying the coming of the Spirit into the world as well as its ability to fashion a new world.

b) St. Luke softens the antagonism which the original account described as existing between the two spirits. He omits any mention of the sin against the Spirit and even replaces the name of the Spirit by the phrase "the finger of God" (v. 20), for he is no doubt addressing readers less alive to the theme of the two spirits. But the gospel tradition has added some elements to this primary source for the purpose of supplying it with various interpretations. First of all the episode of the healing of the deaf-mute (v. 14) and the blessedness of those who hear the Word (vv. 27-28) belong most likely to a source influenced by some catechetical rite (cf. the "finger of God" in verse 20). It indicates perhaps that the Christian ought to place himself under the leadership of one of the two spirits, that he must choose between the one which leads to evil and the one which, by *obedience to the Word,* leads to new life. The second element recounts the victory of the "stronger" (although the original source speaks only of the "strong") (v. 15) and recounts the parable of the offensive return of Satan (vv. 24-26). It wants to instill in Christians a certain intransigency (v. 23) in the choice of the two kingdoms.

Christians who no longer believe in Satan are numerous. The experience which they have of temptation in no way seems to postulate for them the existence of demoniacal powers; sins find insufficient explanation in human freedom. The personification of evil belongs to an era, now ended, where man believed he was the plaything of cosmic forces. The popular mythology of yesterday is today rejected; what was called diabolical possession is now a traumatism, among other things, which depth psychology tries to explain. Has not the Church followed the same evolution in becoming extremely prudent in the use of exorcism?

To affirm that Christ has conquered the empire of Satan is in reality to bestow upon the work of Christ cosmic dimensions. We are then dealing with something basic. Formerly there was a solidarity in sin that affected the whole of creation. Henceforth a breach exists. With Christ the cosmic bond is broken on behalf of the solidarity of love. In other words, in Jesus Christ the creative plan of God succeeds: man becomes once for all allied with his creator in order to help him realize his plan of love. The cosmic history of salvation has its starting point. The day will come when Satan and Death will be hurled "into the pool of fire" (Rv. 20:14); solidarity in sin will then have lost all consistency. There will be no reign of sin!

XVI. Joel 4:12-21 The allusion in the book of Joel to known his-
1st reading torical events are so rare that we find great
1st cycle difficulty in dating his oracles. A plausible hy-
Saturday pothesis dates their proclamation to about 500
before Christ and their definitive redaction to
the 4th century. The events which surround the fall of Jerusalem
and the exile among the nations took shape therefore after these
prophecies.

In the second part of his collection (chapters 3-4) the prophet
predicts that the law of the talion will be applied to the nations;
they in their turn will bear the cruelty which they caused Jerusalem to undergo. In order to do this he presents a series of images
already known but which will later serve to describe the "Day of
Yahweh" (Mt 24, for example): the gathering together of the
nations (vv. 12, 14; cf. Mt 24:30-31), the nearness of the Day (v.
14, cf. Mt 24:33), the darkening of the stars (v. 15; cf. Mt 24:29),
the roaring voice of Yahweh (v. 16), the trembling of the earth
and the sky (v. 16; cf. Mt 24:29b) and finally the eschatological
grain and grape harvest (v. 13; cf. Mt 13:24-30).

a) In fact at the time of the redaction of the prophecies of Joel,
two different ideas about the *Day of Yahweh* were circulating
among the people. The first, recalling the mighty and ancient
deliverances and the spectacular theophanies of yesteryear, dreams
of the day when Yahweh will deliver Israel from the yoke of the
nations. The second, with a more prophetic tone, foresees a day
of punishment for the sins of the people (Am 5:18-20). In the first
two chapters, Joel used the second idea. But the passage which
interests us contains the idea of a Day of Yahweh turned against
the nations and in favor of Israel.

b) Among the numerous elements of the Day of Yahweh, we
must separate the theme of *darkness*. The stars (object of pagan
idolatrous cults) no longer giving light, will plunge the world into
darkness and the entire cosmos will share in the sin of the nations.

The prophet thus defines the essential solidarity of the moral and the cosmic and in his turn he uses an intuition already expressed in the ninth plague of Egypt (Ex 10:22-23; Jl 2:2; cf. Is 5:30; 8:22; 9:1; 13:9-10; 29:18; Zp 1:15).

c) Another essential element: the *divine voice,* shattering when it is directed to the Gentiles (Is 30:31; Ps 28/29), source of blessing when directed to Israel (Dt 8:1-3; Jl 2:19). With Israel it is a dialogue but with the pagans it is a monologue. In contrast to the numerous apocalypses of the Old Testament, Joel is little interested in the elements which provoke alarm but turns his attention to the presence of the God of holiness and to his Word and his will at the heart of events. His message is not less impressive; it is more spiritual.

d) Joel is likewise more sensitive than the others to the *liturgical* aspect of the Day of Yahweh. The voice of God resounds in effect in the very temple of Sion (v. 16) as an expression of the glory of God which resides in the sanctuary. God dwells in Sion, in the midst of a city completely holy (v. 17, cf. Ez 43:12; Is 52:1; Na 2:1; Zc 9:8-9). Joel is one of the prophets who prompted to the greatest degree the idea of the holy city, absolutely pure, destined to emerge during the judgment of the nations (cf. Rv 21:22) as a refuge and a fortress for the just (v. 17). Thus God is holy and the people who are allied with him are called to share in this holiness. For Joel this is the most important outcome of the judgment in the Day of Yahweh.

e) Each day of Yahweh is preceded in Jewish prophecy with destruction or cosmic catastrophe. The invasion of grasshoppers was, in Joel 1, the decisive element of this destruction. Among the other prophets it is presented as marching armies (Am 6:14; Is 5:26; Jr 1:13-15; 46:20-24; Ez 38:4-15). In our passage it is presented with the images of *harvest* and vintage (v. 13) or of the harrow (v. 14: a word sometimes translated as "decision"; cf. Is 28:27; 41:15). These images of destruction reinforce the essential idea of Joel: God who comes radiates a holiness such as all those

who are unclean (and especially the idolatrous) will of necessity
be reduced to nothing and will look like a field of wheat after
harvest or after an invasion of grasshoppers.

Belief in the Day of Yahweh presupposes that the believer accepts that God intervenes in the life of man at privileged moments
throughout their history and especially at the moment which will
mark the end of time and the inauguration of a new world.

But Christian belief in the Day of Yahweh states this idea
rather precisely. In fact Christianity teaches that the Day of Yahweh has already been inaugurated with the incarnation. Christ
does not save man by introducing him to a condition distinct from
the earthly, but by revealing to him what is at stake and by
showing him the way to realize it. The earthly life led by Jesus
up until the cross was indeed the "Day of Yahweh" anticipated by
Israel, for the liberation of humanity is won there by obedience
to the plan of God and in evaluating history. For this to be, one
must live in the Spirit of Jesus and participate in the perfect
response which the man-God gave to the divine initiative, a
response that the Eucharist actualizes in our regard.

XVII. Galatians   The letter to the Galatians answers the attacks
      3:22-29   made by the Judaizers who infiltrated Galatia
    1st reading   and who questioned the teaching of Paul on the
    2nd cycle   unique role of Christ in humanity and more-
    Saturday   over denied him all apostolic approbation. The
first chapters constitute a defense of the min-
istry of the apostle and of his personal behavior. With chapter 3
the author broaches the doctrinal problem which is the subject
matter of the polemics against the Judaizers: is the law still necessary once one had placed himself in dependence on Christ?

The principal argument of the apostle rests on his conception
of the history of salvation. There was first of all the apparition of
God to Abraham, the promises, the faith of the patriarchs and the

blessing through him of all nations. Then came the law, given to Moses by the angels and from which Israel alone will obtain the blessing (Ga 3:1-18).

a) The conclusion is obvious: the law exerts only a relative and transitory influence, only a pedagogical function (v. 24). Since the appearance of Christ, the decisive element in the economy of salvation, the Law had to disappear and give place to the basic regime: that of the promise made to Abraham and attained by faith in Christ (v. 25).

Paul must also prove that Jesus is the *decisive event* which justifies the change of economies. He already did that in the rabbinic fashion, in Galatians 3:15-18, by showing how Christ was "the" descendent of Abraham. But now he declares it more clearly (vv. 25 and 29): in Jesus the promise is accomplished to perfection because he is the man-God. The Son of God (v. 26) constitutes the supreme gift that God could promise and offer to humanity; as man, he is the most adequate answer to this gift of the Father, the heir (v. 29) most fit to enter into possession of the promised goods and to realize the project of God for humanity.

Christ is then the decisive event in the history of humanity because the significance of the latter depends on his obedience to the Father; henceforth, everyone is called to "put on Christ" (v. 27), that is to say, to respond to the plan of God for man.

b) The decisive event in the history of man, Christ renders void the economy of the law. One must also understand how man participates in Christ in order to liberate himself from the law. For Paul, *faith* (v. 26) and *baptism* (v. 27) are two ways of joining Christ; they are not exclusive, for they are in the reach of all (v. 28).

Verses 26 and 27 stress the connection between faith and baptism: it is not one or the other but both together that assure the communion of man with Christ (cf. Ep 2:8; 1 Co 6:3). Faith is the response of man to the initiative of God bound to baptism. Thus we can say that the association faith-baptism corresponds, *mutatis mutandis,* to the complete man-God in Jesus: the gift of God calls for the response of the human partner first of all in Jesus Christ, then in each of the baptized. Baptism truly incorporates into Christ, allows one to be "clothed" with him (v. 27) and offers man a state of divine sonship in the image of that which the Son possesses by nature. These new relations of the baptized with God transform his relations with other men: barriers fall, everyone becomes equal and the blessing of all the nations in Abraham is finally realized (vv. 27-28).

The new Christian economy takes the place of the old. Salvation is no longer a function belonging to a people through rites of circumcision and ablution, not even the function of obedience to the law. In the new economy everything is changed because God had intervened in history by sending his Son who unites in his person the gift of God and the response of faith of the human partner and thus saves humanity. Every man participates in this salvation to the degree that his personality too is at the crossroads of an initiative of God and a response of man, both sanctioned in baptism and in the faith.

XVIII. Luke   For the commentary on this gospel see Friday,
11:27-28   p. 142.
Gospel
Saturday

TWENTY-EIGHTH WEEK

I. Romans 1:1-7   In accord with contemporary convention in
1st reading   letter writing, Paul introduces himself before
1st cycle   broaching the real subject of his letter.
Monday

         a) In his earlier letters this introduction was
rather short (see the salutations in 1 Th and 2 Th). But the doubts
of the Galatians and the Corinthians regarding his apostolic
authority, at the time of his third missionary journey (53–58), led
him to speak of himself at greater length. In referring to himself
as "servant," Paul is aware of taking over an honorific title reserved in the Old Testament for the great patriarchs (cf. Ex 24:31;
Nm 12:7; Dt 34:5; Gn 26:24; 24:14; Jos 24:23). But he calls himself the "servant of Christ Jesus," which is not only a title but
indicates a mission: the extension throughout the world of the
"service" of Christ. Paul also takes pride in mentioning his second
title, "apostle," which Jewish Christians had refused him (1 Co 9;
2 Co 11:13, 23). He had already written many personal apologies
explaining that this title "apostle" was not reserved to the Twelve,
but rested on a personal call (Ga 1:1) and on a mission of "preaching the gospel" (1 Th 1:4; Ph 4:15; 2 Co 8:18). Here he goes on to
say that the vocation depends on the Spirit and the resurrection
of the "son of God" at a time when the apostles are still preoccupied with the "Son of David" and with "carnal" considerations.
    b) The second part of the salutation describes the subject of
this gospel: the son of David, proclaimed Son of God. Paul characterizes it by the contrast "in the flesh . . . in the Spirit," one of
the main themes of the letter to the Romans (Rm 8:1-13, cf. 4:
13-19), but which does not correspond to the modern dualism:
body-soul, or even with the antithesis: human-divine. For Paul
flesh denoted the "world" before the resurrection of Christ, while
"Spirit" is the "new world" strengthened by this resurrection. Here

the contrast "flesh-Spirit" is applied to the terms: *Son of David and Son of God*.

The expression "proclaimed Son of God" is rather striking if it refers to divine sonship, which Paul knows to be eternal (Rm 8:3, 29, 32; 5:10). In fact, he is probably not talking here so much of divine sonship itself as of the messianic title (Ps 2:7-8; cf. Acts 13:33; 4:25-28). Christ is son of David through his ancestors; but, being of the flesh, this title is empty unless God intervenes "in power" to make him Messiah (Son of God) and "give him all nations." To say that Christ is son of David is to assert that he belongs to Israel and that Israel has a central place in the economy of redemption. To say that Christ is Son of God is to stress that the nations now have a "Lord" able to make salvation accessible to them.

Paul insists that his apostolic mission to the nations (v. 5) is the full realization of the universal messianism promised to the "Son of God" in Ps 2:7-8. And Paul is proud of bringing the good news of salvation to the citizens of the world capital.

The thought of Paul would therefore be distorted if we were to differentiate between son of David and Son of God just as we do between the humanity and divinity of Christ. Paul rather shows that the economy of redemption, centered around the davidic dynasty for the sole benefit of Israel, is now displaced by a new order, which invites all nations to gather around the new envoy of God whom Paul is charged to announce.

The gospel of Paul thus presents Christ not only as God made man, but also as son of David and Son of God. Through the Incarnation, God not only espoused human nature, he also took upon himself the concrete human condition, social and political, of Palestine at that time. The Messiah is thus a gift of God, but also the product of human history.

A belief in the son of David proclaimed Son of God nowadays amounts to a belief that civilization and history play a part in the building of the Church and the Mystical Body. It also means a belief in the human aspect of Christ's mission, alongside its transcendence, and an understanding that the Eucharist must have definite human and cultural qualities in order to reveal its mystery more clearly.

II. Galatians
4:22-24,
26-27, 31-5:1
1st reading
2nd cycle
Monday

This difficult text contrasts two trilogies: a) Hagar-Sinai—the earthly Jerusalem (the old economy of salvation); b) Sarah-(Sion)—the heavenly Jerusalem (the new economy of salvation).

a) Paul explains the first trilogy by relating Hagar and Sinai through their geographical position and their slavery (the spiritual slavery of Sinai). But Sinai was in fact to be found in Jerusalem (the Jews had identified Mount Sinai and Mount Sion: Is 2:3; Ps 14/15:1-4; 2 K 22; Ps 67/68:16-18; 98/99:2-6).

The second trilogy is a trilogy of freedom (the second term is omitted: Mount Sion, where Pentecost was fulfilled). The Jerusalem from above does not simply refer to heaven, but to that heavenly city already in the process of construction on earth. Both the rabbis and Christians thought of this heavenly Jerusalem as coming down upon earth (Heb 12:22; Rv 3:12; 21:2); coming down at least in the sense that Christians were already living morally, as though they were in the heavenly city (Ph 3:20).

Paul then establishes the parallel between Sarah and Jerusalem by applying to the Church a prophecy from Isaiah 54:1 on the messianic Jerusalem which was to be amazingly fertile after a period of sterility; Sarah became fruitful after a period of sterility, the Church is the new Sarah, and like her is free.

b) What is Paul's purpose here?

First of all he is eager to know who has a claim on the title: *descendant of Abraham,* which the Jews claim for themselves. In chapter 3 of the letter to the Galatians, he has shown that the

Jews based themselves on an outdated legal system in order to maintain descendance from Abraham. It is faith that ensures true sonship since Abraham has descendants only in faith. The life of the patriarch supplied Paul with an argument that was certainly accommodated, even allegorical, but did illustrate what he had in mind. Yes, the Jews are descendants of Abraham, but as the sons of the slave who is not a child of love but of a legal arrangement allowed to Abraham because of his wife's sterility. Christians for their part are the true descendants of Abraham because they share his faith, that faith which is at the origin of Isaac's birth and because they are born outside every legal arrangement.

c) But very often, and this is the precise situation in the passage which precedes our reading (Ga 4:1-7), when Paul speaks of Sonship from Abraham, he immediately speaks of the *Sonship of God*. In fact, the first involves the second since it is in final analysis the promise of God who was at work in the conception of Sarah and in the birth of Isaac (cf. still Rm 8:14-17; 9:6-7). Also, Paul passes without transition from the espousals of Abraham and Sarah to that of God with his people, that sterile and abandoned spouse whom God will find again in the last days. That is why he introduces the quotation from Isaiah 54 and makes Sarah an allegory of the Jerusalem from above, the idealized type of the actual Church. Thus, in contrast to the Jews who wanted the law to be an irrevocable institution, Paul shows that God is bound, like Abraham, to two successive arrangements, one in favor of slaves, the other of free men. But the least perfect arrangement dissolves before the most perfect, liberty replaces law.

III. Luke
11:29-32
Gospel
Monday

The gospel tradition has retained four allusions to the sign of Jonah (Mt 12:38-42; 16:1-4; Lk 11:29-32; Mk 8:11-12). These different versions are certainly close to the words spoken by Christ himself in a context that allowed easy interpretation of his thought but which today is lost. In any case it is certain that Matthew's interpretation of "the sign of Jonah" is late.

Christ probably wanted to indicate to the Jews that they would not, as far as their conversion is concerned, have access to more signs than the Ninevites (Jon 3:10), the simple presence of the prophet of God and the content of his message being sufficient to lead to conversion (cf. Mk 8:11-12 and Mt 16:1-4). But gradually as the early community asked questions about the personality of Christ, they saw in this manner of speaking about Christ a direction capable of shedding some light on it. Thus they made Christ the awaited sign. In this way Luke 11:29-32 already compared Jonah and the "Son of Man."

The more research on the significant personality of Christ was pursued, the more it concentrated on his paschal mystery. Establishing a parallel between the three days of the Pasch of the Lord, the early community made the "sign of Jonah" the very sign of obedience and the resurrection of Christ. This is the version—rather allegorical—retained by Matthew, but over which Luke did not dally, no more than to retain the theme of the three days for the announcement of the Passion (Lk 9:44), an indication that the theme of the three days is not primitive.

a) The gospel for this day is then the occasion of a statement on the signs of faith. The Jews place themselves on the outermost level: they wanted miracles in order to have faith and be converted. In contrast, Christ proclaims that faith rests uniquely on confidence placed in the person of the one sent. The Christian community had made this even more precise: there is no faith outside the mystery of the death and resurrection of the one sent.

Modern man no longer risks exaggerating like the Jews: a *miracle* embarrasses him and he believes more willingly despite it rather than because of it. An unquestioning belief in miracles could lead man to believe that God is present only in what surpasses man, whereas God is also present in man and in his works.

Furthermore, miracles have no true significance unless they

express the personality of the one who performs them and unless they interpellate the person of the witness. This is why most of the miracles of Jesus are healings, signs of his messianic role and of his goodness (Mt 8:17; 11:1-6), and even of his relation to the Father (the theme of the "signs" in the gospel of John). This is also why they call to an interior conversion (cf. the Queen of the South and the Ninevites) and to faith. They call to it, but do not bestow it. In fact, the Spirit must first work in the heart of man so that he accepts as a beggar and not as a judge, the sign proposed by God.

b) We can however wonder that God and Christ does not give to the Pharisees or to the Atheists of today the *sign* they await. Why does he not write his name clearly in the heavens so that doubt would become impossible? Quite the contrary, it seems the more mankind moves in the direction of progress and secularization, the more it is "desacralized" and the more the signs of God appear rejected.

If God would act in such a manner, he would no longer be the God who chooses to become the servant of man to gain their love and their confidence. It would be an advertising stunt which no one could resist; it would very likely break all resistance. Would he then still be the witness of liberty and in search of a free and confident love? There are truly no other signs except that of Jesus because God chose not to confound man, but to gain his love by dying for him. This is so precisely because he is the God of love who gives no other signs save that fulfilled in Christ Jesus.

The true believer, not misunderstanding the role of miracles, no longer asks for signs because he discerns in the very person of Jesus, the man-God, the presence of God and his intervention. The true miracle is in the moral order: it is that human condition of Jesus, accepted in trust, in obedience and in absolute love and totally radiating the divine presence to the degree that, even in death, God was present to his Son to raise him from it. Indeed it is in this "sign of Jonah" that all the miracles of the gospel reach their highest point, calls to conversion and openness to the salvation of God; sings of his spiritual presence in the struggle against sin and death.

IV. Romans   The first two verses of this passage supply the
   1:16-25   central theme of the letter to the Romans: Paul
   1st reading   considers speaking about the justice God offers
   1st cycle   to anyone who can accept it by faith (vv. 16-
   Tuesday   17). But he will really deal with this question
in Romans 3:21-11:36. Before broaching it, he presents a long preamble (Rm 1:18-3:20) describing the "wrath" of God in face of man's sin. This preamble, which begins here, belongs to the literary genre known as a diatribe and throws a gloom over the situation in order to stress better the light of justice and to set off the dramatic impact of the coming of Christ Jesus into a world destined for ruin.

a) The first verses (16-17) supply a statement for the doctrinal portion of the letter to the Romans. For Paul, the gospel is summed up in a few words: on the one hand *justice* and the salvation of God (and the two words cover the realities in close continuity as in Is 45:21; Ps 35/36:7; 39/40:11; 70/71:2-15; etc.); on the other, the faith of man (Heb 2:4).

The justice in question is not that of the judge who rewards or punishes, but which justifies and saves even the sinner, for it has "force" and power. It is not bestowed upon man without his collaboration. Paul is too Jewish to ignore that to be just is to stand before God in the relationship he has desired. The biblical and Pauline term for justice is, in fact, rich with nuances. It is religious: fidelity to the covenant; juridical: the relation that is fitting between man and God; moral: the appreciation and the judgment born by God; eschatological: the action whereby God justifies the sinner by offering him salvation.

b) This justice is not obtained by the efforts of man, nor by observance of the law, nor by belonging to the race of Abraham.

It is acquired by faith, by listening to the gospel and opening up to its power. Henceforth, Jew and Gentile are on equal footing: like the just man in Habakkuk 2:4, it is in God whom they must confide their salvation.

c) Paul then broaches the question of the natural knowledge of God. He does so like the author of Wisdom (Ws 13:1-3), that is, as a believer formed far more by Scripture than by the sages or by philosophy.

For him, in fact, the problem is not knowing how man can be raised from the created world to the Creator (the position taken by the author of Wisdom), but how man can still ignore God, seeing that he has taken the initiative to make himself known (vv. 19-21). For him, God, in creating the world, charged it with transmitting to man some knowledge of himself (v. 20) because a tragic divorce separates him from the universe. Paul does not exactly attack his contemporaries, but all mankind. In fact, the words of verses 21-22 are in the aorist and designate a sort of collective sin imbedded in the past and continuing to grow worse.

For Paul man's inability to know God from creation is not then an intellectual problem but one of the moral order: by falling back on himself and making himself the center of the world, man progressively lost the ability to read the presence of God in creation. *Sin* has killed his *understanding*. Paul is a reader faithful to the Bible and especially to the first chapters of Genesis which influence the entire letter to the Romans.

The apostle does not state directly whether there is or is not the means of arriving at the knowledge of God in creation. He simply states that sin, which is the wound and the separation between man and the universe, has hindered this.

d) The consequences of this refusal to recognize God are manifest for St. Paul in three categories of aberration: perversion in the relationship between man and God (idolatry: vv. 22-23), in sexual matters (vv. 24-27) and finally in the social sphere (vv. 28-32). Man is free to reject God but he cannot escape the consequences of this rejection. God is not a stranger to the perversion in which the sinner engages, in this sense: that he has established an order which we cannot break without it turning against us. In this respect the perversion mentioned above can be understood as a punishment (v. 18).

The problem of the knowledge of God is perhaps no longer presented in the same way in our era as in that of St. Paul. But the drama is the same.

Modern man is no longer sensitive to the proof of the existence of God from creation: the reality of the beyond seems to him unreachable. Furthermore, the criticism of metaphysics and of religion which he has undertaken is far from being insignificant. The problem of God is not less present to his conscience. Existentialism reveals man as torn even in his ego and the more profound ego from the depth of which the dynamism of being is drawn: this ego which remains alive in agony and death, which is open to God is the very Spirit of God. The two "egos" are separated and man can no longer lay hold of God in him. His lot is like that of the contemporary of St. Paul who does not succeed in finding God in creation. The original wound is found there: it has been reabsorbed only in Jesus, the man who was able to live simultaneously on the plane of his two "egos," both in communion with men and with God, in a perfect integration of himself. Faith enables the Christian to test this integration of the two levels of his personality and to name the Spirit of God the profoundest level.

V. Galatians 5:1-6
1st reading
2nd cycle
Tuesday

Chapter 5 of the letter to the Galatians is the true conclusion to this letter. Paul gives no new insights about Christian freedom but merely recapitulates the essentials of what he said and tries especially to lead his readers to adopt a style of life that will bear witness to the freedom acquired in Jesus Christ.

The reading for this day recalls the general theme of the epistle: the *liberty* acquired in Jesus.

The very first verse affirms our liberation but without stating precisely with what or in what manner we are free. To know this, it is enough to reread the first chapters of the letter: it is the cross that frees man (Ga 1:4, 4:5) and this liberation becomes personal the day each man practices the apostolic preaching (Ga 3:1-5). We discover here in reference to freedom the pattern already developed by Paul in Romans 5:6-11 and in 2 Corinthians 5:14-21 for justification or reconciliation: freedom is something already acquired for humanity by the initiative of God and the death of Christ. But it remains to integrate each man into this mystery of freedom and this is the task of the apostle.

But from what are we freed? In the letter to the Galatians, Paul thinks especially about liberation from the practices of the law (circumcision, days of observance, etc.: Ga 3:10-22; 4:9-10) which he designates under the image of the yoke (cf. Si 51:31-37 and Mt 11:28-30). Nevertheless, evangelical freedom is not only opposed to slavery (Rm 8:21), but to every alienation of man from the sacred.

Freedom and obedience are not then opposed, but the only obedience that is not a slavery is that which yields to the gospel. This is simple: in Jesus Christ humanity has been made free and Jesus is the first to fulfill his destiny in the name and in the dynamism of this liberty of the partner of God.

The Eucharist renews the freest act a man has ever posited: offering his life for love and handing it completely over to the Father. It is the sign which attests to all the assembled faithful that they are truly established in freedom. This communion in the body and the blood of Christ is the way to integrate this freedom in a life still alienated by servitude and to plunge freely into the gift of love.

VI. Luke
11:37-41
Gospel
Tuesday

There are two different versions of the invectives which Jesus hurls against the Scribes and Pharisees. The first is reported by Luke (11: 37-53) and the second, much shorter, by Luke (20:45-47) and by Mark (12:38-40). Matthew has combined the two versions (23:1-32). In the Lucan version, Jesus formulates his attacks during a meal: the evangelist often returns in fact to the "symposium type" (cf. still Luke 14:1).

The first quarrel arises because of the ablutions which normally precede meals. Jesus dispensed himself purposely it seems (v. 38, cf. Mk 7:2, 5), to the surprise of his host; he distinguishes the internal and the external, the within and the without (vv. 39-40). We could draw a moral by intention: it is not what one does that counts, but the intention involved. Fearing, however, a bad interpretation (we would think that good intentions suffice), Jesus quickly returns to an intention translated into action. Here, alms (v. 41).

The modern Christian runs the risk of turning in on himself with a "spirituality of intention." But it is not by means of such a spirituality that we shall reconcile the Church and the technical world. Certainly the submission of our spirit to the will of God confers on our actions a precious value, but to confer primacy to intention alone is equivalent to considering the world and the work of man as a simple occasion for salvation without proper value. Moreover, the tangible reality and the problems which it poses requires at this point every effort of our spirit because it is no longer possible to reserve a zone apart where the moral or religious intention would be formulated. On the contrary, every dichotomy between the within and the without, between the religious and the profane, between activity and the interior life must be rejected. In this respect, the reasoning of Luke (v. 40), even if it is formulated in the Jewish fashion remains valuable: God is more interested in the internal than the external. He rejects every dichotomy.

VII. Romans   In Romans 1:18-3:20, Paul draws a dramatic
2:1-11   tableau of the religious situation of the Gen-
1st reading   tile and the Jew in order to stress in the re-
1st cycle   mainder of his letter the originality of the
Wednesday   salvation which God offers to the true believer.

After the description of pagan decadence (Rm 1:16-25) the apostle brushes over for the present Jewish decadence. It is useful to note that in his mind the association Gentile-Jew does not simply designate two categories of mankind, separate and opposed in the ancient economy of salvation, but a theological association in that it defines the behavior of all men deprived of Christ (cf. "everyone of you" in verse 1), sways between the pagan and atheistic and the Jewish legalistic attitude.

The tableau of human decadence among the Gentiles is so violent that many men—and in every case, Jews—could say: "I am not like the rest of men" (cf. Lk 18:11). But Paul immediately rejects this *judgment* by a series of arguments:

1st, man is certainly capable of making a moral judgment. But this ability has been given to him in order to judge himself, not to pose as a critic in censure of other men nor for proclaiming himself superior to others (vv. 1-2).

2nd, this power for judging ought to lead to the recognition of the fact that if God allows sinners to continue in existence, it is by virtue of his patience and his long suffering (v. 4). Thus others are to be judged as God judges them: with the patience that he exercises in waiting for repentence.

3rd, failing the proper understanding of the divine patience towards sinners, man not only manifests misunderstanding of those who sin but he fails to realize that this respite is offered him also for his conversion. He thus runs the risk of presenting himself before God as impenitent (v. 5), heaping on his head the punishment foreseen for the day of Yahweh (Am 5:18, Rm 9:22).

4th, this ability to judge is still perverted by those who, like the Jews, ease their consciences by imagining that their racial and national privileges will help them to escape unscathed from the judgment of God. This is a false perspective: God abides by a just retribution and does not make an exception for anyone (vv. 6-11).

VIII. Galatians Paul tries to persuade his readers about the
5:18-25 vanity of the proposals which led them to
1st reading adopt the Jewish law and its pseudo-practices
2nd cycle for salvation. Christ liberated the Galatians
Wednesday (Ga 5:1) from all that, why then return to it?

The passage for today compares the fruits of life according to the flesh (the law in his thought is "Carnal") with the fruits according to the spirit. Paul hopes that this comparison will help the Galatians in choosing by making clear what is at stake in their decision.

In St. Paul the "flesh" designates the way that man lives from his own resources, without reference to any particular help from God who is the Spirit.

The apostle thereupon enumerates the *works of the flesh* (vv. 19-21): impurity, the failure to respect the sacred zone in which life is transmitted; idolatry, which disregards the transcendence of the divine domain; and above all, the countless failures to observe charity. For St. Paul the carnal man left to his own resources is necessarily an egoist for whom all means are good which enable him to seize power over others.

The apostle does not hesitate to add to these characteristic traits of the carnal man adherence to the law (v. 18). This addition becomes significant when we remember that it was the law's claim to free man from his uncleanliness, idolatry and egoism. But if it reveals to him carnality, it is powerless to free man from its chains (Ga 3:10-22; Rm 7:7-13; 4:15; 5:13).

Only the Spirit can really give man the way out of the flesh (v. 16). But the deliverance is not automatic: it is the outcome of a struggle where flesh and Spirit confront each other; but the latter makes the conflict and victory possible.

The works of the Spirit are manifold, but this multiplicity is subsumed by Paul under the one idea of charity (vv. 22-23). It is the source of joy, of a joy that is the fruit of hope in the imminent victory (Rm 12:12; 15:13; Ph 4:4-5). Let us note in passing that the Latin text gives twelve works of charity whereas the Greek text gives only nine. Doubtlessly the Latin translator found that one term alone did not cover all the nuances of the corresponding Greek word which led him to multiply certain terms.

But when shall we be truly liberated from the flesh and placed under the guidance of the Spirit? Paul's conclusion is clear: the decisive sign of this liberation will be the imprint of the Lord's cross in our life (v. 24). Consequently, it is not possible to identify a freedom born of the Spirit with any solutions of facility or attitudes not expressed in deeds. True freedom is to be found, like the resurrection, at the end of the way of the cross.

In the economy of the flesh, man undertakes his own salvation and he seeks to make his securities sure. Man according to the flesh even reduces the law of Sinai to a simple means of security and he loses sight of his end which is to lead man to a profound openness to divine guidance.

Christ teaches man to abandon the security which moral precepts provide and he invites him to the unforeseeable encounter with God in the event and in others. This is called obedience to the will of the Father or love of God and the brethren.

By urging the Christian to always more obedience before the event, the Spirit calls him to communion with others in respect for his otherness; it makes him a witness of love and of freedom.

IX. Luke   Luke is here concerned with the discourse on
11:42-46   the curses which Christ pronounces against
Gospel   the Pharisees (Lk 11:37-51). The evangelist
Wednesday   has rather clearly weakened the violence of
                      certain reprimands and has suppressed details
that are too Jewish in origin. Even more, he gathers the curses

into two groups of three whereas Matthew has seven. Finally, he directs the first three curses rather arbitrarily towards the Pharisees and the last three to the Scribes though they are interchangeable.

In every way, the discourse of curses seems better in Matthew than in Luke. In the first gospel Christ, having completed his work, can make an accounting of it. He has counted his enemies and thinks henceforth about the judgment which God is going to render by condemning them and by glorifying him.

a) The first reprimand of Christ concerns the *formalism* of the Pharisees (v. 42). The redaction of Matthew 23:23 is however clearer. Christ attacks the interpreters of the law who quibble without end (the tithe of all little plants), but forget to recall the essential command of justice and goodness. Matthew makes a clear reference to Hosea 6:6. Luke frees himself of this Jewish context: he replaces the reference to Hosea by recalling the duty of love and he adds the tithe on vegetables to the list of harmless details on which the Pharisees debate. Luke no longer then simply compares trifles to the important commandments but, in a general way, the material regulations to the fundamental law of love.

b) Christ then attacks the religious authorities who prefer *honors* to service (v. 43). Luke's version is more percussive for it directly reprimands these authorities in the second person whereas Matthew is content with a description in the third person. It is however adequate in itself, for it aims at the honor which the religious authorities search for, not only in the synagogue in the exercise of these functions but also in public places where nothing ought to single them out. Verse 44 pushes the irony still further: people who claim honors are consumed with vice and to touch them is to contract the impurity that one contracts in approaching a tomb (Nm 19:16).

c) Jesus finally crticizes (v. 46) the casuistry of spiritual directors of people. They have so loaded the law with regulations (from which they exempted themselves) that they made religious life intolerable, whereas the burden of Christ is light and easy to carry (cf. Mt 11:28; Jr 6:6; 1 Jn 5:3-4). The Scribes inhibited the poor, ignorant people who resorted to their light in order to know the will of God.

X. Romans   Paul has just concluded his gloomy picture of
3:21-30a   humanity left to its own devices, and now em-
1st reading   barks on the positive section of his letter; the
1st cycle   revelation of salvation in Jesus Christ (Rm
Thursday   3:21). The section is made up of kerygmatic
                     proclamations, and of analyses and proofs. The
first verses from which today's passage is taken, are clearly a "solemn proclamation," or kerygma. We encounter in it extremely important ideas and phrases, which are not necessarily made explicit: justice (vv. 21-28), redemption (v. 24), propitiation (v. 25), faith without works (vv. 27-28), etc.

a) God's *justice* is first and foremost an event ("and now," v. 21). Already in the Old Testament ("the law and the prophets" of verse 21) God's justice meant not his judgment (over "the good and the evil") but his fidelity to the covenant, and his concern that this should prove fruitful for a humanity conformed to his will, even though this should require from him mercy. In this sense God's justice (v. 21) is contrasted with his anger (Rm 1:18) which proves destructive of the covenant (Rm 1:18). "Now," that is to say in the eschatological age that has arrived, justice is definitively manifested in Jesus Christ. The first man had been destined to be witness to the justice of God and thanks to it surpassed the limitations that death and egoism impose. Now all who live in Jesus Christ can live by the same justice (v. 24).

b) This justice was manifested by Jesus on the cross (vv. 24-25) and above all in the work of *redemption* here accomplished. It was thus that God manifested his justice to the Jews, sinners though they were, by "ransoming" them from Egyptian captivity

(Dt 5:6), by "ransoming" them from the Babylonian exile to which they were reduced by their sins (Is 41:14). However all this is past (vv. 25-26a). Today God is undertaking the ransom of man from death itself (Rm 8:23), and from sin, by offering him through communion with the risen Christ the opportunity of overcoming sin (Col 1:13-14; Ep 1:7). Redemption indeed enables man to go beyond himself, his limitations and his alienation, his sin and his death. Once man lives with the God of Jesus Christ, he can aspire to this.

c) How has God brought about this "redemption"? Paul answers by making Christ the "instrument of propitiation" (v. 25). We cannot say really whether Paul is thinking explicitly of the rite at the expiation ceremony where the high priest poured the blood of the sacrificed victim on the "propitiatory" of the ark (Lv 16:15), or whether he uses the word "propitiation" in the general sense of appeasing the wrath of God. At the risk of making God a sanguinary figure whose desire for vengeance could be appeased only by the sight of blood, the first interpretation seems the more likely. On the day of expiation the sinner was "ransomed" because the victim's blood (a symbol of life) came directly into contact with God on the propitiatory. In some fashion an exchange of life took place: a renewal of man's life by contact with that of God. Christ is a "propitiation," not because he offers himself up to God's wrath, but because he is the propitiatory place where human blood (life) comes into permanent contact with God, even in death. Paul's idea is not that God stemmed his wrath on seeing the blood of his Son, but that the only means of demonstrating the plentitude of God's justice was the blending of human and divine life that the incarnation meant. In verse 25, blood is not a sign of death, nor of divine wrath that has been dramatically appeased. It is, as it was in the Old Testament, a sign of life, life that has been renewed by God, restored and pardoned.

d) This "redemption" or "expiation" is absolutely gratuitous. That is Paul's point when he contrasts the works of the law with *faith alone* (vv. 27-28). He is explaining how man can benefit from the manifestation of God's "justice" that we have in the "propitiation" of Jesus Christ.

In order to understand his view we must remember that Paul distinguishes between justification and salvation (which Judaism did not). Justification, as he sees it, is already accomplished in Jesus Christ, while salvation (and God's judgment) is reserved until the end of time (Rm 5:9). No work of the law is sufficient to gain justification: faith is the only way (v. 30; cf. Ga 2:16; Rm 4:5). For final salvation on the other hand works are necessary (Rm 8:3-4; 14:10; 2 Co 5:10; Col 3:25; cf. 1 Co 15:9-10; Ep 2:8-10). Christian life indeed is rich in works because it is a compenetration of human by divine activity. This guarantees the gratuitousness of salvation, but in a way that differs from the absolute gratuitousness of justification.

**XI. Ephesians
1:1-10
1st reading
2nd cycle
Thursday**   With this passage we begin the series of readings from the letter to the Ephesians that will continue for some weeks. Apparently the letter was written from Rome between 61 and 63, during Paul's first captivity. Subsequent to the great classical letters, the apostle had widened his horizons and deepened his thought. This letter gives us the fruit of all that. It is marked particularly by polemic against the Jews, and the synecretism of Colossae and Ephesus.

The tone is extremely meditative. Two parts can be distinguished, a liturgical (1:3-3:21) and a paraenetic (4:1-6:20). Both are characterized by contemplation of the mystery of reconciliation of Jews and Gentiles in the Church, which is Christ's Body and a sign for all humanity.

Our reading today gives us the first part of the liturgical "blessing" with which Paul opens the letter. It can be divided into the introduction (v. 3), a first strophe (vv. 4-6) which culminates in a refrain about God's glory, then a second strophe (vv. 7-12) culminating likewise in a reference to the divine glory (not present in the liturgical excerpt).

Quite probably this blessing is inspired by a daily Jewish ritual prayer where we find identical themes: divine fatherhood (v. 3), election (v. 4), phrases like "richness of grace" (v. 7), "praise of God" (the refrains in vv. 6, 12, 14), and "in love" (vv. 4 and 6). The differences between the two prayers are important. Where the Jewish ritual thanks God for the gift of the law, Paul gives thanks for the gift of his Son (v. 6).

a) The introductory strophe at once defines the dominant themes not only of prayer but of the whole letter. Thanks are being offered for salvation (here presented as a blessing), which is willed by the Father, merited by Christ and realized by the Spirit.

The salutary *blessings* for which God is praised are: the death (v. 7) and glorification of Jesus (Ep 1:10); the beginnings, through faith and baptism, of divine life among men (Ep 1:13); and throughout the world, thanks to the Lordship of Christ (Ep 1:10). The phrase "in the heavens" which characterizes these blessings designates everything which is neither "flesh and blood" (Ep 6:12), nor the "celestial powers" supplanted by Christ (Ep 4:7-16; 5:23). The phrase "in Christ" is meant to indicate the mediation by which the blessings of the Father are conveyed. In the order of salvation Christ has been substituted for "flesh" and "spirit."

b) The new strophe (vv. 4-6) explains how God's blessing aids man, who has been called to holiness by Christ. This blessing is the *election* made by the Father's love; it transforms men into children of God, "heirs" of the privileges that have been hitherto connected with the observance of the law (Ga 3:18): it links them with the renewing presence of the Spirit (Rm 8:14-17). First among the privileges is holiness. This is the communication of God's very life (Lv 19:2) through the channel of his love, which reaches its culmination in man's adoptive sonship (v. 5).

c) In the second strophe (vv. 7-12) the advantages accruing from the work of Christ are enumerated. The first is *redemption,* where grace abounding is combined with the remission of sins (Rm 13:21-26; Col 1:14). This "redemption" in these terms, or "remission of sins," is the possibility offered to every man of union with Christ, or transcending his limits and shortcomings, while he searches for greater depth, for something beyond the pole of banality. "To him who demands your cloak give also your tunic."

The second advantage is *knowledge* of the mystery (vv. 8b-10). It is called "intelligence," that is to say elucidation in depth and "wisdom," or again religious appreciation. The object of this knowledge is the salvific will of God towards all men (cf. Ep 3:5, 9; Rm 16:25-26). It is a will that has remained hidden for long, but is now revealed in the person of Christ. It is in Christ that every being and every thing finds meaning. The knowledge is knowledge of God's plan: when we cleave to that plan we enter the "universal recapitulation" that Christ accomplished (v. 10).

d) The *recapitulation* in Christ of all things (v. 10) is the most significant detail in this strophe. Some commentators give "re-capitulation" a rather weak interpretation in this context, its purely philological sense: the summing up (as the law is summed up in one commandment: Rm 13:9). Others believe that Paul is investing the word with his ideas about the relations between Christ, the Head, and the Mystical Body (cf. Ep 1:20-23). In this view what we have is an affirmation of the "taking up" of all things in Christ, in whom they have been created, and in whom they are now reconciled (Col 1:15-20) since he has been pro-claimed "Lord" and "Head" of the universe (Ph 2:9-11). It is a cosmic restoration where all creation recognizes Christ as Lord and lives by the very life of Christ. All things belong to God, and return to him through the lordship of Christ. The recapitulation is accomplished through stages. Gentiles are associated with Jews (vv. 11-13), "terrestrial" men with celestial beings. All to-gether will enjoy the same rights and the same life.

From this notion of the solidarity of all beings under one and the same head, by now another idea is beginning to take shape. No longer can some be regarded as subject to others in some sort of dependence. No longer are Gentiles inferior to Jews (Ep 2: 11-12), or men subject to angels (Ep 1:20-2:10; cf. Ep 4:9-10).

XII. Luke   The exegetical introduction for this discourse
  11:47-54   on the curses is found at the beginning of
  Gospel   Luke's commentary at Luke 11:31-41 (the
  Thursday   gospel for Tuesday) (at p. 185) and at Luke
                      11:42-46 (the gospel for Wednesday).

a) The first curse retained by this passage concerns the *persecution* which the Scribes made the prophets undergo (vv. 47-51). It is pronounced in verses 47-48 in words rather similar to those of Luke 6:2, as if the source of the curses found in Luke 6 and Luke 23 came from one and the same source (cf. also Acts 7: 51-52).

Verses 49-51 are a sort of personal commentary added by Luke himself. He alone, in fact, and not Christ, could at the time of the redaction of the gospel place the apostles and the prophets on an equal footing (v. 49). He alone could introduce this commentary by a quotation from the "wisdom of God" which Matthew 23: 34-36 has Jesus pronounce.

b) The second curse deals with the *intellectual autocracy* of the legalists (v. 52). These defined once for all the principles and methods of their science which is self-sustaining, divorced from reality, mere rationalization, and no longer brings light to those who turn to the custodians of science in order to shed light on the meaning of their existence.

It is tragic then for this science that it is so turned in on itself, that it functions outside the real question being asked by lay people and crying for an answer. It is also tragic for that autocratic science that cannot tolerate prophets and that stifles every evolution by impeding the leaven of vitality from developing according to its own laws.

XIII. Romans   After the kerygmatic proclamation supplied by
     4:1-8   Romans 3:21-31, Paul turns to the proof of his
     1st reading   thesis (Rm 4), using as the basis for his state-
     1st cycle   ment the figure of Abraham, so basic to Jewish
     Friday   thought.

The Jewish tradition saw in Abraham the very type of the recipient of *justification* by works, going so far as to have him obedient to a law that did not even exist in his day (Si 10:5). Paul passes over this interpretation in the very name of Scripture by recalling that it does indeed speak of a justification of Abraham, but by faith (v. 3, cf. Gn 15:6). Moreover, for him as for one tradition, Abraham was "impious" (v. 5) before being summoned by God. For this reason Paul does not hesitate to join to the quotation from Gn 15:6 that of Psalm 31/32:1-2 which speaks about the justification of the sinner (vv. 7-8).

As a sinner, Abraham thus found himself empty handed before God. He gained happiness and became just only through grace and pure mercy. He simply believed, that is to say, he accepted to receive gratuitously.

Abraham was born to faith when the ideas he used to define God, such as the idea of justice, suddenly took a new and unexpected appearance. In fact, we do not have faith so long as we think of God in terms of "distributive" justice such as man knows (cf. Mt 20:1-16) or so long as we are satisfied simply to make it superlative (the most just, the best, infinitely just), for the God of faith is not at the end of a progression in grandeur. He reveals himself only as the Totally-Other, in the matter of justice, as one who unfolds a justice so gratuitous and so justifying that it appears scandalous. Abraham the sinner found this God there and believed.

XIV. Ephesians   This passage presents the end of the second
1:11-14   strophe, the third and fourth strophes of the
1st reading   act of thanks which Paul speaks to the Father
2nd cycle   at the beginning of this letter.
Friday

a) The *recapitulation* in Christ of all things (announced in verse 10) is the most significant detail in this strophe. Some commentators give "recapitulation" a rather weak interpretation in this context, its purely philological sense: the summing up (as the law is summed up in one commandment: Rm 13:9). Others believe that Paul is investing the word with his ideas about the relations between Christ, the Head, and the Mystical Body (cf. Ep 1:20-23). In this view what we have is an affirmation of the "taking up" of all things in Christ in whom they have been created, and in whom they are now reconciled (Col 1:15-20) since he has been proclaimed "Lord" and "Head" of the universe (Ph 2:9-11). It is a cosmic restoration, where all creation recognizes Christ as Lord and lives by the very life of Christ. All things belong to God and return to him through this lordship of Christ. The recapitulation is accomplished through stages. Gentiles are associated with Jews (vv. 11-13), "terrestrial" men with celestial beings. All together will enjoy the same rights and the same life.

From this notion of the solidarity of all being under one and the same head, by now another idea is beginning to take shape. No longer can some be regarded as subject to others in some sort of dependence. No longer are Gentiles inferior to Jews (Ep 2:11-12) and men subject to angels (Ep 1:20-2:10; cf. Ep 4:9-10).

b) Another blessing from God is the "setting apart" or *election* of the faithful, made inheritors of the divine life in Jesus Christ (v. 11). Access to this heritage is no longer tied to observance of the law (Ga 3:18) but is acquired by the newness of life inaugurated in man by the presence of the Spirit (Rm 8:14-17). It is then a consequence of that divine sonship acquired by men in Jesus Christ (v. 5) and the foundation of hope (v. 13).

c) Verses 13-14 contain the final strophe of the blessing, with particular reference to the Christians of Ephesus. The chief stages of *initiation into the faith* are mentioned: evangelization (v. 13a), the salutary content of this missionary gesture, conversion, the sacramental reception of the Spirit's seal (v. 13b), and finally the presence of this Spirit, the pledge of life eternal in the whole texture of life. The strophe is designed to reassure Paul's correspondents that they do share in every truth in the spiritual blessings that have been celebrated in the early portion of the hymn.

XV. Luke 12:1-7   This passage presents various statements of the
    Gospel   Lord which the oral tradition had already
    Friday   brought together before the gospels. Matthew
                      has integrated them in the discourse on mis-
sion (Mt 10). Luke uses them as an introduction to the directive given by Christ to his disciples in the situation in which they are led to confess his name (Lk 12).

Verses 2-3 gather together sayings of Christ which the evangelists had some difficulty interpreting correctly. Matthew 10:26-27 makes of it a declaration by the Lord according to which he was able to transmit his message with all the desired clarity (Mk 4:22; Jn 16:29-30) and he would entrust the task to his disciples. Luke 8:17 applies them, by contrast, to the vitality of the gospel and seems to destine them for its adversaries whose machinations will end by being unmasked. He thus prepares the continuation of Jesus' discourse on the counsels in time of *persecution*.

In verses 4-7 Jesus reminds his disciples that one enemy alone is deadly: Satan, but that God has his fate in hand and that the Father jealously guards all his own.

Despite the diversity of these statements, Luke has been able to give them a certain unity and he uses them to elaborate a doctrine on the difficulties and contradictions of the life of a Christian in the world. He draws from it the necessity for the disciple to go to the heart of Christ's message in order to discover new resonance there; he stresses the solidarity of the master and his disciples in the contest and recalls the confidence necessary in this divine assistance within the options taken in faith.

The building of the Kingdom cannot in fact happen without the rending of man or without the confrontation with a world that thinks it can procure the means of salvation of itself. The dialogue between the Church and the world which Vatican II wished to reestablish does not do away with difficulties or opposition. Even if the people of God one day come to express their faith in a secularized world, opposition will remain alive, for the desire to save himself is too profoundly written in the heart of man to tolerate the practice of the evangelical beatitudes.

By celebrating in the Eucharist the victory of the love of Christ over hate, the Christian knows at what point sin, in him and in others, is an obstacle to the Kingdom and he offers his will to triumph over his own pretensions to autonomy so that God can help him remain faithful to the gospel message.

XVI. Romans Paul continues his analysis of the bonds be-
4:13, 16-18 tween faith and justification, beginning with
1st reading the example of Abraham. In his first argument
1st cycle (Rm 4:1-10) the apostle has shown that the
Saturday patriarch was impious and a sinner at the time
God justified him. He now develops two more arguments.

a) The question at hand is knowing why it is faith that procures justice and not works. Paul replies that faith justifies better than the works of the law because it has been relieved of the bearing by which God enters into the encounter with man. It is not a question of preferring one or the other: the secret of their qualification is found in God. If he came to man with a contract, works would then be the most adequate human response. But he comes to him with a *promise*, with a gratuitous gift by which he intends to keep the initiative; consequently the works of the law are useless, at least in the process for the realization of this promise.

Man believes he can obtain through his works the object of the promise (v. 14), but he claims to gain by his own works what is in reality a gift. He thus changes the nature of God's activity and automatically provokes the rupture (v. 15), as the heir who would like to secure his inheritance before time.

b) The third argument is barely outlined (vv. 16-17). The promise was made to Abraham at a time when he was not yet circumcised and when God foresaw a *universal fatherhood* for him (Gn 17:5). It is then contrary to the will of God to limit the posterity of Abraham to those who are circumcised. Every believer has Abraham as father and furthermore God is powerful enough to make the dead themselves benefit from the promise, as those who have not yet come to existence (v. 17).

A religion of the promise is rather remote from the spontaneity of the man who, in quest of his salvation, seeks security. One must have encountered the living God and have taken one's bearing on his fidelity in order to have a foreboding that the awaited salvation belongs to the order of promise, that is, the order of love.

But how encounter God and his promise? It takes time for the reciprocal relations of love and fidelity to deepen.

The journey is however marked out. The man who reflects on himself and on his existence happens now and again to discover in himself an "ego" at two levels: the normal "ego" and the profound "ego." The first is the source of activity and involvement; it succeeds or fails to suffer from its limitations or to settle down in unconcern. This "ego" can test its limits only because there exists an "ego" more profound which participates in the absolute and in transcendence.

The road which leads to God passes by this consciousness of the two "egos." Certainly man succeeds only very rarely in living at the depth of his profound "ego" and in leading his life as he wills. A sort of rupture separates the two "egos" in a rather "original" way.

Even when he manages to rejoin his profound "ego," the man who grasps his participation in the absolute or at least his thirst for transcendence can nevertheless be disappointed in this return to himself. He makes himself absolute and no longer perceives anything beyond himself. On the other hand, if he experiences this transcendent "I" as unexpected in his being, he will be tempted to see there the gratuitous gift of "someone." He will come to it no longer in a possessive manner but as the encounter with a gratuitous gift and with a promise, with a divine person and with grace.

Jesus Christ is the first man in whom God has been able to reveal himself totally in the profound "I" and who has been able to respond perfectly to this initiative of God in him.

XVII. Ephesians   Following the traditional style of Jewish
        1:15-23   thanksgiving, at the end of this hymn of bene-
    1st reading diction (Ep 1:1-10, 11-14), Paul has an epi-
    2nd cycle   clesis, where on behalf of his hearers he asks
    Saturday   for the grace of understanding the divine plan.

a) The *wisdom* that he seeks for his listeners (v. 17) is the supernatural gift that was previously known to the sages of the Old Testament (cf. Pr 3:13-18); but in the Christian understanding it is considerably amplified. It is no longer just the practice of the law and knowledge of a divine plan for the world. It is now more than an explanation of the world: it is the revelation of human destiny (v. 17), of man's heritage of glory (Ep 1:14), which contrasts so strongly with the misery of human existence (Rm 8:20). Finally, it is the discovery of God's power which is already manifested in Christ's resurrection (v. 20) and is the guarantee of our own resurrection.

b) Paul dwells a moment on this divine *power*. He uses three synonymous terms to describe it: power, vigor and force (v. 19). It is more than the power used by God in creating the earth and imposing his will upon it (Jb 38). This power even reverses that order, because it is able to make of one crucified the Risen Lord (v. 21b). In this sense the power is hope (v. 18), because it means confidence about the activity in this world of the God of Jesus Christ.

c) Nor is the manifestation of this power of God altogether reserved for the world to come. Even now it brings fulfillment. It has set up Christ in the mystery of the Church, his "plenitude," as the head of all being (vv. 22-23). Paul prays for the gift of wisdom for his audience, so that they may understand first of all how the Church is the sign of God's power displayed in Jesus Christ. It is indeed an unheard-of privilege to have the Lord of the universe as its head, and to be his body. It is not subject to the Lord as the universe is, because it is already united with him indissolubly, as the body to the head. It is the *pleroma* of Christ, the receptacle of the graces and gifts he bestows on all humanity. The phrase "all in all" suggests that the receptacle is without limits. Nor are these graces reserved for the Church only. They belong to humanity, to the growth of all humanity (Ep 4:11-13) until man becomes the "perfect man," man that is assembled in Christ and enjoying the plentitude of divine life.

XVIII. Luke   This gospel like that of Friday (Lk 12:1-7) be-
12:8-12   longs to a section of sayings which seems to
Gospel   have been redacted prior to the gospels.
Saturday   It is made up of two parts: the first verses deal with the fidelity of Christ towards those

who will be faithful to him (vv. 8-10); the rest of the verses stress that Christians should not allow themselves to be shaken by fear when they are persecuted (vv. 11-12).

Luke's version seems the most original (cf. also Mt 10:19-33 and 12:32; Mk 8:38; 3:29; 13:11; Lk 9:26, 21:14-15).

a) The first verses state a cause-effect relationship between the attitude of *fidelity* of the Christian towards Christ and that of Christ towards the Christian at the time of the gathering which the Son of Man will hold to determine those who will be part of the Kingdom of God. Verse 10 contains a correction of this relation between the fidelity of man and that of God. It admits that some do not recognize the divinity of the Son of Man, since it is hidden within him, but it does not admit that one can remain blind before the clear manifestation of the Spirit (that is, of the risen Christ). We can then see in this verse the echo of the enthusiasm of the early communities and of Luke in particular before the works of the Spirit (Acts 2, etc.).

b) Furthermore, it is this same Spirit-Paraclete (cf. Jn 15:26; Acts 4:8, 31) who will work wonders by sustaining the persecuted before tribunals and by inspiring them with what they should say, as he did for the prophets (Jr 1:6-10; Ex 4:10-12). Here still the echo of the enthusiasm of early Christians is revealed in the cases of which they were the object.

TWENTY-NINTH WEEK

I. Romans
4:20-25
1st reading
1st cycle
Monday

Here Paul concludes his analysis of the link between faith and justification, beginning with the example of Abraham (cf. Rm 4:1-8 and Rm 4:13-17). He has already shown that Abraham was a "sinner" at the time of his justification. He was called to be father of a multitude before he was circumcised, before he had observed the works of the law, faith alone had "justified" him. But what is this faith?

a) Faith is first of all a *hope* surpassing all hope (v. 18). The patriarch's faith maintained him in the conviction that God can suspend all determinism in nature where the future naturally stems from the past, and bring about a new and unexpected future. Thus Abraham did not rely upon himself, shutting himself in his own past. He relied upon God as one who could renew everything. Believing as he did, Abraham did not consider his physical state which seemed to belie his hope. He trusted God to find a way of resolving the seeming contradiction.

We should remember that Paul is taking a theological rather than an historical stand in the whole matter; because in actual fact, Abraham will subsequently be capable of giving a son to Agar and six children to Keturah (Gn 25).

b) The faith of Abraham concerns the person of God himself rather than the content of his promise (in this case, changing natural laws). It is *personal*. It presupposes an awareness of man's capacity to shape by himself his future (v. 19) and the confidence which the power of God can make of that which seems good to him. Moreover, it opens up to an act of thanks (v. 20), being thus contrary to the views of atheists and idolators (Rm 1:21). All this explains why Abraham attaches himself to the person who was promised rather than what was promised; later the patriarch will be ready to deprive himself of the object of the promise, his own son, without relaxing his attachment to the author of the promise.

c) Paul, who was concerned with a theology of faith rather than the history of the faith of Abraham, seen in the attitude of the patriarch, a third component: faith in the *resurrection* (vv. 19 and 24) or, more exactly, personal faith in Him who raised up Jesus. It is impossible to have faith in a miracle or in the resurrection without a prior act of trust in the one who works them.

By giving life to the worn body of Abraham God anticipates Christ's own resurrection and Isaac, the son sprung from the barren loins of Abraham, can be compared to Jesus issuing from the tomb. True, the two events can only be compared allegorically in their material content, but they are joined by the faith they presuppose.

The true "yes" of God's promise is the Risen Christ. In him God gives himself to man, a gift that is not merited. In him man is enabled to join God in complete openness and confidence. The order then both of promise and of faith is the reciprocity in Jesus Christ of two personal fidelities.

**II. Ephesians
2:1-10**
*1st reading
2nd cycle
Monday*

The beginning of the letter to the Ephesians reminds its readers of the divine power placed at their disposal. Paul has contemplated the supremacy of Christ over all the forces of evil in the world gained by Christ at the Ascension (Ep 1:15-23).

In contrast the apostle depicts the weakness and death promised to the earthly and sinful condition. In no other New Testament passage have we such a depressing picture of the demonic element in human existence (Ep 2:1-3). But the author assumes such a negative tone only to emphasize the hope introduced, once the power of God has made of Jesus Christ the Lord. The verses read in the liturgy for this day aim at showing this.

This *power* of God is manifested for the first time in the person of Christ who has been raised from the death he suffered and is seated on the throne of Lordship (v. 6). It is verified in God's attitude towards us: although dead in sin, we rise again because of the extraordinary power of his love which will one day enable us to share the glory of his love. This is the same insight which Paul had in writing to the Romans 6:3-11; 8:11-18: the power of God will save us, but in the future.

But here in Ephesians 2:4-7 Paul is affirming that the power of God has already made us rise again, already given us in Christ a share in divine glory. Of course it is only in the "ages to come" (v. 7) that the power will be fully revealed. But it is at work already through the grace that wipes out our sins and guides our lives provided we receive it "in Christ Jesus," that is to say, with faith in his person, sharing his fidelity to the Father, through the mediation of his sacraments.

III. Luke
12:13-21
Gospel
Monday

The parable of the foolish rich man (vv. 16-21) certainly belongs to a very ancient tradition. We have it also, in a more primitive form, in the aprocryphal gospel of Thomas (n. 63). The discussion that Luke has associated with the parable (vv. 13-14) must also for the same reason be regarded as quite ancient. But we probably owe to the evangelist the association of the discussion and the parable by the addition of verse 15. Luke however was not content to add the introduction: he also provides the conclusion in verse 21.

a) The discussion between Jesus and the two brothers is concerned with an inheritance. The older wants to keep it undivided, as was the custom. The younger on the other hand wants to withdraw his share (cf. Lk 15:11-15). Jesus' intervention in the discussion is to the effect that he has no wish to exercise distributive *justice.* The gospel was not created to sacralize pleadings. His reason is very clear: he has no authoritative mandate to treat these subjects.

He is judge as Son of Man, but with a justice that in no way resembles the distributive justice of man (cf. Mt 20:1-15). It is a justifying justice and a sign of gratuitous love.

There is generally speaking an eschatological tone in which Christ says, at least by implication, that this matter will not be for his judgment. He refuses to allow the disciples the right to join the gospel with mere options, to sacralize that which ought not to be sacralized.

b) Luke however gives the incident a more moral emphasis. Concerned as he was with *poverty* and with the particular difficulties of the rich in living the community life of the Kingdom, he tries to convince his readers of the danger of money. He also introduces verse 15 where Jesus gives a second reason for his refusal to judge: terrestrial goods are not of sufficient importance to require the judgment of the Son of Man. He then proceeds with the parable of the foolish rich man, adding a significant conclusion (v. 21, "for himself" . . . "in the sight of God").

We must not take it however that Luke is putting forward an ethic of poverty without eschatological reference. Jesus is not trying to frighten his hearers with thoughts of a sudden death that could ruin their hopes. The death in question indeed is the eschatological catastrophe which will be followed by judgment. The lesson becomes clear: if one displays an attachment to goods at a time when only attachment to God can save men from the imminent catastrophe, this is "foolishness" (in the biblical sense of the word: an inability to recognize God and attach oneself to him: Ps 13/14:1).

We are then far removed from the worldly and moralistic teaching of the Old Testament (Dt 6:10-13; Ws 16:20-21; Ec 11:10-19). Luke's account raises the question to the eschatological plane and extols an attitude that is the sign that the Kingdom is an already acquired reality which one must now reckon with (as indicated by the moral ideas in Ep 4:30-5:2).

Texts such as this gospel have been used as an example for the accusations of Christian preachers against the terrible power of money. Money, however, is not Satanic; it is the use which man makes of it. Nor is it a power, rather it is man who makes himself its slave or who uses it to suppress his brothers.

Today, money is also the symbol of man's work, of a progressive economy, of the love we owe to the poor and the hungry. It is the symbol of the prosperity of a nation but also of the financial aid which this latter sacrifices for the promotion of the Third World.

Money is Satanic when by using it man has nothing in view but himself; money is a blessing when man or the state that uses it directs it towards the happiness of others. In this respect, the gospel about the amassing of wealth becomes especially realistic when one considers the innumerable "granaries" and "silos" in which rich countries store their surplus wheat from one fat year to the next while poor countries count the grains of rice alloted to them.

IV. Romans
5:12, 15b,
17-19, 20b-21
1st reading
1st cycle
Tuesday

In the letter to the Romans Paul presents a kerygmatic type of proclamation (cf. Rm 3:21-31) and a scriptural or dialectical analysis (as in Rm 4). Here in chapter 5, he embarks on a new kerygmatic demonstration. This justification about which he has been speaking since chapter 3 is seen in the early verses of chapter 5 as a reconciliation (vv. 10-11) in order to show that man has no right to justice and that no work of his has any value because he is fundamentally sinful ("feeble," "sinners," "enemies": vv. 6, 8 and 10).

This justification-reconciliation is brought about by Jesus Christ (vv. 2, 6b, 8, 10). In this context Paul points out how the divine initiative of justification and man's response to it are summed up in Jesus even prior to any impulse of Christian faith.

a) The first question that arises concerns the meaning of verse 12, in particular *original sin* to which Paul seems to allude. Paul's style (he usually dictated) is not quite precise. Verse 12 begins with a conjunction (*dia touto:* because of this), and a comparison (*ôs ei:* as if), which remain incomplete. Thus, one cannot determine whether death, which he personifies almost in a mystic manner, is physical or spiritual. Neither can we tell whether the relative *eph'* ô should be translated *"in whom* all have sinned" (the Augustinian understanding of original sin); or *"because* all have sinned" (an allusion to personal sin only); or again *"from the moment when* all have sinned" (personal sin being somehow a ratification and augmentation of all mankind's sin, because from generation to generation it repeats and proclaims the basic revolt of humanity against God, throwing into direct relief the spectacle of an enfeebled and quasi-impotent mankind).

Furthermore we do not know whether Paul understands the word sin (*anastein*) in a classical sense (the *act* of sinning) or in a passive sense such as we sometimes meet in the Septuagint (*state* of guilt: Is 24:5-6). The actual state of exegetical research does not yet permit us to form a doctrine of original sin from this verse alone. Finally we must not forget that, as in the preceding chapter concerning Abraham (Rm 4:18-25), Paul's reflection on Adam is more that of a theologian than an historian (cf. also Rm 7): he searches for the fundamental structures of human existence and calls attention at least to a collective responsibility and a dominion of "death" over humanity.

b) The parallelism between Adam and Christ (vv. 15b, 17-19) does not however attribute equal importance to the two figures. One must be careful not to regard Christ simply as the person capable of redressing the debacle for humanity that began with the first man. The obedience and the sacrifice of Christ not only cancel the disobedience and the sin of Adam and of the many;

Christ has become Lord of the eschatological life (cf. the "how much more" of verse 17). There is more here than simple restoration or expiation: this means the beginning of a new economy.

c) This last point is essential for Christian *anthropology*. If it were true that Christ simply redresses the debacle begun by Adam, Adam would be the primary figure because we could not comprehend Christ apart from him. But if what Christ brings ("life") is radically different from anything that Adam, left to his own resources, was capable of bringing, then we see Adam in terms of Christ. "Adam is no more than the figure of him who was to come" (v. 14b). Adam and Christ are not then two persons of equal dignity, as if the sin of the one and the justice of the other are counterbalanced. Then we see that Christian anthropology is essentially rooted in the notion of man in Jesus Christ, who enjoys the promise of life, and Adam enters in only as the object of a backward glance on an ancient past, a simple image of reality. In the Christian view humanity cannot be defined in terms of Adam; only Christ, and not just Christ of the cross, but Christ become Lord, possesses the key to the mystery of man.

There is a similarity between Christ and Adam: each is connected with the many by an extraordinary bond. But there is no question of the old and the new, of the first and the second. There is only Jesus Christ and those who prefigured him, figures who find their meaning only when the one they herald has come. The two terms of the Adam-Christ antithesis are so unequal in their very brotherhood that it makes very little difference ultimately for Christian faith whether science one day demonstrates the truth of polygenism and tears away the veil from the allegedly mythical thinking of Saint Paul in his commentary on Adam. For us the only important point is that there is no way for humanity to find the meaning of existence except in the light of Christ's lordship. Where we come from is not important so long as we know where we are going.

V. Ephesians
2:12-22
1st reading
2nd cycle
Tuesday

The author of the letter to the Ephesians completes in this passage his treatment of one of the principal fruits of redemption: the reunion of Jews and Gentiles in the one Church of God (vv. 11-18). The conclusion (vv. 19-22) recalls an ancient baptismal hymn.

a) Christ is *peace* in a double sense. He has inaugurated a new humanity in which the differences between Jews and Gentiles are wiped out (vv. 14-16) and he has also, by his death on the cross (v. 16) and his gift of the Spirit (v. 18), made peace between God and man.

Christ also proclaimed and realized the peace that was foretold and preached by the prophets (Is 57:19) by restoring normal relations between men and between them and God so effectively that the distant as well as those close have heard and accepted his message.

b) Addressing himself especially to the Gentiles Paul enumerates for them the special benefits of this peace: they are no longer "strangers" but fellow citizens of the new people and members of the household of God (v. 19).

This image of the *household* of God gives Paul the opportunity of composing a kind of hymn to the Church, the temple (v. 21) and the new dwelling place of God (v. 22; cf. Mt 16:18), whose construction was begun by the Word of the apostles and the prophets. Paul attaches a great importance to the role of this Word in the construction of the Church; already in the organization of liturgical assemblies he gave it first place (1 Co 12:28), priority to all their religious phenomena.

But if the Word of the apostles and the prophets in their conversion of hearts is the foundation of the Church, Christ is the cornerstone of the building. The expression is borrowed from Isaiah 28:16. It concerns a messianic image (cf. Rm 9:33; 1 P 2:6; Barnabas 6:2) which designates the most important stone, the one on which the entire structure stands, assuring it solidarity and conferring cohesion and harmony.

c) The image of the household conjures up that of the *structure*. Israel is par excellence the construction of God who "built" it all along as a secular work, preserving it from its enemies and assuring it his fidelity by sanctifying it (Ps 88/89: 3-5; Jr 31:4, 28; 24:6; 18:7-10) with a kind of permanent miracle. In order to build his people, Yahweh used "builders" (Ps 117/118:22): the leaders of the people and the religious elite. But these have not observed the instructions: they have rejected a stone, Christ, to which God attached special importance (Acts 4:11; Mk 12:10-11) and have cast aside living stones, the pagan nations which God intended to incorporate into the building (Jr 12:16). Christ should have been the final stone of the building. But once the Jews rejected him the building collapsed and the destruction of the temple revealed the ruin of the building—Israel (Mt (23:37-38; 24:2).

However, God continues to build his people; he simply replaces the team of builders with Christ (Mk 14:58; Jn 2:19) and his apostles (Mt 16:17-19). The personified character of this edifice will be recalled: it involves a personal action of Jesus (cf. the expression "in him" of verses 21-22), entrusted to other individuals: the apostles on one hand, Christian converts from paganism on the other (cf. "you," v. 22). For the first time Paul talks about the participation of all the faithful in the building; until now he had strictly reserved the privilege to the apostles (1 Co 3:5-17; 2 Co 10:8; 12:19; 13:10; Rm 15:20). Moreover, the structure is in perpetual making because of the diversity and the kinship of ministries, but always under the unique impulse of Christ.

By presenting the Church as a structure in which everyone collaborates, Paul does not envisage an enormous construction, all structure and institution, for to him this building is not an end in itself: it prepares for God's eschatological dwelling among men and allows itself to be judged by it.

The Church defines itself by complementary expressions. It is temple and dwelling and yet it is still in construction. It is solidly founded and established and yet still unfinished. It is the personal work of God and Christ, but cannot rise without the collaboration of the faithful. Its structure cannot hamper its dynamism; the care placed in founding it is not enough for it to be fully the resting place of God in Spirit. It remains weak and incomplete so as to continually to allow itself to be erected by Christ on the foundation of the Word.

VI. Luke Christian vigilance is presented as a virtue
    12:35-38 capable both of revealing the arrival of a thief
    Gospel (Mt 23:43-44) and of recognizing the Lord
    Tuesday who comes to his own (Acts 13:33-37). Saint
Luke unites the two themes: the coming of the thief and the return of the master (vv. 35-38) which leads to a single conclusion (v. 40).

a) In Luke the parable of the servants who await their master differs from the account presented by Mark 13:33-37. The porter, symbol of Peter in Mark, is not the only one to keep watch: all the servants are charged with doing so with him (v. 37). New details are also introduced. Thus, the injunction to let your *belts be fastened* (v. 35) has probably no relation with the posture prescribed for the paschal ritual. It is concerned with a parable (where only the general meaning is involved) and not with an allegory (where all the elements are important). The expression "to fasten one's belt" indicates working (Jn 21:18). The servants must then conduct themselves during the night as if they were working in broad daylight.

The detail about the return from the nuptuals (v. 36) appears additional: it belongs solely to the anecdote and not to the real meaning of the account (contrary, for example, to Mt 25:1-13).

b) In contrast, the essential element of the parable consists of the *reversal of situations* which is brought about at the time of the bestowal of rewards (vv. 37). From servants, the slaves become masters whom the master himself serves at table. This manner of presenting the reward is popular in the eschatological literature of the poor of Israel. These latter were awaiting in effect the Kingdom as an occasion for avenging their actual misery (Lk 6:20-26; 1:52-53).

c) Luke goes beyond this image: the simple stipulation of poverty is no longer sufficient for obtaining the Kingdom; necessary is that *vigilance* which for Luke is manifested especially in prayer (21:36; 18:1; 22:39-46). There is here an overtone unknown to Mark 13:33-37. The bearing of this parable is then more moralistic than eschatological.

d) It is also clearly *eucharistic*, for Luke was able to write it only by thinking on the word of the Lord which he himself introduced into the account of the Last Supper (Lk 22:24-27) although the other synoptics place it elsewhere.

VII. Romans 6:12-18
1st reading
1st cycle
Wednesday

After chapter 5 Paul goes from kerygma to the analysis of certain objections: from "proclamation" he passes to dialectic. The objections that are presented to him are clearly indicated in Romans 6:1-15; 7:1. This reading is then placed between two responses which can be summed up in a single question: how can Christ establish a humanity truly freed from sin?

First of all Paul considers the sacrifice of Christ, the reference point for Christian sacrifice. That is where the Christian really dies. Is it possible to imagine that anyone returning after offering his sacrifice for sin would commit sin again after leaving the altar (v. 15)? This is not only a psychological or moral conclusion: the sacrifice of Christ has really drawn into his death those whom he had freed from sin and made to pass to the service of a new

Lord (v. 15). The Christian has then been freed in order to give himself to a new master, not in order to live for himself, for the liberty that is acquired is not license or libertinism, but service.

VIII. Ephesians   These verses bring to a close the doctrinal por-
3:2-12   tion of the letter to the Ephesians. Paul is con-
1st reading   sidering the "mystery" of the admission of the
2nd cycle   Gentiles into the Church and the apostolic
Wednesday   ministry that accomplishes it.

a) In this context of the "mystery" (vv. 3-6) of the reunion of all men into the Kingdom, Paul sings of the *cosmic* bearing of his apostolate.

The intervention of the apostle is first of all decisive in the order of time because it falls to him (v. 9) to reveal the decision made from all eternity by God, but hithereto hidden. However unworthy he feels of such a mission (v. 8), Paul makes clear the mysterious indications of the gospel he was to preach to be found in the work of the creator. This makes him a co-worker in salvation-history.

His intervention is no less decisive in space. It affects not only men but heavenly principalities and powers (v. 10), those forces hostile to the Kingdom (Ep 6:12; 1 Co 15:24) now subjected to the Lordship of Christ (Col 1:16; Ep 1:21), and led to discover in the gospel of Paul a mystery of God's will of which they were totally unaware.

b) Paul's emphasis on the victory of Christ over these angelic powers (Ep 2:2; 6:12) is developed all the more because Christians of pagan origin had not completely rid themselves of fear where such powers were concerned. Was it not such powers which controlled the evolution of the world, procuring for men the "earthly blessings" of collective and individual well-being? Paul is not content with proclaiming their downfall. He makes it known that, thanks to Jesus Christ, they are supplanted by the

Church in the dispensation of such blessings because of admission into intimacy with the Father (v. 12; cf. Ep 2:18).

The sinful world had been under the domination of these angelic powers committed to their cult and their intervention. Now it is supplanted by a new world, a regenerated humanity, which knows no other mediator but Jesus Christ (v. 11), no other blessings but those of the Church (v. 10).

IX. Luke   We have here the continuation of Jesus' par-
  12:39-48   able on vigilance. After that of the master of
  Gospel   the house who stands in fear of thieves and
  Wednesday   that of the servant who awaits his master,
                  Luke recounts a third, rather similar, but
which he reserves especially for the apostles, after having Peter
ask Jesus for a parable directly related to them (v. 41). Here,
moreover, we are dealing with a steward and not just a simple
servant.

This interpretation of the parable as indicating the *vigilance* necessary for the apostles does not appear primitive. In relating this parable Christ was probably thinking about the leaders and the Scribes who, at that time, willingly bore the title servant. He thus announced to them an unexpected proof that would permit them to verify their fidelity.

However, the Christian community transformed this parable into an allegory in order to show the Son of Man returning to judge his own and more especially those to whom he had confided the greatest responsibilities. We most likely owe to this reinterpretation of the primitive parable the addition of verse 46b which would be an allusion to the lot of Judas and then the addition of Peter's question (v. 41).

Vigilance is a virtue of the Christian people because Christ regards time as not merely a juxtapositioning of successive moments but an organic sequence whose meaning will one day be revealed. The Christian is a "watcher" because he is sensitive to every moment of a time which can be decisive for a new stage or for a greater maturation, and because he knows it as unbroken and the bearer of a still mysterious meaning. He places himself then in a "now" which engages the future and asks questions about the past. He modifies time in order to make it the measure of his destiny, thus giving it all its meaning.

Consequently it is essential that temporality is more visible in the sacraments. Baptism presupposes that time has meaning, that it has measured the faith and the conversion of the candidate and has become in some manner the echo of its destiny. The Eucharist is, in its turn, written in time so that certain moments during the course of which it is unfolded, reveal the coexistence of the eternity of God and of the time of man. That is why the president of the assembly must be a "watcher," capable of grasping this coexistence and of proclaiming it.

X. Romans **6:19-23** *1st reading* *1st cycle* *Thursday*	This reading repeats practically the same lesson as the preceding passage (Rm 6:12-18). Before baptism Christians were slaves of sin and "free" in respect to justice. Baptism reverses the situation, freeing them from sin but bringing them into subjection to justice (v. 19).

The *fruit* theme introduces another nuance to the text. In the preceding verse (v. 21), the fruits represent evil and shameful actions and finally eternal life (vv. 22-23).

The fruit image could be expressed in modern dress in terms of efficiency. The fulfillment of God's plan is realized in fact in a history in which all have a unique and irreplaceable role to play. Following Christ and in living unity with him (the bondage theme: v. 20) the Christian is an efficient man. His actions produce fruit. He does not perceive the gift of God as something to be received passively: God gives himself only to partners. To be sure, he is the first to intervene but his intervention becomes real only in a truly reciprocal activity.

The terrain in which the Christian bears fruit is not the closed field of certain virtues but this very world which has made an inventory of the resources available to man for his future. The fruits of the Kingdom are also the fruits of the human community. Sin can also reappear there. But the Christian is urged to seek an efficiency measured by purely human standards, more tangible than the efficiency of the gospel. Sacramental efficiency, that of the Eucharist in particular, is unfolded in him so that both the principal author of this efficiency, the Lord Jesus, and the conditions for its display, sometimes mortifying and often contested, may appear.

XI. Ephesians
3:14-21
1st reading
2nd cycle
Thursday

Paul had just revealed the mysterious plan of the Father (Ep 3:8-13): to make all men co-heirs of glory in Christ. Before such a "mystery" Paul feels quite full of pride: is he not the herald of this good news to the Gentiles (2 Co 3:6; Col 1:23; 1 Th 2:4; Ep 3:8-13)?

Finally, overwhelmed by such responsibility, he bends his knee (v. 14) in order to address a prayer to God (vv. 14-19) and an act of thanks (vv. 20-21).

a) Paul directs his prayer to the Father (v. 14) and he explains it. Every human family (*Patria*, v. 15) looks back to an ancestor, but humanity is divided into several families, races and nations: into Jews and Gentiles to be exact. But under the common Father there is only one, universal, unified family. From all these various ancestries the Father, through Jesus Christ, reassembles his children.

b) Paul's prayer is that there should be collaboration between man's higher faculties (the interior man: Rm 7:22) and the power of God's Spirit (v. 16). But the second intention is more explicit, that God should dwell in man, according to the prophecy of Ezechiel 36:26 (v. 17).

This theme of God's *dwelling* in our hearts is perhaps the precise key to these final verses (length, breadth). We should seek the source of the symbolism in the description of the new temple in Ezechiel 40, where the prophet had been asked to give the dimension of the future eschatological temple. In fact Saint Paul, a few verses earlier (Ep 2: 20-22), had just been saying that this temple of God, erected on the fundamental Rock which is Christ and constructed in the Spirit, is here and now the assembly of Christians built up in the charity and love of God. Each individual Christian accordingly is a stone in the edifice, and the foundation on which he is solidly established is the charity of God and his redemptive love (Rm 5:1-11; 8:35-39; 2 Co 5:14-19). Paul recommends us to study this impenetrable and mysterious plan of God, visible in the bringing to birth of the new man by the gift of the Spirit, and in God's indwelling in his new spiritual temple. He bends his knee before God, now, just as he would have in the former temple, because in each instance the love of God is at work.

c) At the end of a prayer which asks God for the most important graces, the author reminds his readers that the *richness* of God will surpass any possible demands we can make upon him (v. 19), just as in the case of Jesus Christ (vv. 20-21). Our whole passage in today's liturgy revolves around the theme of God's richness. We are given several synonymous expressions: plenitude (v. 19), transcendence, infinity (v. 20), power, glory (v. 16), energy (v. 18), etc. This divine "richness" in Pauline terms belongs more to the order of love (v. 17) than of knowledge.

XII. Luke
12:49-53
Gospel
Thursday

This passage combines two sayings of Jesus that present some difficulty in interpretation. The first we have only in Luke's version (vv. 49-50). The second also appears in Matthew 10:34-36, in a form on which Luke's text appears to depend.

a) Verses 49-50 follow the rules of Hebrew parallelism:
—fire and water (baptism)
—the yearning and distress of Christ
—kindling the fire and consuming baptism

The association of fire and water is characteristic of the description of the *judgment* in Jewish apocalyptic literature. This is when God will bring the old, corrupt world to an end and substitute for it a new world that will remain faithful to him (cf. 2 P 3:5-7). Doubtless Jesus is referring to this belief, but he stresses the fact that it is he himself who will be the object of this judgment. He will be consumed with fire and plunged into water. It is then in his person that the ancient world will be purified to become the new world. This is what he yearns for most ardently, with the greatest distress: the passion. The Son of Man does not come to judge and condemn, but to take on himself the judgment of the world and enable the universe to be transformed.

b) This transformation of an ancient world into a new world was wrought in his person when he was offered in death. But this has repercussions on every member of humanity. Each one must be converted and substitute new attitudes for his ancient ways. Some will accept *conversion,* others reject it. Through the very center of Jewish families themselves the line of division will run between those who remain loyal to Judaism and those who become loyal to the Lord.

XIII. Romans   The first problem raised by this excerpt from
    7:18-25a   one of the most important chapters of the let-
    1st reading   ter to the Romans is the significance of the
    1st cycle   constant use of the pronoun "I."
    Friday   Paul probably cannot himself be questioned,
                      for he has preserved from that period of his
life when he was under the regime of the law, a rather favorable impression which corresponds to nothing so far expressed (cf. Ga 1:14; Ph 3:5-6). There can no longer be any question of a portrait

of the Christian who, although already purified, is always exposed to sin, for the problem will be raised only in chapter eight.

We are most likely dealing with a description of humanity itself evolving throughout the history of salvation and here personified in a fashion rather common in Scripture (cf. for example Jr 20:7-11). Thus we are dealing less with a psychological introspection than with the expression of an historical situation conforming to the laws of a literary genre which reunites public, liturgical "confession."

Many exegetes until now saw in Romans 7 an outline of the history of salvation in three stages:

1st, from Paradise to Sinai; a time for man where there was no responsibility because the law did not exist, which brings the natural law into disrepute (v. 9);

2nd, after Sinai when the law unfolds the responsibilities of man and makes his lot mortal (vv. 14-24);

3rd, since Christ (Rm 8).

In reality Paul seems to envisage the stages of the history of salvation as follows. The first stage would be that of Paradise before the order concerning the tree of knowledge (v. 9; cf. Gn 3:3). The second would represent the state of all humanity, Jewish or not, victim of "original sin," that is, its constant orientation towards sin (our reading). The third would be that which Christ begins.

a) Once admitted, the exegesis proposed above makes this a less difficult passage to understand. Every man is born into a situation in which he cannot avoid commiting sin and being drawn down into death (cf. Ws 1:12-15). Intellectually, in his most profound "I," he is certainly capable of grasping the will of God, his goodness and his spirituality (vv. 22-23), and this value judgment, which is practically connatural, keeps him from taking refuge in bad faith. But at the same time somewhere in the earthly condition left to itself (the body or the flesh of verses 24-25), he is led almost inevitably to *sin* before even having been able to deliberately choose it and at a time when his profound "I" does not cease taking him to task for it. Death (to be understood here as nonparticipation in the eschatological Kingdom) comes then to sanction this splitting.

Although this divided man grasps God as an absolute (the law of God, v. 8), it is for him only an abstraction which he is unable to transform into reality (vv. 16-18). Consequently, God cannot become the object of love and so cannot help man to join actively the inclination of his profound "I."

So, even before man makes a decision, evil is already in him (vv. 21): more than a simple external solicitation, temptation expresses the inner bondage which encloses the conscience. It is this evil prior to the decision which perverts the mechanism of the conscience and the primacy of reason (v. 23). It asserts itself even before man decides and man cannot free himself from it without God. Now, God for him is only a notion and not a living, challenging being: that is not enough to let in salvation by God.

b) This evil that is prior to the decision (*originatum*, as the Scholastics say) is, for the apostle, the true *sin of the world*. Then he is asked what its origin is and he turns to the *sin of Adam* (*originans*, as the Scholastics say), especially in chapter 5. He goes then from the better to the less known. He does not stop however at the sin of Adam as the tradition of Genesis 3 reports it, but beginning with the old Adam, he presents the new Adam, Jesus Christ (v. 25), the only man who was able to control the "sin of the world" in him and who communicated this victory to his brethren.

This reading describes all at once the condition of man left to himself (the old Adam) and that of man redirected towards God by Christ (the new Adam).

Man is created in the image of God, but he remains fundamentally a being to be saved, and only the intervention of God can allow him fullness to which he tends. The first "law" which God has given to the first man was to renounce fulfilling himself and making himself god by his own powers (Gn 3:3-5). But man preferred to save himself and he installed himself in this contradiction, so admirably depicted in Romans 7.

Man perceives more or less that he is made for the absolute, he the limited; for the divine, he the profane. He tries to resolve this paradox by turning his human nature into the absolute, and the means of salvation he elaborates, into something sacred, instead of simply recognizing his condition as creature.

With the appearance of the man-God on earth, the paradox of the human condition is definitively surmounted. In him, man accepts the condition of child of God without ceasing to be a creature. Consequently he can accept totally this condition made by obedience and death, knowing that henceforth this is the condition of divine sonship. His filial yes to the most banal and ambiguous circumstances of the life of man replace from now on the sacralizations and absolutizing not due to the old Adam.

The Eucharist reassembles into the family of the Father the members of the true humanity, assuming their human and earthly responsibilities in the filial yes which founds the universe in Christ.

XIV. Ephesians 4:1-6
1st reading
2nd cycle
Friday

Previous readings from the letter to the Ephesians have indicated the importance in the whole letter of the theme of unity. It appears again, more explicitly, in this passage.

a) Paul pleads above all the humility, gentleness and charity (v. 2). These are precisely the virtues by which Jesus established his lordship over the world, and succeeded in unifying it (Ph 2:6-11; Jn 13:14-16; Mt 11:29; Col 3:12-13). All are in *communion* with the same sources of salvation (vv. 4-6).

b) The unifying principle is described by Paul in three affirmations, each with three elements. The Spirit which animates Christ's Body and the hope it kindles (v. 4). The Risen Lord, the faith which professes him and the baptism which makes us sharers with him (v. 5). Finally, the Father, over all, through all and with all (v. 6).

What we have here is a trinitarian formula. The secret of *unity* for men lies in the common life of the three persons. The Father is mentioned in the third place instead of the first (cf. Ep 1:3-14), because the unity in question is built by the gradual ascent of humanity, through the Spirit and Christ, to the Father himself.

In order to show how divine life is the principle of unity not only for humanity but for the individual person, Paul juxtaposes a theological virtue with each person of the Trinity. The Spirit sustains hope (1 Co 12:13; Ep 2:18; Rm 8:26-27). Christ kindles faith (Rm 10:8-17). The Father is "within all" to kindle love and communion (2 Co 13:13; Ph 2:1).

XV. Luke	The judgment of God will not be delayed and
12:54-59	Christ even desires its accomplishment (Lk
Gospel	12:49-53). For the last time he alerts the
Friday	crowds to regulate their affairs in view of the
	judgment to come (vv. 57-59) and to learn to

read the signs of its imminence (vv. 54-56).

Jesus reproaches the Jews for not knowing how to read the *signs of the times*. They do know how to appreciate meteorological phenomena (vv. 54-55); why then do they not have enough lucidness to interpret "the present time" which is the mission of Christ among us (v. 56). The signs of the exceptional times in which they live are numerous, and Jesus has often interpreted these for them: his miracles (Lk 7:21-23), his power over Satan (Lk 11:20), his manner of fulfilling the Scriptures (Lk 4:18).

Christ then invites his hearers to see in the accomplishment of his mission the signs of the time of salvation. But these words do not lose their meaning because his earthly mission is achieved.

Today still the signs of his presence are not lacking for anyone who knows how to interpret them. Each man encountered is for the Christian a sign of God (Mt 25:31-46). Now this encounter carries a collective dimension which men of today are more and more conscious of and it is carried out in a concrete way across conflicts, struggles and demands. To the degree that these situations are lived as the ground for a more authentic love for others, they engage our relations with God and they can be for the believer the signs of the coming of the Lord.

XVI. Romans   Chapter 8 of this letter to the Romans is the
   8:1-11   third kerygmatic statement in this letter. It
   1st reading   forms the sequel to Romans 3:21-31 and Ro-
   1st cycle   mans 5 and has as its objective the profound
   Saturday   study of Paul's gospel: God bestows justifica-
                      tion on us through Jesus and through faith. It
describes above all the actual state of the Christian, already justified by faith, but before cooperating with his salvation, because of what Christ had accomplished in him (v. 3) and what the Spirit revives and transfigures (v. 14).

a) The first four verses supply the principal elements of this Christian life suspended between the justification already acquired and the salvation yet to be realized. The first is the law of the *Spirit of life* (v. 2). It is rather astonishing to witness Paul resorting to a law, he who in the preceding chapters is so vividly opposed to all legalistic bondage. But he refers to Jeremiah 24:7; 31:33 and to Ezechiel 36:26-28 (cf. 2 Co 3:1-6; Rm 7:6). For him the new Covenant is in fact the gift of a "law" which is the gift of a "new heart," of a "new Spirit;" even more, of the "very Spirit of Yahweh." The new Covenant can be declared "law" if we admit that it presently designates the activity of the Spirit in man in view of leading him to the eschatological life.

b) The second instrument of the Christian life is a *power* given to our flesh in Jesus Christ and with which the law was powerless (v. 3). The law bestows the insight needed to understand, but not the ability to accomplish the good perceived (Rm 7:16, 22). The new Christian law gives both the insight and the needed ability. This ability is required "because God has condemned sin" in the flesh, an expression in which we are probably meant to see an allusion to the moment when God judged the world by raising his Son on the cross (Jn 12:31-32). Just as Ezechiel 36-37 announces the gift of the new law of the Spirit along with a judgment about enemies (Ez 35, 38 and 39), Paul associates the gift of the Spirit to the condemnation of the powers of evil.

c) How can these instruments aid the Christian in accomplishing the "justice of the law" (v. 4) even when Paul has shown that the Christian was dead to this law? Simply because the Spirit establishes a new law, that of love in which all the precepts of Moses are summed up. The Christian is no longer "under the law," rather he fulfills all its commandments if he practices the law of love. The text of Jeremiah 31 and Ezechiel 36, cited above, which announced the new Covenant, insisted on its legalistic character and it is clearly these texts that Paul is thinking of when he speaks about the Christian fulfillment of justice and the law in love.

d) *Flesh* designates the way which man selects for himself in being preoccupied by self-sufficiency, failing to look to that special help from God who is the *Spirit*. The law, even if it is a gift of God, can belong to the order of the flesh when man changes its nature by making it the vehicle for presenting himself before God with his titles and merits. "To live in the flesh," is to desire this same autarky which was Adam's failure and that of the mere observers of the law: it amounts to being consecrated to death (that is, isolation as far as God and the eschatological life is concerned). "To live in the Spirit" is to acknowledge that he "dwells" in us and to want our whole being to be open to the initiative of God so as to be led by him to life and peace. If he dwells in us, it is as master (the authority theme in verses 7-9), and he is to all appearences the guest of a dead body (v. 10) as he already was in the buried Jesus.

XVII. Ephesians Paul is here commenting on Psalm 67/68:19
4:7-16 (vv. 7-10) which describes the mountain of the
1st reading Lord on the heights of Sion whence he dis-
2nd cycle tributes his blessings to the people. He sees
Saturday the fulfillment of this psalm in the ascension
and then shows how at the side of the Father,
Christ provides the Church with his gifts (vv. 11-16). These are
evidently the last verses which will hold our attention.

a) The gift of the risen Christ to his Church is above all that of a *hierarchy*. The Lord gives to some, apostles, prophets or evangelists (v. 11) and to others, pastors and doctors. All are charged with "organizing" the people (vv. 11-12).

This hierarchy has as its goal to lead humanity, through the Church, to its adult status: that of the Body of Christ, united in the same faith and knowledge (vv. 12-13), thanks to the "joints" (the ministers) who insure cohesion and growth for it (vv. 15-16). The Church effectively leads humanity to adulthood because the Spirit which it gives, and which it can offer only by its hierarchical structure, aids it in better placing itself in view of nature and history and in freely making a value judgment, thereby permitting it clearly to be involved.

The hierarchy by the joints which it establishes and causes to function in the Body, thus promotes the maturity of humanity. In contrast, false teachers retain it in an infantile state (vv. 14-15) both weak and, for lack of good "joints," given over to dispersion.

b) The joints which connect the Body of Christ, made up of Christians, exercise their function only because a basic joint unites the Body to the *Head* who is Christ (vv. 15-16), transmitting to the Body the necessary vital influx. Paul reserves the term "Head" (cf. Col 2:19) to designate the relations of Christ with the people of God; he uses rather that of "Lord" to signify his relations with creation and humanity.

The apostle moreover uses the term Head in two different ways: as a sign of the authority he exercises through the ministers over his Body (the Hebrew meaning; cf. vv. 11-12), and as the seat of the vital power (the Greek meaning; cf. v. 16). Christ is then Head because as Lord of the world he governs the Church by ministerial mediation and because, as holy, he sanctifies each Christian by sacramental mediation.

c) But the image of the Head and of the Body is not enough to account for the root of the universal mediation of Christ in humanity itself. Thus Paul introduces the idea of Christ, the *universal man* (v. 13). His knowledge of the Scriptures allows him to pass from the personal to the universal: in fact, the Servant of God in Isaiah and the Son of Man in Daniel 7 (compare vv. 13-14 and the commentary on them in v. 27) appear in this personal and collective ambiguity. Paul can thus conclude that Jesus, the Son of Man and the Servant, was not an individual person but is in some way identified with every man (cf. an approach to this mystery in Mt 25:31-46).

But by what right can this Jesus, born in the 1st century, of the Jewish race, claim to represent all humanity, even the unjust, before God?

The solution can be glimpsed by acknowledging that the human being is fulfilled only in openness to others: it is always the other who allows actualization of our being and touches it in its very essence. Certainly man never comes to the realization of this constituent universality by himself; he glimpses it only spasmodically and he lives it only in outline form. But a person reaches his divine "self" by his resurrection, and nothing hinders that the realization of himself equals the most perfect universal opening. The Risen Christ is this man and the universe is really his "fullness" (v. 13).

XVIII. Luke   After he reminded the Jews about the neces-
    13:1-9   sity of reading the "signs of the times," Jesus
    Gospel   immediately supplies them with two episodes.
    Saturday

    a) The first "sign of the times" is the suppression, elsewhere unknown, of the Galilean revolutionaries (v. 1). The second is an incident that happened close to the fountain of Siloam which killed eighteen (v. 3). These individuals were killed by surprise. Others could have died (vv. 2, 4b).

Jesus reads the signs of the times in these diverse incidents, for death has seized these people by surprise, as a thief or like a master returning unexpectedly (Lk 12:35-40). The judgment of God will likewise fall unexpectedly on him who expects it the least.

Hence the lesson is clear: do *penance* (v. 3, 5) and you will not be surprised by decisive events.

b) The parable of the barren fig tree is above all an invitation to do *penance*. But Luke's version probably reproduces more than just the words of Jesus.

From Luke 12:35 on the gospel presents a series of accounts directed to the theme of eschatological waiting; the servants await their master, the master fears the thief (cf. Lk 12:35-40), the steward waits his protector (Lk 12:43-44). And Jesus comes, but to bring fire (Lk 12:49-50). Time presses to be reconciled with one's enemies (Lk 12:57-59).

The year of grace granted to the fig tree appears then as the last chance offered to men to be converted (cf. Mk 1:15). Recent incidents in the political life of Israel (Lk 13:1-5) confirm in effect the urgency of conversion.

c) This parable, pronounced perhaps at the beginning of Jesus' public life, was made into an allegory by the early community. It becomes an allegory when it introduces the vinedresser who softens the severity of God and when it fixes at three years the period of time during which the tree was inspected. Christ then appears as the intercessor par excellence who prays for his people throughout his ministry (cf. Rm 8:34; 1 Tm 2:5; Heb 7:25; 12:24), and the fig tree symbolizes the chosen people: Israel and the Church (cf. Hos 9:10; Jr 8:13; 12:10).

Consequently the first meaning of the parable is modified: it is less concerned with calling men to penance than with turning towards God and Christ to discover their longsuffering and their respect for delays (cf. Ps 102/103:8-10; 2 P 3:9).

We are sometimes surprised at the place that death occupies in the announcement of the Kingdom and many atheists and even Christians reproach the Church for brandishing the scarecrow to lead men to conversion.

However, death is the most compelling sign of the times, one which every man must at all cost interpret. The penance to which Christ invites his disciples does not involve simply an examination of conscience that would prepare for entry into the beyond, but more exactly in a willingness to die, which is for each man the most decisive proof of his condition as creature and, all things considered, the acceptance of this condition.

To interpret the "sign of the times" which is death, is to agree to go beyond its proper project; it is to believe in a stronger sense the nonsense of death and the nonsense of life. It means searching out the meaning of each moment.

THIRTIETH WEEK

I. Romans
8:12-17
1st reading
1st cycle
Monday

In the preceding verses the apostle insisted on the priority of God's action in the sanctification of man, basing himself on the "flesh-spirit" antithesis (cf. vv. 12-13). It is not the works of the "flesh" that saves but the presence of the Spirit in man which turns him towards

a new life.

a) The first dimension of this existence is the status as *son of God* (vv. 14-15). God has given his Spirit to man so that he may be able to enter the Father's dwelling. There is then no longer any reason why a spirit of fear should prevail (meaning here a personal disposition). This is the normal reaction of a man who believes that God's benevolence depends on his own efforts. One must simply live as a son and this relationship banishes all fear.

The privilege of the child of God is to be able to call God by the name Father (*Abba* may possibly be a reference to the *Our Father* which some of Paul's hearers may still know in Aramaic, v. 15). The child of God has not then to construct a religion where, if he is a Jew, a ledger of accomplishments must be assembled for a Judge-God; or if he is a Gentile, he must depend on the rites that give security against some awesome power. He simply calls God his Father, with all the familiarity that this implies, and with emphasis always on God's mercy.

b) The second principle is that of being an *heir* of God (v. 17). If a man is a son he has the right to family life and the goods of the household. We should not understand the word "heir" in the modern sense (disposition of goods after the death of the father), but in the Hebrew sense of "taking possession" (Is 60:21; 61:7; Mt 19:29; 1 Co 6:9). Paul's thought is based on the Old Testament notion of heritage, but it adds a new, clarifying dimension by linking it with the notion of sonship. Henceforth the heritage is the possession of men according to the measure of their link with the Son par excellence, who alone is entitled to the divine goods by nature. What the child of God is heir to is the divine glory, the effulgence of God's own life in the person of Christ.

The heritage however does not come without suffering. We are heirs with Christ if we suffer with him. Suffering is the road to glory, not as some sort of meritorious performance but as evidence of life with Christ, the pledge of our being co-heirs with him in glory.

c) The Spirit of God in us is not simply the teacher of truth; his proper role is to move and animate all our being (v. 14); he has then an ontological dimension which can only be perceived by anticipation in the mystery of the very person of Christ and of his Pasch (v. 17). In fact, the obedience of Christ even to death manifests that he recognizes that he depends basically on God and that, in this dependence, he discovers his own stability as creature consecrated to suffering and death. But this obedience as creature to his state is at the same time in Jesus the obedience of the only Son to his Father: it has then an external echo which, glorifying man, fulfills beyond all his expectations his most intimate aspirations.

Now, in the Spirit the Christian, without denying any aspect of his human condition and his dependence, finds himself established in divine sonship and thus capable of giving his obedience a quasi-divine dimension which glorifies him, him too. The role of the Spirit in him is to make firm both this sonship and this divine echo of obedience (v. 16).

In the process of justification then the Trinity is at work. The love of the Father makes men his children. The Spirit takes possession of them to bring them more and more to a filial way of life. Finally, the Son who is the only child by nature, the only heir by right, comes down to earth. He takes upon himself the task of making the human condition and suffering the road to sonship, thus demonstrating to his brothers what the conditions of inheritance are.

As the prophets announced, the gift of the Spirit imbues all hearts with a filial love for the Father and with a fraternal love for all men. The law itself has a new look. It is no longer a heavy yoke, for man has received the Spirit of the last days which liberates him from sin and arms him for a victorious struggle against the works of the "flesh." This envoy of the Spirit is bound to the suffering and to the resurrection of Christ: because he is the Son of God, this man has given the perfect response to the previous initiative of the Father and has led the envoy of the Spirit to all those whom God calls to adoptive Sonship. Thus united in a living manner to Jesus Christ in his Church, man becomes a child of the Father's family offered in the Eucharist.

II. Ephesians   After he considered the plan of God for the
   4:32-5:8   world (Ep 1-3), Paul passes to the description
   1st reading   of Christian behavior as the vehicle of the
   2nd cycle   divine intentions to the world.
   Monday

a) It is, to be sure, charity and mutual pardon that will be the most authentic sign of the will of God. Paul first explains it by showing how they are the *imitation of God* (vv. 1 and 2). This is an idea already affirmed by Christ (Mt 5:44; 6:12-14; 18:21-27).

b) Love and pardon are not only a way of imitating God who saved men when they were sinners; they are also a means of participating in the *sacrifice* of the cross. Paul adopts in fact a sacrificial and liturgical vocabulary (v. 2; cf. Ps 38/39:7; Dn 3:38; Ex 29:18-25; Lk 1:9-17) in order to show how charity is constituative of the offering of Christ on the cross and of the part which the Christian takes in the realization of the salvation of the world.

c) After indicating these principles, the apostle comes to their application and emphasizes especially the struggle against impurity, eroticism and the cupidity of his contemporaries. These three *vices* have in common the will to dominate and ruin others

(I Th 4:6; Col 3:5; I Co 5:10-12) by leading everything to self. Sexuality is not then an autonomous power but an instrument for the salvation of the world. Impurity on the other hand is a vice which is an obstacle to the plan of salvation and thus draws the anger of God (vv. 6-7).

III. Luke
13:10-17
Gospel
Monday

The cure of an old woman, sick for eighteen years, follows immediately the parable of the barren fig tree. The vision of the two passages is then the same.

Jesus frees the old woman from a long history of diabolical possession. There is no doubt that his power can do so, but it is especially because his *goodness* wills it. In fact Jesus accomplishes his miracle even before the sick woman had expressed her faith or made a request. He anticipates her request and reaches his very hands to the old woman who is stooped over and too resigned to hope for anything from others.

The goodness of Jesus prevails over formalism and legalism (vv. 14-17). The law can only aid love in training itself; if it fetters love it must be rejected.

IV. Romans
8:18-25
1st reading
1st cycle
Tuesday

Baptism makes us sons of God (Rm 6): how then can suffering and failure have a hold on us?

The biblical tradition sheds little light on this point for Christians. In fact, sages limited to the observation of the present and of nature, admitted that it was presumptuous to understand (Jb 38) or better they concluded that the universe is absurd (Ec 1:2-9). The prophets saw imperfectly a solution in the eschatological future, as the end of a catastrophe which would annihilate the universe and humanity (Is 51:6; 65:22-23; Ps 101/102:26-27).

Saint Paul brings about a synthesis of these currents by harmonizing the solidarity of man with nature and the hope of a new world.

a) Paul begins by referring to conclusions from wisdom literature. Our body belongs to the *present world* (v. 18): thus it shares its sufferings. Creation, that is to say, the matter to which our body is closely bound, is in effect subject to vanity (v. 20), we would say to the absurd—not because of the sin of man, in general, but because of the very laws of a limited creation (Is 40:26; 48:13; Ba 6:56-57; Si 16:27-28) which forces it continually to begin anew its cycle (Ec 1:4-11) and contains it within limits too narrow for it (Jb 38:8-11; Ps 88/89:10-11; 103/104:6-9).

b) But Paul quickly passes on to a more prophetic vision. For him it is not without reluctance that nature, personified by him, complies with these laws and limits from which it hopes to escape one day (vv. 19-21). Now, this *cosmic hope* is not empty and the solidarity between our body and the cosmos in suffering and decay is found there too. Our body in fact possesses its secret, for it enjoys already the pledge of glorification (v. 23) which will resound over the cosmos (v. 21).

By expressing this solidarity in hope for a new world, Paul is faithful to biblical thought (cf. Is 65:17-25; 11:5-9; 55:13); however he modifies more than one important point. Thus the paradisaical state promised to the universe is no longer tied to the salvation of the people of Israel, as in the Old Testament, but to the revelation of our divine sonship (vv. 21-23). The day this is accomplished in all men, even to transfiguring their bodies, it will transfigure the whole of nature, freeing it from the slavery of "vanity" and adapting it to the new status of humanity.

Far from placing Christian hope in a sort of immortality of the soul separated from the body and from the world, the Greek idea, or beyond the world and life, the Gnostic concept, Paul defines it in view of the present. What we hope for is not a beyond but a within, which can only be attained by living life in the world. The apostle has moreover demystified the "beyond" of death by reminding the Christian that he is already dead by baptism, that he is already in some way in this beyond about which he dreams and which he can join in discovering the "within" of life.

V. Ephesians   This excerpt is taken from a section where the
   5:21-33   apostle is describing the new life "in Christ."
   1st reading   He has shown the influence of this in the tex-
   2nd cycle   ture of moral life (Ep 4:17; 5:20). Now he il-
   Tuesday   lustrates it in some specific institutions such
                      as conjugal life (Ep 5:21-33), the family (Ep
6:1-4), social intercourse (Ep 6:5-9). It is natural that Paul should think of marriage "in the love of Christ," and tell Christian spouses that genuine love for one another is a reflection of Christ's love. The Christian is always a sign of that love of the brethren and of God, of which Christ was the perfect exponent, and which each member of his body is called upon to manifest (v. 30). This will sometimes be difficult to do and it will often be good to have recourse to memory and the Spirit of Christ in order to love as he did (vv. 25-28). In any case married couples are asked to continue in their own state the mystery realized by Christ in his Church.

a) But Paul thinks that Christian marriage reflects more precisely the love of Christ for the Church.

This image of marriage between God and his people mirrors something very deep, a love of God for man that is a love of sharing, a love as unique as conjugal love. And if Paul passes from the image of marriage between God and Israel to that of marriage between Christ and the Church, it is to emphasize that the love of God for humanity achieves its plenitude in Christ, something that was decisive for the history of humanity. Thus he qualifies the kind of love that should animate Christian unions. The little ecclesial cell which is set up in every Christian household ought to be shaped by the love of Christ and the universal Church.

b) It is *baptism* that brings about the association between the Christian household and the espousals between Christ and the Church. Christ's union with the Church is achieved by his redemptive death (v. 25) and baptism which makes us members of Christ (v. 30) is our avenue of entry to the mystery of Christ and the Church.

The word which accompanies the baptismal rite (v. 26) is none other than the Word of God made manifest in the Christ event, and the word with which this event is proclaimed in kerygma and catechesis. The faith which joins us to the paschal event of Christ automatically associates us with his work of love for his Church which is the "great mystery" (v. 32) of God's salvific plan for humanity.

c) But Saint Paul pushes the likeness of the conjugal cell to the nuptials of Christ and the Church very far. Thus he appears to transfer to the husband the prerogative of *Christ-Head* and thus confuses the symbolic role of Christ-Head (Ep 1:18-20; 2:19; Col 2:10) with the juridical title of head attributed to the husband.

At this point Paul is in danger of leading the thought of his readers too far. It is true that the love of the Christian couple is a sign of the love of God (manifested in the Christ-Church espousal). But a simple image (the espousals of Christ and the Church) cannot place particular roles on a couple as if the husband alone was fitted to play the role of Christ (mediator . . . head: cf. v. 23; cf 1 Co 11:3) and the wife that of the Church (warmth, receptivity, cf. v. 27). A symbol, although it is beautiful, can have material repercussions in the diversification of roles. It is the love that unites Christ and the Church which conjugal love should reflect, not the roles suggested by the image of their nuptials.

Paul is too influenced by Judaism and by the juridical structure of the household with which he was familiar. He could not see the female spouse in the role of Christ exercising the mediation for her husband, or the husband in the warm receptive role of the Church.

His wish to see Christ's love for humanity in the love of a Christian couple is perfectly valid; that is the whole meaning of the sacrament. However, he lived at a time when the man was always the mediator in the family; this was only a partial and provisional idea; Paul is somewhat too attached to it to the point of wanting to redeem, for the Christian situation, a role as mediator proper to the groom, figure of Christ and a receptive role proper to the spouse, figure of the Church.

VI. Luke **13:18-21** *Gospel* *Tuesday*	An excerpt from the parabolized discourse of the Lord on the development of the Kingdom of God. Like Matthew 13:31-33, Luke relates two somewhat parallel parables: that of the mustard seed and the yeast.

a) This assemblage gives some insight about the vision which the evangelists had: they clearly wanted to stress that the sign of God grows by an extensive growth (the mustard plant to which birds come to nest) and by intensive growth (the yeast in the dough).

b) The parables however do not stop at the growth but at its final stage: the tree shading the birds and the raised dough, which gives them an eschatological value. The eschatological *abundance* is manifest in the exaggeration of certain traits: the mustard tree cannot become a giant tree, no housewife could manage to use three measures of flour. Moreover, the tree is a classic image (Dn 4; Ez 17:22-24; 31:3-9), of a kingdom come to its apotheosis.

c) Perhaps the two parables also serve to encourage the small flock which surrounds Christ: the fragility of these means is no reason why the Kingdom of God cannot be inaugurated.

St. Luke, like the other evangelists and St. Paul, is amazed when he describes the riches in which Christians participate or which he calls the power of the Spirit at work in Christian communities and in evangelistic activity. The first Christians know themselves as filled with all sorts of blessings.

But the nature of this messianic abundance must be well understood. The satiety which it engenders has nothing in common with the satisfaction of the secure; on the contrary, it is the source of responsibility, it is wealth offered to free wills, called to get themselves ready by taking their bearing on Jesus Christ. The abundance of the Kingdom is a totally gratuitous gift of God, but we do not receive it passively. It commands a task and is developed in growth. To say that we have abundance as our share is to affirm that all is accomplished in Jesus Christ since his resurrection, but at the same time all remains to be accomplished. The eschatological kingdom is a work in the making, an edifice to be constructed, a project of catholicity to be progressively realized.

In other respects the fundamental law of this growth in and towards abundance is, paradoxically, a law of poverty. Saint Paul was the first to insist on the contrast between the wealth he possesses and the poverty we attribute to him. The growth of the Body of Christ is accomplished through our weakness and sometimes even under the appearance of failure. In every way the essence of what happens is invisible to the eyes. The realization of the project of catholicity is effected under the sign of the "seed" and of the "yeast." The true growth escapes our glance. By looking from the outside at the development of the Church man can give a verdict of failure. But the true failure would be that the Church reacts as a power of this world and that the efficiency which Christians dream of, borrows from this world its norms and resources.

Finally, the abundance of the Kingdom and the active growth which it creates constitutes the ultimate source for growth of human values consistent with the gospel. There is here below a true "abundance" which deserves to be sought by man: the brotherhood between all men. The pursuit of all other riches must be subordinated to the search for this brotherhood and this peace.

VII. Romans   To the Jewish or pagan concept of a law or a
   8:26-30   rite that gives security, something that he des-
   1st reading   ignates as "flesh" (Rm 8:1-10) because man in
   1st cycle   these circumstances has recourse to overly
  Wednesday   human means, the apostle opposes the Christian notions of life in the Spirit. It is something
brought about by divine intervention, but it comes to fruition
and accomplishment in human activity (Rm 8:11-17). The things
that militate against life in the Spirit are numerous, suffering and
death above all (Rm 8:18-23). Yet, for Paul the solidarity of man
and of the cosmos in their close victory over death is the object
of hope and of certitude (vv. 24-25). Certainly this hope itself is
expressed by difficulty in prayer, the most expressive place for
hope, but the Spirit inspires the prayer of the faithful (vv. 26-27)
by recalling for him the marvelous conditions of his election (vv.
28-30).

a) It seems that verse 24 must be translated: "it is by hope that
we are saved" and not only by: "our salvation makes the object
of our hope." In other words, *hope* has an active part in the realization of salvation. This is an essential theme in the letter to the
Romans. The letter to the Galatians describes the birth of the new
life by the reception of grace in faith; the letter to the Romans
describes it also in its growth by the cooperation of all the moments of grace in hope. It is then only faith, which by its advance,
realizes salvation. Faith welcomes justification as the free initiative of God; hope transforms this justification to salvation with
the aid of grace. It becomes in us endurance (v. 25) in order to
resist difficulties, and love, diffused in us by the Spirit, unites us
to God.

The ancient Jewish hope confides in the love of God who had
promised his intervention; Christian hope refers to God for whom
love is already at work and who by justifying us, reveals himself as
our Father. Briefly, hope truly realizes salvation which consists in

this confidence and this opening to the love of God throughout the growth of the new life in us.

Certainly, this love of God is not yet manifest, and that is why there is hope (v. 25), but is already present and active.

b) To physical and material suffering the misery of our spiritual life is added, especially in the area of *prayer*. Some Pharisees sought solace for this in a flood of language (Mt 6:7; Lk 18:10-12). The believer in Christ consoled himself with the certainty that the Spirit dwelling in him guaranteed his spiritual life.

The question is not one of knowing how to pray; having subjects for prayer is sufficient for this. Nor does it concern knowing how to speak, a quite common accomplishment. What is important is praying "as we ought" (v. 26) and only the Spirit can bring this about, because only the Spirit knows God's plan (v. 27). The most authentic prayer then will spring from the petitioner's deep disturbance, combined with certainty about the Spirit's role. The essential role is that of intercessor (v. 27) and interior mover, enabling a man to realize his greatest potential, his full status as child and heir of God.

Agony in prayer is a normal characteristic of the interval between our justification in baptism and its full realization in the glory of God. Spiritual life now is no longer just the product of human effort, but the progressive expansion in us of the life of the Spirit (v. 26).

There is then no prayer possible except in an eschatological perspective, in virtue of the promise given by the Spirit to the adoptive children of the Father.

c) The thrust of man and of the cosmos towards glorification will carry the plan of God to fulfillment. Corruptibility in one or spiritual weakness in the other can never jeopardize the project of a God who is faithful to his purpose (v. 28), and who finds in Jesus Christ a perfect partner. "Those who love God" then are assured of glory, not as a merited reward, but because they, in turn, have become his partners. God "knew them in advance" with that biblical knowledge which is communion and sharing of life. He transforms them into children of God conformed to Jesus Christ (v. 29).

Divine *predestination* does not mean election of one and rejection of the other. It means that God is the first to know and to love. His love is realized in Jesus even before men come to it. Predestination is concerned with his plan of love and its way of operation. We are not dealing with a time element at all, as if everything had stopped once for all: precedence accompanies the very unfolding of time and each stage of the Christian life (v. 30): the call (by preaching), justification (by baptism), glorification (by death) are marked by the attentive initiative of God who calls, justifies, glorifies and disposes the instruments of this call with that justice and that glory in the person of Christ and in the Spirit who dwells in the most profound area of our being.

VIII. Ephesians   Following his remarks on conjugal love,
6:1-9   Paul recalls some other precepts also referring
1st reading   to the domestic life of the time. He addresses
2nd cycle   children (vv. 1-3), parents (v. 4) and slaves
Wednesday   (vv. 5-9).

a) The obedience of children is based on several motives: the law of the decalogue (v. 2; cf. Ex 20:12; Dt 5:16); the promise of happiness bound to the observance of this law (v. 3); finally the new thrust introduced by Christ in humanity ("in the Lord": v. 1).

The first two motives are supplied by Jewish ethics: obedience to an external law and the promise of a reward are valid motivations but imperfect in the Christian regime where the basic motivation is in the theological order: to offer to the Spirit of the Lord the possibility of shining on all mankind in order to spiritualize it.

b) Scripture rarely recalls for parents their *duties towards their children* (v. 4). Paul asks them above all to avoid a tyrannical authoritarianism. The education of children must be accomplished in such a way that here too it is the "Spirit of the Lord" who acts.

c) Then the apostle recalls for slaves their duties towards their masters (vv. 5-8) and for these latter their obligations to their servants (v. 9).

This passage is inspired by Colossians 3:22-25. On all sides slaves must practice the same virtues: fear (v. 5) and purity of intention in work (v. 5). However, these virtues are not directed to masters, but directly to Christ.

Likewise, the masters will avoid all violence towards their slaves by reminding themselves that these last are the property of the Lord and not theirs.

The dynamic presence of the Lord intervenes at every moment and in all human relations in order to confer on morality a new dimension which transcends previous motivations: the Christian attitude is as the bearer of Christ and sign of the progressive extension of his reign.

Of the three points broached by Saint Paul in this passage, the duties of parents towards their children will be especially stressed. They are particularly difficult to specify and to practice in the actual world, especially when children have attained the adolescent years which are those of struggle and during which they reject the constraints of education and especially of religion.

In these circumstances parental duty involves above all confidence in the "Spirit of the Lord." What does this mean?

Adolescence is the period of struggling with traditional values. However, it is transitory and does not necessarily involve the definitive rejection of these values; it is even necessary so that these latter will be personally accepted. Then the duties of parents are clarified: to rise above their anxiety, to place confidence in the Lord who works in the future adult, to guide their children towards the future in place of keeping them in structures of the past (which "would exasperate" them, as St. Paul says). Certainly a severe trial which nevertheless allows parents to prove their own faith and to live a new life "that is inspired by the Lord."

The adolescent often rejects many religious practices. They do not see their relation to faith and are satisfied with considering them as the expression of a sociological conditioning which they reject. This reaction is perhaps unjust and incomplete, but it is healthy since it excludes what is perceived, at least subjectively, as formal. It also prepares for a more personal way of living and involves progress which will be realized perfectly only in personal adherence to the Lord.

IX. Luke 13:22-30 Gospel Wednesday   Circumstances that Matthew (7:13-14 and 22-23) passes over in silence, in order not to break the altogether artificial continuity of the sermon on the mount, are preserved by Luke (13:22-23). In Luke 13:24 the image of the narrow gate is not combined with any other, whereas Matthew rather confuses it with the theme of the two ways (7:13-14). The gate in Luke is that of the eschatological banquet (a primitive note very likely) while Matthew seems to envisage the gate of a city which comes at the end of a moral "road." He is replacing the primitive eschatological emphasis with a moralizing and cate-chetical one. In Luke 13:26-28 Christ alludes to the attitude of his hearers (v. 26) while Matthew has in mind the charismatic Christians of the primitive communities (Mt 7:22). This suggests a later redaction for Matthew. In verses 28-29 of Luke we seem to have the original context. There is a reference to the eschato-logical banquet predicted in verses 24-25 and the whole ambience is typically Jewish.

a) Thus the basic theme in the passage is the *eschatological banquet* of Isaiah 25:6. The crowd will press for entry but the door will be too narrow to admit all. The less vigilant will remain outside (v. 28; cf. Mt 25:10-12) and appeal in vain to their pre-vious association with the master of the house (v. 26).

The selection process at the door is not separation of Israel from the nations, but a choice of the more deserving from both groups. Those united at the table are Jewish patriarchs and prophets (v. 28), together with the more deserving from all nations (v. 29). So that the banquet will reassemble both Jews and Gentiles, with equal rights, in the new Kingdom. The Gentile uncleanness which prevented the Jews from sharing meals with them is no more (cf. Ga 2:11-14).

b) With Luke 13:22-30 should be compared those other passages where Jesus speaks of the *convocation of the Gentiles* to the Kingdom, always set in an eschatological context. We have the themes of banquet (Mt 25:1-12), the regathering of the flock (Mt 25:31-32), the building of the temple to include the nations (Jn 4:21-23, 12:20-23), and the return in power of the Son of Man (Mt 24:29-31).

Christ considered the conversion of the Gentiles as an eschatological initiative of the Father. Thus he was not concerned to call them during his public life (Mk 7:24-30; Mt 10:5-6), remaining in this faithful to the economy of salvation that is "first for the Jews" (Rm 1:16).

c) The first lesson would seem to be that Jesus' statement is a warning to his hearers who do not read the signs of the times (cf. Lk 12:54-56; 14:16-24), and fail to grasp the decisive nature of his ministry. This lack of understanding will entail their immediate *exclusion:* not even fidelity to Moses will avail them if they do not recognize his message. However, this will not prevent fulfillment of the ancient prophecies about the eschatological assembly of the nations. The Gentiles will enter and the Jews will find themselves outside (cf. Mt 10:15; Lk 10:13-14; 11:31-32).

d) Matthew actually affirms that it is because of their faith (Mt 8:11-12) that the Gentiles will replace the Jews at the banquet. But Luke seeks another explanation: it is works and the practice of *justice* that will admit Gentiles to the banquet (vv. 23-27; Cf. Lk 8:21; 11:28). As he sees it, God is not an accepter of persons. The decisive factor will not be membership of the chosen people (Acts 10:34-35) only the practice of justice will be acceptable.

The two evangelists are not at one in their interpretation of Jesus statement. Matthew is endeavoring to explain why the first Christian communities are more Gentile than Jewish. Luke has a more universal outlook. Salvation is attainable by all men: there will be no automatic salvation on the basis of membership in the chosen people.

The Christian is also included in Jesus' warning. Membership in the people of God certainly makes him a missionary and a sign of salvation, but this salvation will depend on personal justice. The Christian is a "savior" but is not himself automatically saved.

X. Romans **8:31b-39** *1st Reading* *1st cycle* *Thursday*	Chapter 8 of the letter to the Romans ends with a hymn to the love of God. The first two strophes especially sing about the content of this love (vv. 31-32 and 33-34); the final two verses allude to his adversaries (vv. 35-39).

a) Like Job 1 or Zechariah 3, Paul pictures to himself Christians brought before the tribunal of God (cf. Rv 12:10). Motives for judging are not lacking, for combat for the faith and the struggle against evil are not always crowned with success but often uncover weakness and cowardice.

But who is going to make the accusation? Three persons can do so: God himself (vv. 31-33), Satan ("the accuser" according to the etymological meaning of this name: verse 33) or Christ (v. 34). And Paul asks which of the three would be able to condemn Christians.

God? But he has already spoken for them by handing over his Son (v. 32; cf. Gn 22:16). Could he go back on his decision and withdraw the benefit of the death of Christ?

Satan? Yes, he is by nature the accuser of men before God, for he tries to convince him not to place confidence in beings who do not merit such love (cf. Jb 1)! Paul probably is thinking of

Isaiah 50:8-9 where the Servant of Yahweh defies his accusers: who can accuse him when God pardons and justifies always.

Christ? Can he condemn to death those for whom he died (v. 34)? Can he condemn, he who was "raised" as savior (v. 34)?

b) This final interpretation demands some explanation. The word "to raise" which, in this verse, designates the *resurrection* expresses in the Old Testament God's choice of a king or a prophet destined to save the situation at a particularly critical moment in the history of the chosen people (Jg 2:16, 3:9; 3:15; 2 S 3:10; 1 K 9:5; Ez 34:23; Is 41:2, 25).

The theology of the resurrection which appears in this passage is then very early: God, who had promised to "raise" a savior each time the people would face misfortune, "raised Christ from the dead" (Acts 2:32-33; 13:23) in order to make a Savior of him. Salvation is then bound to the resurrection and to baptism which gives a participation in it.

c) In reading the final strophes we think of Job's arraignment before the tribunal of God by Satan. Having made the accusations, Satan is allowed to use trials in order to test their validity. Likewise, for Saint Paul, the Christian's *trial* is part of the great campaign by angelic powers against humanity. God trusts man and makes an alliance with him. But the celestial powers who have hitherto held man in thrall, try to convince God that his confidence and love are misplaced. Humanity is only capable of deception.

The catalogue of trials is the one Paul has often used to describe his own misfortunes (1 Co 4:9; 15:30-32; 2 Co 4:8-11; 6:4-5; 11:22-28; 12:10; Col 1:24). His own experience helps him to understand the plight of Christians in general. He also instances the case of Israel persecuted by the Gentiles (Ps 43/44, the vocabulary of which colors the whole account of the Maccabee martyrs: 2 M 7). Thus, "the existence of faith is lived on the edge of death."

But the attitude of the great judge of human affairs cannot be swayed by accusations from the celestial or spatial powers (v. 38), by the forces of nature (v. 39), by trials or by death itself. In fact

God does not rest content with showing confidence in man, rather his love enables the Christian to resist trial and to liberate himself from all alienation (vv. 37 and 39b).

We could say that the Judge, so to speak, has already decided to declare the defendant innocent and gives him the weapons to resist accusations and avoid snares which await him. God's love binds him to the defendant and gives him an *assurance* that nothing can shake. Truly man is liberated from all forces that could interfere with his destiny. If he refuses to allow sin mastery over him, the judgment for him will be a resounding victory.

It is not because the plan of God toward man is ambitious that all trials will be avoided by him. Thus, we cannot doubt the fidelity of God towards Jesus who experienced the most tragic trial. God leads man to glory but at the very center of his earthly condition.

XI. Ephesians 6:10-20
1st reading
2nd cycle
Thursday

Paul compares the moral life with a divine "armor." Since victory over death and over Satan, the Lord has at his disposal an exceptional power that henceforth enlivens the life of the Christian and strengthens it as armor (v. 10).

a) Verse 11 speaks about the *armor* of God, alluding to the struggles which God waged against the enemies of his people. Yahweh was often represented as vested with armor (Is 11:4-5; 59:16-18; Ws 5:17-23). Thus Israel learned that it was not by its own power that it fought but with that "armor" with which God would vest his risen Son and with which he presently invests us (Rm 6:12-14; 13:11-14; 2 Co 6:7; 10:3-6; 1 Th 5:8; Heb 4:12). From this aspect the armor theme is parallel to the "clothing" theme (Ga 3:27; Col 3:12). But by passing from the Old to the

New Testament, the armor theme no longer carries any religious implications.

b) In verse 12 Paul raises the spiritual combat to its true dimensions: it is not a struggle in which simply "flesh and blood" is at stake, that is, human adversaries, but a struggle with *cosmic reverberations,* undertaken by Christ in order to triumph over the forces which dominate the world and alienate man (Ep 1:21; Col 1:13; 2:15, 20). Our moral life thus becomes an episode of the struggle which Christ leads against Satan for the definitive lordship over the new creation.

It is useless to describe each of the weapons making up the panoply set forth by Paul. The author simply wishes to point out their divine source.

XII. Luke   This gospel brings together two statements of
   13:31-35   Christ for which Luke furnishes in all likeli-
   Gospel   hood the original version. He is moreover the
   Thursday   only one to report the thoughts of Christ about
   Herod (vv. 31-35). These two statements were
brought together by Luke or by oral tradition, probably around the key-word Jerusalem or because we have seen in each of these two texts an announcement of the Passion of Jesus.

a) In all likelihood Herod Antipas sent the Pharisees to intimidate Jesus by allowing him to see his death beforehand (v. 31). Political hypocracy won for Herod the epithet fox (v. 32). Jesus responds by revealing that, and this with a premonition of his approaching death, he can only remain faithful to a mission which is not yet complete. Today passes but there is still tomorrow and also the day after tomorrow (vv. 32-33) and on the road which leads to Jerusalem many miracles and other good works must take place.

Luke understands the word "to fulfill" or "to accomplish" (v. 32) in two different and superimposed senses: to accomplish his mission and to fulfill himself. In other words: to accomplish his mission by *death* itself. There we have a doctrine close to that of Saint John (Jn 19:20) which could indicate that Jesus, conscious of his failure, could envisage no other possible accomplishment except in death where he refers to God the concern for prolonging his mission by new means and thus accomplishing it perfectly.

b) The second statement of Jesus (vv. 34-35) closely related to the first, wants to make clear that Jesus presses beyond to his death and that it will be possible to pursue his mission after it. This mission takes the form of a *substitution of "he who comes"* (himself) *to the temple* of Jerusalem as the instrument of reassembly (v. 34). Thus, the taboos and interdicts which prevent the temple from exercising its mission and which prevent Jesus from accomplishing his own, will be abolished and the Son of Man will be able "to come" (v. 35) and to realize the plan of God.

**XIII. Romans
9:1-5**
*1st reading
1st cycle
Friday*

The early chapters of the letter to the Romans analyzes the role of faith in human justification, something that neither the Gentiles with their philosophy nor the Jews with their privileges could allow.

By 57 Paul had already traveled the roads of the Near East sufficiently widely to realize that he could not count on an early conversion of Israel (Gal 4:29). Why had Jewry revolted against the faith and become a persecutor of the gospel? He faces the question and our reading today indicates the pain he feels about his own nation, and his amazement that so many privileges have been conferred on the chosen people in vain.

Just as Moses would rather himself disappear than have the people destroyed (Ex 32:32), Paul is ready to become anathema if only the multiple privileges can come to full flower for his people. The privileges are enumerated and he affirms that they cannot be ultimately in vain, characteristic as they are of the New Israel.

a) *Israel's privileges* will always remain with her, even in her situation outside the Church. For Paul there can be no doubt about this (v. 4).

The privileges are first of all those of the Word: the covenants, the legislation and the promises (v. 4). The covenants with Abraham (Gn 15:18) and David, the promises that were made, the law of Moses (Ex 20) and the commentaries of later Judaism are the Word of Yahweh (which he has never withdrawn). They are the expression of God's presence with Israel which transcends the limits of the Law and never cease to give indications of the Messiah through the medium of the promises.

Next come the privileges of the liturgy: the power to render cult to the true God and the privilege of the divine presence in the temple (Ex 40:34). Cult had indeed been transformed now by the spiritual sacrifice and the glory of the resurrection; but the Jews still retained their liturgical prerogatives and would continue the quest for a cult in spirit and in truth.

b) Finally there are the privileges of blood. Israel was of the blood of the patriarchs, Abraham in particular. This blood and strain in the body of Jesus of Nazareth had brought salvation. The basic Jewish privilege lies in the fact that *Christ was born from its flesh* (v. 5). Yet Israel refuses to recognize that her flesh could produce a divine person, a God to be blessed throughout the ages. This is the drama of a people who refuse to accept the greatest privilege there is!

Understood in this way the last verse is indeed one of the most important in the New Testament. It affirms the fleshly reality of Christ, sprung from the race of patriarchs but preexisting nevertheless in divine glory.

Israel still preserves these ancient privileges today, but it does not authenticate them in the man-God as the new Israel. The baptized proclaim in fact that God has revealed himself to mankind in a flesh equal to its own and in the daily witness of each Christian.

XIV. Philippians After the greeting for this letter (vv. 1-2)
1:1-11 drawn up either in 56 at Ephesus or in 62 at
1st reading Rome, Paul formulates a solemn act of thanks
2nd cycle (vv. 3-11) built on the traditional scheme of
Friday the Jewish *berakab:* blessing (vv. 3-8) and
epiclesis (vv. 9-10).

a) The motive for this thanksgiving is the generosity of the Philippians and the part which they have taken in the apostolate of Paul, the measure of confidence for the future (v. 6). Since God has begun to pour out his grace on the community in so striking a manner, the future cannot be doubtful: the grace of God will not be lacking where his love is already manifest.

b) The *growth of charity* among the Philippians is the object of the epiclesis of Paul. The apostle here understands charity in the general sense: the love of God and the love of the brethren, in a word, the entire Christian existence. The growth of this virtue is revealed in the appearance of a series of fruits such as *understanding (epignosis)* which is not speculation but experimental and loving understanding of the mystery of God (cf. Col 2:2; 3:9-10; Ep 1:17; 4:13; Rm 3:20) and *comprehension,* a sort of refinement of understanding which leads to discerning the best (vv. 9-10) and to quickly adopting the attitude that fits in the most moving circumstances of life.

c) This growth and fruition of Christian life permits the faithful to present themselves pure (or whole) on the *day of the Lord,* without weakness (or reproach) and filled with justice (vv. 10-11). These Jewish expressions would have concealed a mere legalistic justice if the apostle had done so: it is necessary to be "filled" with this justice which "comes by Jesus Christ." The term "filled" always indicates in St. Paul the action of the Spirit already at work until the day of the Lord (Rm 15:13-14; 2 Cor 7:4). As to the justice that "comes by Jesus Christ," it is divine justification granted to men by the mediation of the Savior (Rm 5:9).

Paul's act of thanks (we would prefer to say in order to form a link with the Mass, his eucharistic prayer) is concerned with the growth of the community. In this he is faithful to the teaching of Jesus who spoke about the growth of the seed into a cluster, slow and ambiguous growth, but constitutive of the coming of the Kingdom of God.

Today more than ever Christian communities must forget that they are already the Kingdom in order to remember that they are "not yet" such. Consequently they must agree to search for the Promised Land to which they have not yet fully entered and discover in union with all of restless and searching humanity the dynamism needed to begin that new march in the desert of that new growth. The Eucharist of each assembly will be able to return to the themes dear to Pauline Eucharists.

XV. Luke 14:1-6 Chapter 14 of Saint Luke is entirely concerned
    Gospel   with our Lord's "table-talk," a common literary
    Friday   form in the classical world. The first verse in-
             troduces the chapter giving the time, circum-
stances and place: it was in the home of a Pharisee on the Sabbath. Luke goes on at once to record the healing of a man with dropsy (vv. 2-6), then he presents a parable on the choice of seats (vv. 7-11) and another on the choice of guests (vv. 12-14). Finally comes the parable of the feast (vv. 15-24). In order to insure unity for the passage Luke presents Christ as speaking first to the guests, then to his hosts and lastly to one of those at table.

In the "table-talks" found in contemporary pagan literature, the authors presented the diners united around the master of the house and they stressed the presence of the aristocracy and philosophers (cf. Plato's *Symposium*). Luke also begins by describing Pharisees of repute, but he immediately brings a man with dropsy on the scene, thereby indicating that the meal of Christ is never a banquet for an elite.

During the banquet each diner had to make a speech, either in praise of some subject under discussion or a description of some outward manifestation. Christ's words follow this same plan: he chooses humility as his subject, described its manifestations (vv. 7-10) and concluded with a definition (v. 11).

Luke assembles the diverse elements of chapter 14 in thinking especially about the difficulties which Christian assemblies experienced. As these assemblies broke away from the temple and risked adopting as a model pagan meetings, it was imperative to give them precise rules reflecting the gospel. Luke 14 does this just as James 2:1-4 and 1 Co 11:20-21 do.

The lesson is presented in a setting of Jewish moral teaching which is fond of indicating the possible consequences of certain attitudes. Thus, to take the lowest place is a way of arriving at the highest. In this way we may perceive the influence of wisdom literature (Pr 25:6-7).

Luke's intention in reporting the two accounts which form the gospel for today (he is moreover the only one to do so) is to form a theology of the Sunday assembly. Christ pulls down all barriers of legal impurity which the Jews had erected around their assemblies: his is open to all, it is an assembly of salvation only if all the participants feel at ease.

XVI. Romans 11:1-2a, 11-12, 25-29
1st reading
1st cycle
Saturday

The Church is the new Israel because in her the promises are accomplished and the spiritual privileges of the chosen people given reality. She is however largely made up of former Gentiles; the Jews are only a small minority, a very little "remnant" (Rm 11:4-5; cf. 9:27-29).

The patrimony of Israel is then presently that of the Church, but why should Christians enjoy it and not the

Jews? What is the meaning of the rupture between the Church and Israel in view of the history of salvation?

a) Paul's first observation is that it is not God who took the initiative in the rupture. He remains faithful always to the people he has chosen (vv. 2, 29) and it will continue to be the object of the promise even in the rupture because God is present to it.

The continuity of God's presence with his people and the sanctifying influence of the promise, indicate that the rupture is not a complete disaster, but a mistake (v. 11). Furthermore, even outside the Church, the chosen people still have a *raison d'être,* a positive purpose. They bear witness dramatically to the failure of human attempts to achieve salvation. As such they are a reminder to the Church that she must remain faithful to the promise and to the grace of reconciliation (vv. 12 and 15a).

b) Verse 12 at first glance is rather astonishing. How could a mistake by Israel enrich the Gentiles? Paul was able to write this phrase only after having remarked that he was first expelled from the synagogue in each village through which he passed before going to the Gentiles (Ac 13:44-52; 17:1-9) and stated that the persecution by the Jews against converts was waged at Jerusalem before there was founded, at Antioch, the first truly Gentile Christian community (Ac 11:9-26). But the apostle was able to write this phrase only in an eschatological climate; yes, the Lord is going to come, but he delays his return because of his mercy, in order to give men time to be converted (1 Tm 2:4). The actual unbelief of the Jews prolongs the granted delay, allowing a greater number of Gentiles to enter the Kingdom (v. 25). Conversely, the witness of Gentiles converted to the Church ought to bring about the conversion of Israel (by "jealousy": vv. 11, 14) and if it does not happen, it is perhaps because the witness is not pure. Thus the salvation of Israel and the Gentiles are similar because each is saved only by pure mercy (Rm 11:30-32).

When Israel is converted to Christ it will bring to that moment something the Gentile could never bring. It will welcome Christ as the fulfillment of a history that the Jews were the only ones to live. It will demonstrate, as nothing else could, that salvation is the gift of God's mercy. This people, who had their origins in an initiative of love, are pursued by that love even in withdrawal. They live because God is faithful to the Word. The Christian can hasten the return of Israel by laboring to build a Church that will be worthy to welcome her, a church, that is, which derives all its strength from the divine initiative.

**XVII. Philip-
pians
1:18b-26**
1st reading
2nd cycle
Saturday

For his beloved Philippians Paul provides news of his imprisonment. Our reading has some reflections on the fate that has become his lot.

a) The apostle is filled with joy (v. 18b) for the concrete help which his Philippians bring him and because he is assured of the assistance of the Spirit of Jesus Christ. Even if his imprisonment ended in death, Christ would not be less glorified (v. 20; cf. 1 Th 5:10). Is it not by his death that Christ has glorified his Father and has been glorified himself (cf. Jn 17:1)? If the apostle dies, resurrection will come to crown his life (vv. 21-23; cf. Ga 2:20).

b) For Paul the true life is a *life with Christ* (v. 21). What is involved here is a traditional Jewish idea filled with numerous images, some more emotional than others: it means association with the Kingdom of the Messiah, sharing with him the eschatological banquet of the poor, setting on thrones round about him, judging the qualities of the members of the Kingdom, sharing the tent of the Messiah, sharing with him the joys of Paradise.

All these images are more or less explicit in most of the writings of the New Testament. Paul himself, good Jew that he is, shared this hope and described it at length in the letters to the Thessalonians. He wants moreover to participate in this life with Christ here and now because the Lord's coming is at hand.

But when he writes to the Philippians the perspective changes completely. Now he is seriously contemplating death. He compares life and death and balances their respective advantages (vv. 22-24): to go or to stay, to be with Christ or to continue laboring for the gospel. He makes his choice: he will remain here (v. 25) even though he is persuaded of the advantages of death, because it means being with Christ.

To share the messianic kingdom envisaged by the Jews one must undergo death and the emptying it involves.

XVIII. Luke   This gospel is dealt with in conjunction with
14:1, 7-11 Luke 14:1-6 on the preceding Friday, p. 227.
Gospel
Saturday

THIRTY-FIRST WEEK

I. Romans
11:29-36
1st reading
1st cycle
Monday

Paul concludes his analysis of Israel's destiny by recapitulating, rather hesitantly, his argument (vv. 30-32), and rendering thanks to God (vv. 33-36) for his mercy and his plan of universal salvation. This also brings to conclusion the doctrinal portion of the letter. There can be no doubt that he had in mind the salvation history of all humanity from the fall of Adam and the promise to Abraham right up to justification in Christ, and the final gesture by God that will save Israel.

a) Paul sees all human history as a sort of counterpoint between Jews and Gentiles. The Jews were the first to obey but they disobeyed afterwards. The Gentiles, who disobeyed to begin with, obeyed when the time came (vv. 30-31; cf. Mt. 21:28-32). But, over-arching this ebb and flow and providing the key is the *mercy* of God (v. 32). It enables every man to learn by sin the vanity of his own will, and to open himself to God's gratuitous love, which is the only solution to the human predicament.

b) The act of thanks for God's mercy and human conversion is principally inspired by Psalm 138/139 (vv. 6, 17, 18), which celebrates the immense knowledge of God that baffles human comprehension. He goes on to allude to Isaiah 40:13, one of those oracles that gave people hope about God's salvific plan for his people at the time of return from exile. Finally he quotes Job 41:3, but according to a version that differs from the original and celebrates the faith of the poor man who is undaunted by events, however incomprehensible.

c) Paul is deeply distressed by Israel's refusal to accept the plan of God and the "mystery" of the conversion of the pagans. Its pharisaic mentality and its national pride are wounded to the core. All he can do is avow his *lack of understanding* and place his confidence in the wisdom of God.

This handing things over to the Lord is not resignation. The apostle knows the behavior he must adopt and he proves it in his mission to the Gentiles. He is in the dark but some light does shine through, that of the plan of God which is always operative in terms of his great mercy.

**II. Philippians
2:1-4**
1st reading
2nd cycle
Monday

The Philippians, among whom Paul sojourned during his second missionary journey (about the year 50; cf. Ac 16:11-40), were one of his favorite committees. Relations were always cordial and affectionate, and the Philippians showed great solicitude for Paul during his imprisonment (Ph 1:7, 13-14, 20; cf. 2:25; 4:18). He asks them now to crown his happiness by cementing yet more their brotherly ties and by giving evidence of greater humility in their relations with one another.

a) In his exhortation to unity, which is so pressing that it may very well indicate threatened factions in Philippi, Paul appeals to the basic values that he shares with his hearers. First, their "consolation" in Christ, the Lord's presence which strengthens their faith; the "persuasion" in love which is common to them both and which comes from God; the "communion" in the Spirit which enables them to share the graces of the new covenant; finally the "tenderness" and "compassion" of which all have had occasion to bear witness "in Christ."

The apostle then asks that the *fraternal love* at the very center of the community be on the same level as the love which unites the community to its founder. It is at times easier to love as a group the same leader than to love another! The expressions which describe this fraternal love are many: here we mention especially "united in spirit and ideal" (v. 2) which is not so much concerned with unity of doctrine as it is with intention and disposition in the pursuit of a common end, yet that "unanimity" which prevents the party spirit from asserting itself.

b) But fraternal love can be established with depth only if each person brings to it humility, struggles against vain glory (v. 3), avoids self interest (v. 4), but imitates the abnegation of Jesus (v. 5.)

The term which Paul uses to indicate mutual humility usually signifies in the New Testament the humility of man before God (Ac 20:19; Ep 4:2; Col 2:18). What this says is that fraternal humility can be attained only by a spirit of faith and through imitation of Jesus.

He alone who lowered himself to the point of forgetting that he was God (Ph 2:6-12) can lead his faithful to forget their titles of honor and superiority in order to be united in fraternal unanimity.

III. **Luke**   Chapter 14 of St. Luke is given over entirely
    14:12-14,   to the Lord's "table-talk," a common literary
    15-24   genre in antiquity. Luke relates the conversa-
    Gospel   tions that took place during a meal in the
    Monday and   house of a Pharisee. He then describes the cure
    Tuesday   of a man with dropsy (Lk 14:2-6), the question
                      of choosing seating places (Lk 14:7-11) and
a word on the choice of guests (Lk 14:12-14), and finally the parable of the banquet (vv. 15-24). Luke presents Christ as making these remarks in that order to the guests, to the host and to one of the guests.

Chapter 14 of Luke is then a rather artificial anthology of various statements grouped in the framework of the literary genre known as the "symposium." Luke is especially concerned with the difficulties which the Christian assemblies were then experiencing. They had abandoned the structure of the temple assemblies, and so it was imperative to form precise rules less they be unduly influenced by pagan practices. Luke 14 deals with this as well as other texts such as Jm 2:1-4 and 1 Co 11.

a) One of the problems the early communities had to face most frequently was the sort of reception the poor should receive. To begin with, Luke gives an answer framed in the rabbinic and sapiential tradition (vv. 12-14). Remembering the consequences which particular attitudes could have, it was better to invite the *poor*, just as it was better to put oneself in the last place (vv. 10-12; cf. Pr 25:6-7). However, he quickly goes beyond this interesting morality to more eschatological perspectives and he relates the parable of the banquet (vv. 15-24).

Aware that Christ was inaugurating the final times, Luke compares them, in conformity to Jewish tradition, to a feast of the poor (Is 55:1-5). It is clear that he sometimes leaves himself overwhelmed by the optimism of certain sources concerning material poverty, the only valid title, according to these sources, for access to the Kingdom (Lk 12:13-21; 16:1-15, 19-31; 14:12-14; 20:45-21; 4).

Matthew (22:2-10), who wrote after several years of church experience, realizes on the contrary that sociological poverty does not necessarily form a better claim than another for salvation (cf. the correction that he adds to the beatitude of the poor: Mt 5:3). For him the problem consists in knowing why certain of those who are admitted to the banquet (therefore already called, already Christian) cannot stay there because of their faults.

It is therefore possible to think of three steps in the evolution of the parable of the feast. Jesus lets it be known that the messianic feast, expected since Isaiah 55:1-3, is a reality and that the invitations are already sent out. On the basis of problems that had arisen in the primitive Christian community, Luke interprets this passage on the sociological conditions of poverty which are necessary for obtaining the Kingdom. Matthew finally puts a new nuance on these last by adding an allusion to a necessary "righteousness."

b) The evangelist and the primitive tradition probably preserved these accounts and others (1 Co 11:21-22; Jm 2:1-4) because of the problems which arose in the liturgical *assemblies* of the first Christians. At a time when large numbers were judged unclean and so were excluded from cultural reunions, both Jews and Gentiles (Mt 21:14; 2 S 5:8), Christians gradually began to understand that their assemblies ought to be open to all. First, to all social categories without distinction, and that is the reason for the interest indicated in the New Testament texts in parables such as Luke 14; then to all races (Rm 10:12; 1 Co 12:13; Ga 3:28; Rv 7:1-9); finally, even to sinners which led Christians to preserve numerous details from the life of Christ in which he took his meals with sinners (Lk 7:36-50).

The Christian assembly is not then a reunion of the elite; it is bound to be infected with mediocrity and its president must take this into account.

Unlike Matthew, Luke mentions the excuses of those who were invited. He also makes much of the fact that the servant had to make two appeals: first within the city, then outside it. The first Christians wanted to make of their assemblies a prefiguring of the kingdom where the sons of the City (Israel) and those outside the City (Gentiles) would be seated at the same time.

There is a twofold intention present in the Lucan redaction of the parable of the banquet: we are in the last days, the time when the poor and pagans precede the rich and the Jews at the messianic banquet, for it is open to the whole world.

The Church is the sign of the universal gathering willed by God and poverty, the necessary characteristic of those who respond to the invitation. At a time when the modern world challenges the ability of the Church to assemble men of every race and mentality, it is imperative that Christians are aware of the responsibilities they accepted when they received baptism.

The Church is not a people of the earth and its gathering together cannot be done sociologically. The believer is both the assembled and the assembler only to the degree that he confronts death as Jesus of Nazareth did, in perfect obedience and in the gift of self to a brotherhood without limits. The Christian effects this assembling of the world in dispersion among men. The building of the community of people and the elaboration of the encounter of cultures do not allow him indifference. But a true dialogue must necessarily be initiated between interlocutors who have really nothing in common. Insecurity is total and detachment is indispensable. Love and poverty are consequently indispensable for building the fraternal city here below. The Christian must live them and thus witness the announcement of salvation.

In assembling her faithful in the Eucharist, the Church does not form them into sociological communities called "Christian," distinct from human communities. The Christian must know that he will not find in the eucharistic assembly the security and warmth that he cannot find in his task as universal assembler, dispersed in the world. He does not abandon this fundamental condition in coming to the Eucharist. Only then will the eucharistic assembly be the sign par excellence of the ecclesial assemblage of all men in the Kingdom.

IV. Romans
12:5-16a
1st reading
1st cycle
Tuesday

Paul has just begun the parenetic portion of his letter (Rm 12:1-2). He now analyzes in succession the attitudes adopted among Christians (Rm 12:3-13), towards others (Rm 12:14-13:14) and towards the weak (Rm 14). The advice he gives to Christians in the matter of mutual charity is of the utmost importance because Christian Jews at Rome, founders of the Church, seem to have been expelled from the capital over a period of years. In their turn, they found themselves in a Church of Gentile origin, with usages diametrically opposed to their own. The danger of schism was menacing and we can understand the interest which Paul brings into his letter about the relationship between Jews and Gentiles and about tolerance.

The passage read in the liturgy today envisages all together the relationship between Christians and those with non-Christians. Paul has just spoken about the use of charisms in the light of the common good: he now describes the manifestations of charity.

a) Paul often speaks in praise of *charity* when he intends to deal with charisms (cf. 1 Co 13). For him it is charity that allows all the children of the same Father (v. 10) to live as brothers, without pretensions or pride, in concern for the good of others (v. 9), led by a love which goes as far as tenderness.

As in a family, this love is not brought to life on command. It is fervent, zealous, spontaneous (v. 11).

b) Charity is likewise marked by the *last days*. The end of verse 11 should probably be translated: "Note the times in which you live" rather than: "He whom you serve is the Lord." Paul asks that the times in which one lives be weighed, a time that is dominated by the resurrection of Christ and expectation of his return, but also by persecution (v. 12), for the resurrection of Christ places Christians outside the world. This difficult situation entails the practice of charity in particular activities: hospitality towards refugees (v. 13) and concern for the problems created by this trial.

Paul goes beyond the bounds of solidarity among the persecuted in order to invite his own to bless even those who persecute them (v. 14; cf. Mt 5:44-45).

c) But it is not enough simply to love one's brethren and one's persecutors. All men must be loved regardless of the situation in which they are found. In this respect Paul outlines the Christian teaching on *tolerance*, the secret of which is to be conformed to the sentiments of others, with joy as well as with pain (cf. Si 7:34; 1 Co 9:19-22; 2 Co 11:29). Thus the encounter of the believer and unbeliever rests on the interpersonal relations which very much involve the realm of psychology (v. 15).

Finally, avoid thinking oneself superior to others, for faith is far from conceit (Rm 12:3) and the truth that it discovers remains a truth to be caught and conquered, a fact that makes the Christian very close to all who search (v. 16).

V. **Philippians**	This hymn to the kenosis and glorification of
2:5-11	the Lord is made up of three strophes:
1st reading	Verses 6 and 7a: Two mentions of God:
2nd cycle	contrast between God's state and that of a
Tuesday	slave, and the theme "he has emptied himself."

Verses 7bc and 8: Two references to man and the theme "he lowered himself."

Verses 9-11: Contrast between slave and Lord, the obedient and exalted one.

The whole hymn parallels the customary Pauline development about Christian charity. It lies in self-emptying, after the example of Jesus (2 Co 8:9; Rm 15:1-3).

a) In contrasting Jesus' divine state with the *servile condition* of Jesus, Paul does not mean to say he abandoned his divinity or that he became man only in appearance. The problem of natures does not arise, nor is the context incarnational. In the first strophe, for instance, it is not said that Jesus was God but only that he possessed a rank of equality with God. Likewise, in the second, the humility of Jesus is not denied, but it is stressed that the Lord allowed himself to be confused with men (v. 7; cf. Rm 8:3). He could have appeared on earth as Lord demanding divine honors, but he did not. Saint Paul frequently requires that our charity should display that renouncement of self of which Christ gives us a living example (2 Co 8:9; Ga 4:1-5; Heb 11:24-26).

There is an allusion in the hymn to the Suffering Servant (compare verse 8 and Is 53:7; 53:10; 53:12), but it sharpens that image by its use of the typically biblical contrasts: "Lord-slave" and "lowered-raised" (Lk 1:52; Mt 23:12; Lk 18:14; 2 Co 11:7).

b) But the gradual descent into humiliation is paralleled by a *triumphal ascent* in glory. Again the imagery here transcends that of the Suffering Servant who is "raised up" only (Is 52:13). Christ goes further because he gets the title of Lord (Ps 109/110), one that entitles to the honor of "genuflection" and "proclamation." These rites were reserved for God alone. Kings had already prostrated themselves before the Suffering Servant (Is 49:7), but "because of Yahweh." Before Christ, on the other hand, men prostrate themselves as before God, all the time glorifying the Father.

In our different cultural context the passage of St. Paul on the kenosis of Christ could easily be misunderstood. It might seem that the thirty years spent in the human condition were parenthetical, an accident, as if God the all-powerful, the judge, had for a brief moment forgotten himself, for love indeed, but hastened then "to recover" his proper lordship. Thus Jesus would simply be abdicating his privileges for a time to serve the poor; some sort of facade instead of the plenitude of divinity, would be the image presented during the public life. Indeed, his gesture in sharing human poverty might seem a patronizing one, a sort of luxury, open to resentment by humanity.

It is important to affirm that the God revealed in Jesus Christ is the true God who continues to serve. And so much so that we can certify that it is the fact of taking the condition of a slave that unveils God, because to be God is to serve. Christ's obedience is not only obedience to his terrestrial condition. Nor is it submission to the decree of a God external to him; it is fidelity to all that divinity implies. So it is that Jesus is forever the victim of what he accomplished, in his own person first of all and then in those who want to imitate him.

VI. Luke
14:15-24
Gospel
Tuesday

The commentary for this gospel will be found with that for the preceding Monday, Luke 14: 12-14, p. 234.

VII. Romans   Paul has just reminded his listeners that they
   13:8-10   should obey the civil laws, even those of a
   1st reading   pagan and persecuting state. It is not only by
   1st cycle   the sacred law of Sinai that God's will is
   Wednesday   manifested but by profane law as well.

There is no real conflict between the law of Moses and civil law, any more than there is between the principles of "rendering to Caesar what is Caesar's and to God what is God's" (Mt 22:21). The Sinai law is no more than civil law interpreted in the light of communion with God. When it commands believers to love one another, it also endorses the demands of civil law about adultery, theft and covetousness (v. 9). Its superiority to profane law consists in the fact that it makes *love of one's neighbor* the key to all human behavior.

When he makes the second table of the Decalogue (Ex 20: 13-17; Dt 5:17-21) the basis of the duty of charity towards the other, Paul is following a spiritual tradition that had already reduced all the law of Moses to the double commandment of love for God and one's neighbor (Mt 19:18-19; 22:34-40; Ps 14/15; 111/112; Zc 8:14-17. Likewise, when he reduces all the commandments of civil law to the obligation of love for one's fellowmen, he is interpreting that law in the same way as the Jews interpreted the Mosaic law.

Among Christians nowadays there is sometimes poor respect for civil law, especially penal and fiscal laws. A certain moral casuistry maintains that it is not wrong to evade fiscal laws or purely penal enactments. Paul however rejects such a deformation when he asks the Christians to regard civil regulations as a way of loving the brethren.

The Christian accordingly sees civil law as a means of extending Christ's loving Lordship over humanity. He can only disobey insofar as these enactments contravene the law of love. It does not matter whether he approves or not of the political authority, they are not representatives of God and the Lord (Rm 13:4) by virtue of their origin, but because they are collaborating with the lordship of Christ in inculcating respect for the second table of the decalogue. That is why we pray for governments during eucharistic celebrations.

VIII. Philippians 2:12-18
1st reading
2nd cycle
Wednesday

This is a commentary on the liturgical hymn on the kenosis and glorification of the Lord (Ph 2:1-10). Jesus appears here as a model of the humility and the obedience which Paul holds out to his readers.

a) Paul encourages an *obedience* with "fear and trembling" (vv. 12-13). This expression is borrowed from Isaiah 8:13 (cf. Ps 2:11; 1 Co 2:3; 2 Co 7:15; Ep 6:5), and designates the certitude we have of God's presence and the confidence we place in the power of him who can realize all he demands of men.

The opposite of this obedience is "grumbling" and "arguing" (vv. 14-16; cf. 1 Co 10:10; Nb 14:2; 17:6-15), that is to say, the inability to recognize the will of God in the circumstances of life (Heb 3:7-19).

b) The practice of obedience as understood here involves a spiritual *cult*. In verse 17 Paul seems to wish God to accept as a sacrifice his apostolic life and his daily difficulties just as he does the obedience of his readers.

IX. Luke 14:25-33
Gospel
Wednesday

This piece is made up of rather disparate elements. For its proper understanding it is necessary to refer to verses 34-35. These parallel Matthew 5:13 and give us the *logion* about salt, the original context of which had been lost in the synoptic tradition. Luke makes it into a kind of parable in order to accommodate it to the lesson of verses 28-33, which are proper to him and concern the renouncement of all goods. Verses 26-27 are added as an introduction. They, too, belong to another context (cf. Mt 10:38; 16:24; Lk 9:23, and he gives another personal touch (the woman: v. 26) to reinforce the ascetic dimension.

a) The inauguration of the Kingdom is imminent. Consequently one must develop the necessary dispositions to surmount the obstacles that stand in the way of entry. The first one recommended is *prudence:* one must know what one wants. The man building the house without the wherewithal to complete it (v. 30), the soldier who goes to war without calculating the cost (v. 31), the salt which loses its savor (v. 34); all these symbolize the man who begins to believe in the Kingdom, but stops halfway. In Luke, it should be noted that salt is the symbol of prudence, whereas in Matthew it indicates the disciples' role in the world.

b) As Luke sees it, elementary prudence consists in knowing how to renounce all one's goods (v. 33) and all human attachments (vv. 26-27). This *renouncement* must be total and it is urgent in view of the imminence of the Kingdom. It also dispenses one from the normal responsibilities of terrestrial communities (1 Co 7).

In reality, of course, the coming of the Kingdom did not change the face of the earth. Christian tension came to consist more in pilgrimage and delay. Was Luke then wrong in asking for total renouncement? The true lesson of this gospel lies at a deeper level. The Kingdom is not "near" in a temporal sense; it is near in the sense that the Christian must utilize his goods or live with his fellow men through the mediation of Christ. This link is more "immediate" for a man than any one he can possibly have with person or things. But to be relevant, the relation of man with man or with nature is in no way rejected.

X. Romans
14:7-12
1st reading
1st cycle
Thursday

In this chapter Paul deals with the relations between Christians who have different attitudes on certain points of religious practices: days of fasting (v. 5), abstinence from meat and wine (vv. 14, 17, 21) observed in the case of certain foods (vv. 14, 20). In fact, certain Christians ("the strong") thought that their faith emancipated them from such practices; others, more timid and conservative ("the weak") felt they had to follow their religious scruples. The reading for today is especially directed to the "weak" who do not have to judge the "strong."

a) A fundamental principle for maintaining charity among Christians is that each one act for the Lord (vv. 5-6), in the assurance of being, regardless of circumstances, *servants of the same Lord* (vv. 7-9). Neither life or death changes any aspect of this dependence, and *a fortiori,* questions of religious practices.

b) "Conformists" have the tendency to condemn "progressives." Paul tells them that they do not have the right to judge, for *judgment* is a divine prerogative (vv. 10-12; cf. Rm 12:14-21). Furthermore, if the strong adopt a very free behavior, it is in the name of a liberty granted by God (v. 3-4).

Paul does not insist that the conservatives and progressives share the same opinions: it is not at this level that unity is accomplished, but more profoundly, in the awareness that each serves the same God.

Our modern society tends to become more and more pluralistic. By this is meant that Christians will have opinions that are more and more diverse, not only in profane, political or social matters but even on moral, religious and liturgical issues. Is there any reason to lament or consider this development with anxiety and to wish to maintain uniformity towards and against everything at all costs? Such an attitude would risk losing sight of the fact that Christian unity is based on another level where faith alone is essential and the glory of the one God whom we serve.

In reality at this point each one should be able to count on the love and respect of others to whom he should not fear to show himself as he is, with his weaknesses and his strengths, willing in return to give to all the same love and respect. The parish Eucharist which brings together Christians of diverse leanings is the terrain par excellence where the conflicts and tensions inherent in pluralism must be recognized and dealt with.

XI. Philippians This chapter 3 of the letter to the Philippians
3:3-8a is probably a note which Paul calls to the
1st reading attention of the Christians of Philippi and
2nd cycle which was then joined to other remarks, thus
Thursday forming the letter we now have.

The apostle invites his readers to be on guard for their adversaries (vv. 1-2) and to direct their lives on the basis of the spiritual values proposed to them (vv. 3-7).

a) Paul characterizes as "dogs" the *adversaries of the gospel* (vv. 2-3). This title which the Jews used for the Gentiles (Mt 7:6; 15:26; Mk 7:27) probably designates Christians who returned to idolatry and those who returned to the impurity from which they had been converted (cf. Rv 22:15; 2 P 2:22). The "workers of evil" represent preachers who have turned the gospel from its simplicity by making it part of their school of thought and their gnosis (Ph 1:15; 2:21; 2 Co 11:13) and "those who mutilate" refers to Christians of Jewish origin who have returned to the prohibitions and rules of the old law (1 Co 7:19; Ga 5:6; Rm 2:25-29; 4:9-12).

b) The last adversaries, those "who mutilate," seem the most formidable, for Paul again supplies the Philippians with arguments to combat them better.

He recalls first of all that since Jeremiah the true *circumcision* is that of the heart (v. 3; cf. Jr 4:4; 9:24-25; Dt 10:16). He then declares that he himself possesses all the desired titles, Jew of

Jew, since he is circumcised (vv. 4-5), but he considers all these advantages as derisive before the grace of Christ and membership in his Kingdom (vv. 6-7).

XII. Luke This parable belongs to a group called para-
15:1-10 bles of "mercy" which deal with the lost
Gospel sheep, the lost drachma and the lost son.
Thursday Apart from a brief parallel in Matthew 18:
12-14, this group is proper to Luke with whom
the entire work stresses the importance of mercy in the life of
Christ: the pardon given to sinners (Lk 7:36-50; 22:48, 61; 23:34),
pity shown to the unfortunate (Lk 6:24; 8:2-3; 10:30-35; 11:41;
12:13; 16:9, 19-25; 18:22), his attention to the weaker sex (Lk
7:11-15, 36-50; 8:2-3; 10:38-42; 18:1-5; 23:27-28).

a) Severe pharisaic laws about purity and ablutions had excluded sinners and publicans from the sacred meals. To such ostracism Jesus opposed the *mercy* of God, who seeks always the salvation of the sinner. He is following the wishes of the Father when he carries to the limit the search for the sinner. We see this clearly in the parable of the lost sheep, where Luke, unlike Matthew 18:12-24, compares the shepherd's joy to that of God and the angels (vv. 6-7). It is not however stated that the sinner is more loved than the others; the joy over the recovered member is not to be confused with love for all men.

The parable of the lost drachma is identical in structure. This repetition is due doubtless to Jesus' wish to secure the attention of the women who surround him as well as the shepherds, but it is also a common procedure in Hebrew parallelism.

b) To justify the order in which Luke presents the parables of mercy we must turn to Jeremiah 31. For the early Christians, the Old Testament was the only available Scripture. Through reading certain passages they recalled the words of Christ and noted them in the margin of the text. That is why the order of the passages in the Old Testament became the basis of the order of certain readings in the New Testament. Now, in Jeremiah 31: 10-14, like a shepherd God gathers together his dispersed people and announces that there will be joy among the assembled (cf. Lk 15:4-7). In Jeremiah 31:15-17 a woman cries over the loss of her children whom she shall recover again (cf. Lk 15:8-10). In Jeremiah 31:18-20 Ephraim is converted and becomes the beloved son of God (cf. Lk 15:11-32). Finally, the conclusion of Jeremiah 31:31-34 is also valuable for the parables of Luke: the new covenant rests essentially on *forgiveness* and mercy.

c) The primitive parable of the lost sheep stressed the behavior of the shepherd, off in search of his sheep (see the parallel version in Matthew). Luke adds a verse, verse 7, which shifts the perspective to the behavior of the sheep by speaking of *repentance*. He thus gives the parable a more moralistic and theocentric direction. The original version stressed the priority of the divine gesture and its absolute gratuity; Luke, the evangelist of conversion, insists on the human attitude. Actually, the opposition is less than it appears since to repent, for St. Luke, is nothing else but the acceptance of a life dependent on the forgiveness and the mercy of God. To repent is to accept forgiveness as the source of one's life; it is to acknowledge that all one is, is from another.

Modern man is somewhat unsympathetic to the classic theme of divine mercy. The word itself has fairly sentimental, paternalistic overtones and the idea, the impression of religious alienation, as if the Christian who willingly turns to the mercy of God is dispensed from true responsibilities.

The Bible presents a more profound idea of mercy. This term describes love in its fidelity and its tenderness. In a word, it designates a profound attitude of one's being.

The experience of the miserable and sinful condition of man is at the origin of the notion of the mercy of God. It is an invitation to conversion and like an exhortation to witness love to others and especially to pagans (Si 23:30-28:7).

On this point, Jesus is faithful to the insight of the Old Testament. He shows the mercy of God in its greatest intensity, joining with it the practice of human mercy in order to make of it an undertaking involving both God and man, the active response of the second to the attentive initiative of the first. He gives evidence of an infinite mercy to sinners and to the excommunicated.

Christians are first of all invited to a spiritual experience of the divine mercy towards themselves, for God accepts them as they are. Never do they feel abandoned: God is always there, always present to their searching. Recourse to the paternal benevolence is always possible. However, the sinner is truly repentent only if he heeds not only the call to conversion but also the demand of mercy towards others. In the same way the Church understands the divine mercy which makes her what she is only when she casts aside the obstacles engendered by the ecclesial institution in order to rejoin the poor and sinners, at the same time respecting their dignity.

As memorial of the death of Christ, the Eucharist recalls that one man alone has been merciful to a divine degree. To commune at his table is then to benefit from this mercy of the man-God, but it is also to be its witness.

XIII. Romans 15:14-21
1st reading
1st cycle
Friday

In bringing his letter to its conclusion, Paul makes still another apology for his ministry, but in terms which surpass the personal situation in order to rise to a doctrinal level. Several verses of this reading will in fact be used as a basic "theological source" for a definition of the Christian priesthood.

a) First of all Paul excuses himself for interfering in the life of a community which he did not directly found (v. 15). He has no intention of building on the foundation of another: there are too many areas to be conquered for the gospel for him to cause trouble in the jurisdiction of another apostle (vv. 20-21). Then why this intervention at Rome? Is it because he has to depend on this community to enable him to go on to Spain (vv. 22-24)? Perhaps, but more so for a doctrinal reason: *apostolic collegiality.* Paul feels that he shares with the Twelve the responsibility of an envoy on mission and that this charge is collegial. This conviction appears in verse 19 where the apostle describes his missionary activity as starting from Jerusalem, which is wrong historically (cf. Ga 1:15-18; Ac 9:19; 26:19-20), but doctrinally correct. Deeming himself an apostle completely apart, Paul justifies himself as an envoy on mission "from Jerusalem to the ends of the earth," as our Lord said to the Twelve (Lk 24:47-49; Ac 1:8; Jn 20:17-23). Jerusalem is the place where the apostolate was founded and the symbol of the collegial unity for this apostolate. It is on this basis only that Paul refers to the capital of Israel and it is by virtue of this collegiality that he defines his right to intervene in the life of a community he did not found.

b) The notion of *apostolic ministry* has in this context a very precise meaning. This ministry is a "liturgy" (v. 16) and the one who exercises it is a "priest." The apostle preaches the Word in the sense that he expresses the presence of the risen Christ in the heart, in events and in things. He is a priest not because he is a specialist in sacrificial rites like the priests of the temple but because in revealing the paschal meaning of all things he leads his hearers to an attitude of faith, of conversion and involvement which forms the content of the spiritual sacrifices of the new Covenant.

XIV. Philippians
3:17-4:1
1st reading
2nd cycle
Friday

This passage in the letter to the Philippians is at the heart of the polemic which Paul wages against the Judaizers who by their insistence on the place of circumcision "place their glory in their shame" (v. 19) and who, by their abuse of dietary prohibitions, "have as their

God, their belly" (v. 19). This passage belongs, as does the entire chapter, to a particular note by Paul which was inserted later on into this "collection" of notes which make up the letter to the Philippians.

a) Paul is aroused against the teaching of false teachers (Ph 3:4-14). He asks his readers to choose now between the flesh and the Spirit: either follow the Judaizers or imitate Paul, their apostle. On the one hand, the earthly city makes a man a slave of matter; on the other hand, the heavenly city (cf. Col 3:1-4) is where all is risen and transfigured.

The apostle then refers to the theme of the *two ways:* that which leads to death and that which leads to life (Mt 11:26-28; 30:15-20; Pr 8:32-36; Mt 7:13-27).

b) The apostle then does not fear identifying the choice of the good way with imitation of himself (v. 17; cf. Th 1:6; 2:14; 2 Th 3:7-9; 1 Co 4:16; 11:1; Ga 3:12; Ph 4:9). This invitation rests on the conviction that he is the father who has given these Christians birth in the faith, not only by his teaching but still more by his example (1 Th 1:7; 2 Th 3:9; 1 Tm 4:12; Tt 2:7). Initiation into the faith is accomplished in a twofold fashion: by the Word and by life.

XV. Luke 16:1-8
Gospel
Friday

This gospel presents numerous problems. The words of Jesus recounted are certainly authentic, but we do not have the context that would clarify them. This was lost and in the primitive community there were many different attempts at explanation.

Doubtless Jesus is referring to some cheating episode that would clarify matters if we knew about it (vv. 1-7). The context however eludes us. We just have verse 8: "The owner then gave his devious employee credit for being enterprising!"

Who is this master? Not the master of the servant, but Jesus (*o kyrios*). We notice an identical change in the meaning of a word in Luke 18:6. There "Lord" indicates Jesus, not the judge.

a) Verse 8 then does not belong to the account of the cheating episode. It is Luke's addition. But why should the Lord commend this servant? Wherever we can penetrate in the synoptic tradition to the actual text of Jesus' sayings, we often find that he wants to convince his listeners that the judgment is inaugurated. This being the case, there is no time to lose. One must foresee tomorrow (Lk 12:54-56), and be sufficiently *warned* to deal with one's adversary before the judge intervenes (Lk 12:58-59). The servant profited by the respite to make sure of his future and be among the survivors. For Luke apparently this is the primary lesson of the parable. One should make use of the short time remaining in order to insure the future.

b) A second interpretation was developed in primitive Christian circles: "The children of this world are wiser than the children of light" (v. 8b). This is a sad affirmation. In ordinary affairs (it is terrestrial affairs that are meant) Christians are always going to be at a disadvantage, because they cannot resort to the tactics others adopt. In this view the parable expresses Christian *resignation* when confronted by power tactics and efficiency that are unlawful for them.

Too often the "children of light" are overly concerned with intention and principles. They run the risk of making Christianity an ideology and diminish the real efficacy of the Kingdom of God.

XVI. Romans
  16:3-9, 16,
  22-27
  1st reading
  1st cycle
  Saturday

The link between Chapter 16 and the letter to the Romans and in particular the Pauline origin of the doxology (vv. 25-27) are still under discussion, although the arguments in their favor are gaining ground. In reality the Jewish or Pauline themes in this doxology seem in every way serious indications that it was composed by the apostle himself. We will be concerned solely with this doxology; the other elements of the reading for today are the greetings.

a) The revelation of the *mystery* seems to be the principal theme of this doxology. This theme is in general, in the Pauline writings, that of the access of the Gentiles to salvation, at the dawn of the last days (v. 26; cf. Ep 3:8-9; Rm 11:25; Col 1:25-27). It is conceived by the wisdom of God, the "sage par excellence" (v. 27), who can foresee the outcome of a history centuries back and into the future age (same idea as in Dn 2:20, 28).

This mystery, until now hidden in time (v. 25b; cf. Pr 25:2; Is 45:5; 1 Co 2:6-8), is manifested now, first by Jesus Christ and by his death for all men (basic theme of the letter to the Romans), then by Paul and the gospel he must proclaim to the world (theme of the beginning of the letter: Rm 1:5). But the mystery remains the secret of the world to come: the establishment of a humanity reconciled with God and with itself. God's wisdom realizes this mystery in the cross of Christ; the apostles are its witnesses and those who make it a reality.

b) Yes, the mystery of God still remains hidden. The fact that the verb "to hide" is a past participle, proves that this mystery remains sealed to us as for those too who have already received a part of his revelation. The mystery of God remains *silent* even after his revelation. It is his secret even if it is revealed in Jesus Christ, and it is not by reservation or disdain but because of the irremedial distance between God and all that is not God. Even when known by men, God remains unknown.

XVII. **Philip-**   These verses are among Paul's final remarks
      pians   to his correspondents at Philippi. The commu-
      4:10-19   nity had probably helped him during his im-
      1st reading   prisonment.
      2nd cycle
      Saturday   a) The apostle thanks his beloved disciples
                      and explains the significance of their gesture.
Their generosity consists above all, according to the principles often expressed in the letters of Paul, in an authentic *sacrifice*. It is in this way, both spiritual and charitable, that the only worship acceptable to God is celebrated today (v. 18).

b) Paul also makes his sacrifice on the occasion of these acts of charity towards him. He gives thanks to God for this generosity but he affirms at the same time his *detachment* (cf. 1 Tm 6:6-10). He does not refuse the gifts he is offered. He does not practice a severe asceticism, rather he is able to deprive himself or to profit by good things according to the circumstances. In every way he gives no importance either to abundance or penury but rather to the fulfillment of God's plan and the exercise of his mission.

Christianity is the only religion that considers life itself as worship. The Old Testament prophets (Is 1:10-15; Am 5:21; Is 58: 1-12; Mi 6:5-7; Jr 7:3-5) had already criticized ritual that was isolated from real life, thus indicating considerable progress over other religions for whom life was insignificant and had value only in relation to rites and consecrations.

The coming of Christ modified this idea radically. Jesus is not a specialist in ritual (Heb 7:13; 8:4); but his life and his death have cultic value because of the oblation he made of it in the service of man and his Father. In his turn and like St. Paul, the Christian can confer on his life a liturgical value (Rm 12:1-2; 1 Co 10:31; 1 Co 6:19; 3:16-17). The new liturgy for this worship is that which, by its word, converts hearts (Rm 15:6) so that they might offer the spiritual worship (v. 17).

XVIII. **Luke**   After the parable of the wily manager (Lk
       16:9-15   16:1-8), Luke introduces a series of diverse
       Gospel   statements which can be used both as com-
       Saturday   mentaries (vv. 9-13) and as a transition be-
                    tween it and the parable of the beggar
Lazarus (vv. 14-15).

a) Besides the conclusion of the parables proper to Luke (16:8a) and the second, added by the early Christian community (Lk 16:8b) other Christian circles provided yet another interpretation, stressing especially the *use of money* (v. 9). The main point was not the ensuring of the future by the manager but the way he used the money: he did not seek to raise money but, on the contrary, he distributed it to merit heaven. A definite inclination towards allegorization is needed to accept such an interpretation, but this last was so obviously in the general outline of St. Luke that we can admit that the evangelist retained it (cf. Lk 6:29-35; 12:33).

b) Verses 10-12 supply a completely different interpretation from the preceding. Here the manager is taken as an example of what should not be done: if you want to be an administrator of spiritual goods, be at least *honest* in the administration of material goods.

c) Finally Luke adds a supplementary text borrowed from another context (vv. 13; cf. Mt 6:24) and which is clearly foreign to the spirit of the parable. One cannot serve both God and money;

a choice is necessary. Luke, who considers the Pharisees as greedy men, immediately illustrates this necessity by putting on stage members of this sect who are convinced that they can serve God without taking leave of their money. These people live a double life (vv. 14-15): faith cannot be present in the heart of such a hypocrite. On the contrary, an undivided heart is needed to approach God and *poverty* alone can insure the validity of this option. Thus, Luke is now able to introduce an idea that is particularly dear to him; he can now recount the parable of the rich man and Lazarus (Lk 16:19-31).

THIRTY-SECOND WEEK

I. Wisdom 1:1-7
1st reading
1st cycle
Monday
The Book of Wisdom is chronologically the last of the Wisdom books (1st century). The author, faithful to Jewish culture, is however influenced by Greek thought (for example, the themes of divine philanthrophy in verse 6 and the role of God in the cohesiveness of the world, verse 7) from which he does not, however, adopt any philosophical system.

The theme of the first five chapters is the most characteristic of the research of the sages of Israel: the final lot of man and the means placed at his disposal for reaching it.

The basic means for attaining his final end is *wisdom,* which the author here compares with the spirit (vv. 5-7). This divine force animates man and the universe to which it confers its cohesiveness (v. 7). But the animation of the cosmos is mechanical whereas the inspiration of man depends on his liberty and his will for communion with God.

This collaboration involves different aspects but it implies an identical demand: to be conscious of the presence of God on the level of one's loins (the passions), of the heart (intelligence) and of ones words (contracts) and open to his influence (v. 6). This is called "loving justice" (v. 1), that is, to live in communion with the will of God; it is "to have integrity of heart" (v. 1), that is, it implies unifying one's life solely around the quest for God (in contrast to duplicity; v. 5). This also signifies "giving one's faith" to God (v. 2), which consists in taking the hand which God extends when there is question of adapting oneself to events. Finally, it involves renouncing sin (vv. 3-4), namely, the will of man for promoting his salvation by his own means. This last attitude separates from the Spirit, but also from the world since its cohesiveness is the work of the same Spirit (v. 7).

II. Titus 1:1-9   The epistle to Titus, one of the last letters of
1st reading   Paul, was probably written between the years
2nd cycle   65-68. The apostle wrote it either just before
Monday   or during his final imprisonment. More so
than the letters to Timothy, it indicates an
evolution in the structure of the Church at the end of the apostolic era. The local churches were organized so as to unite their
members in the participation of the same faith and grace, and the
development of the hierarchy raises the problem of recruitment
of responsible individuals and their qualifications.

a) Paul follows the same method everywhere in the establishment of local churches. Once he evangelized the city and converted disciples, the apostle leaves them to themselves for a
while. Then he returns one or more times to confirm them in
their zeal and finally he definitively organizes the community.
With this in view he institutes a council of elders or the *presby-
terium* (Ac 14:21-23), thus adopting in part the organization of
the Diaspora Jews. This college manages the community, especially on the administrative level and the economic. These elders
were called "presbyters" or "bishops" (compare verses 5 and 7;
cf. Ac 20:17, 28), the first involving perhaps more the notion of
dignity whereas the second involves responsibility. In any case,
it is not necessary to seek the actual distinction between bishops
and priests and all its implications.

b) Paul, however, adopts an original policy towards the presbyterate. The presbyterate was often chosen from the local Jewish communities (cf. the identical process in Ac 1:15-25 and
6:1-7). The presbyterate of the communities founded by the apostle was designated by the apostle himself (Ac 14:21-23) or, in his
absence, by one of his disciples, authorized for this task (v. 5). The
local community has a hierarchy for reasons which go beyond
itself. As a sign of the universal community, it is not sufficient to
itself, and its leaders are responsible on the local level because

they are so on the universal level. Titus' mission involves the choice of just such responsible individuals.

c) Paul calls them "stewards," a term of evangelical origin (v. 7). He thus recalls the parables of Christ on vigilance which is the charge for those who are to take their place among his own (Lk 12:42; cf. 1 P 4:10; 1 Co 4:2). He also demands of them qualities which will guarantee this virtue.

The stewards of the house of God must above all be perfect stewards of their own household. They are to be "men of one wife" (as we say: "a man of one book": v. 6), their children must receive Christian education and they themselves are to be "irreproachable" (1 Tm 3:4-5). Paul also recalls the councils given by Christ and he transmits them to the members of the presbyterate (v. 7; cf. Lk 12:42-48; 1 Tm 3:2-3).

d) An important evolution must have taken place between the formation of the hierarchy at Corinth and the formation of that at Crete. In the first case, those who possess the charisms of teaching and of the Word have the advantage over the community and the gift of governing or administrating takes a secondary place (1 Co 12:28; Rm 12:6-8; Ep 4:11). In the second situation, the charism of governing is raised to the first place and associated particularly with the gift of *teaching* (v. 9). The problems which the explanation of the faith involves on the one hand and its defense on the other oblige those responsible to take on the duty of teaching, for they alone can listen to the universal Church and bear witness to the unity of faith. Perhaps Paul is returning to the organization used by the Qumran community.

III. Luke 17:1-6 This gospel reading is made up of fragments
    Gospel   which seem more in place in the gospels of
    Monday   Matthew 18:6-22 and Mark 9:24. It speaks
                        about scandal to little ones (vv. 1-3a) and for-
giving the brethren (3b-4).

These fragments are probably extracts from a discourse by Christ on the conditions for entrance into the Kingdom. Luke holds up two essential characteristics of *charity:* first of all, respect for "little ones," that is, the mass of Christians, ignorant of the subtleties of casuistry and doctrine and so quickly scandalized by the positions of an "elite"; and then the attention granted to those who are sorry for the wrong they have caused their neighbor.

IV. Wisdom   The author is writing probably during the
  2:23-3:9   persecution inflicted on the people by Ptolemy
  1st reading   Lathyrus (88-80 B.C.). Judging from their
  1st cycle   ways and customs, their nonconformity and
  Tuesday   their refusal to collaborate with the political
                        society of the epoch, the Jews irritated the
Gentiles who sought to suppress a people so contentious. It is fitting then to reveal to the members of the chosen people the significance of the process of which they are the object.

a) The idea of terrestrial *retribution* which was still alive in the pious circles to which the author addresses himself, hardly responds to the new conditions stirred up by the persecution. How can a just man, faithful to God, see his life cut down by the mere will of men? A teaching of this kind could not quiet the anxiety of the faithful who are brought prematurely to their death. The author also proposes a new doctrine, drawn from Hellenism, according to which the soul lives on after death. Such a belief does not belong to prior biblical revelation. It even has a note of duality about it which a Jew could not admit, but it permits the author to explain that death is not an end but an intervention by the devil (v. 24) who can in no way tarnish the plan of God (v. 23). There is no place then for anxiety: all is not ended with death and the one who with good reason seeks retribution for his merits must rely on God (v. 9) to recompense him after death (vv. 1-4).

Consequently, all changes if there is a beyond to death: the just will enjoy the awaited retribution and persecutors will find themselves before their victims, now their judges (vv. 7-9).

b) The faithful can then enter into death with *confidence* and reliance on God. Thus death is already conquered by the very attitude with which it is approached and which is a means of affirming the incorruptible character of the soul (v. 23) and the will of man to triumph over Satan, its author (v. 24). This attitude is also *sacrificial* (vv. 5-6), in the measure in which it transforms death into a passage towards God and makes it a free and voluntary act.

V. Titus 2:1-8, 11-14
1st reading
2nd cycle
Tuesday

The Christian exhortation presented by Saint Paul imitates in many ways Greek morality. The apostle speaks in turn to the older men (v. 2), the older women (v. 3) and the younger women (vv. 4-5), the young men (v. 6), missionaries (vv. 7-8) and to slaves (v. 9). He invites them to live in conformity with the Word of God (cf. Ep 5:21-6:10; Col 3:18-4:1 or 1 P 2:11-3:7).

All social classes and generations are mobilized by St. Paul in view of the essential task of *education* in the *faith* in face of heresies and the relaxation of morals. Everyone must be conformed to holy doctrine (v. 1) and propagate it. Thus, the older women, widows for the most part, will dedicate themselves to the Christian education of the younger women (cf. 1 Tm 5:3-8) and the young men to the deepening of faith, at least by the mastery of themselves. The missionaries will take upon them the responsibility for teaching the faith and for a life conformed to this teaching (vv. 7-8).

The urgency of this education in the faith asserts itself as soon as the newness of Christianity is perceived (vv. 11-14) and it is this newness which must guide the apprenticeship in the Christian faith.

In an epoch when a new humanism is being formed, catechesis proposes still too often a faith tied to outdated concepts of man.

It will be able to educate in the faith only in allowing itself to be educated by the world and in abandoning some of its monopolies.

Furthermore, the Church, which often limited the education in the faith to childhood and adolescence, is today called to undertake the "recycling" of older people. Consequently, it must bring into play new methods of education for adults: schools of preparation for marriage, a catechumenate for parents, institutes for catechesis etc.

VI. Luke 17:7-10   Luke shows the most originality in that sec-
    Gospel   tion of his gospel which describes the journey
    Tuesday   to Jerusalem (9:51-19:28). Many elements here
                     are peculiar to him; others have been clearly
reworked. From chapter 14 onwards he is warning his readers against the Pharisees particularly, and against riches. He wants to turn their attention to the feeble and the poor.

The parable of the worthless servant (vv. 7-10) was perhaps originally delivered by Jesus in order to castigate the Pharisees who believed they had rights before God. Luke suggests that it was addressed to the apostles (cf. v. 5) to teach them modesty. The transference however is somewhat awkward because no apostle seems to fit the description of verse 7 ("who among you. . .").

a) The master-slave image is often used in the gospels to describe the relation between God and his servants, the Scribes and the Pharisees (Mt 25:14-30). God is represented as a demanding master, little concerned with the wishes or well-being of his slave. But the parable stresses above all the fact that the Pharisees, those believers who measured their merits and rights against God, are in fact servants incapable of rendering proper service. To their assurance and calculation of merits is opposed the pure and simple faith (v. 6) of the poor and the little ones. An attitude of *unconditional confidence* in the Lord is contrasted with the murmuring of those whose concept of religion is confined to merits and a right to reward (cf. Mt 20:13).

b) Transferred to the other context, where the apostles are addressed (v. 5), their *ministry* is represented as *worthless* (v. 10). It would be wrong to regard this as Jesus' intention. God has need of men, and Christ has need of his Church. The lesson concerns the element of Pharisee and authoritarianism that is in all of us. When we are given credit for something that could only come from God, we should beware of regarding the function we exercise as a right to life eternal, of glorifying ourselves instead of "glorifying the Lord" (1 Co 1:31; 9:16; 2 Co 10:17; Ph 3:3; Ga 6:14).

VII. Wisdom This text serves as an introduction to the sec-
      6:1-11 ond part of the book of Wisdom (1st century
   1st reading before Jesus Christ). For the first time a Jewish
   1st cycle author affirms that Gentile kings receive their
   Wednesday authority from God, a position which does
              not fail to raise certain controversies.

Ancient traditions saw the davidic kings as representatives of God, empowered for this function by royal anointing, but no one dared to propose that Gentile kings also held their power from Yahweh. He often made use of these as instruments of his policy towards the chosen people (1 K 19:15; Is 45:1; Jr 25:9; 27:6; 43:10), but it is far from the idea of a God who accidentally uses someone for the accomplishment of his design to that of a God who confers on rulers their power. In other respects the apocalyptic strain thought that the kings of the nations held their power from Satan whom they supported.

To elaborate his teaching, the author is without doubt inspired by Proverbs 8:15-16 and by Daniel 2:21, 37; 5:16-21. He confines himself nevertheless to generalities, speaking of "kings," "princes," "judges" who dominate even to the "ends of the earth" and over "a multitude of subjects," without envisaging their manner of accession to power, or their justice or competence. He has their authority depend on the sovereignty of God over the universe (v. 3) and sees there a mandate for which God will demand an account (v. 5). He does not consider the king of nations as the supporters of Satan or as persecutors, but he cautions those who imagine they owe their *authority* to their geneology or to their personal daring whereas it comes from the Wisdom of Yahweh. Good or unjust, the Gentile king receives his power from God, and Wisdom commands him to give an accounting.

VIII. Titus 3:1-7 This is the conclusion to the parenthetical
    1st reading statement in the letter to Titus. Paul wants to
    2nd cycle base Christian involvement in the world on
    Wednesday a proper theological foundation.

Paul invites Christians to show themselves as good and conciliatory before non-Christians (v. 1-2) since they were not so long ago like them (v. 3) and because the goodness of God is manifested in the first as well as in the second (v. 4). How can a Christian be a sign of the *love of God for men* yet despise them? All the more so since the goodness of God is gratuitous and confers no title of glory on the Christian (v. 5).

But this goodness of God is expressed especially in the *baptized* (v. 5) who actualize the mystery of salvation manifested in the birth of Jesus (v. 4) and which suggests a new life to man (v. 5) in order to become sons of God and heirs of his life (v. 7). Baptism is not studied here for its own sake but in view of its principal effect: the inner regeneration which makes man a new being and the Christian in particular, an "epiphany" of salvation in the world.

This passage, one of the most precious which the New Testament presents in view of placing the Church and Christians in dialogue with the world, affirms that all men benefit from the salvation of Christ, the new Adam and the recapitulation of humanity.

But this solidarity of all in Jesus Christ must be applied to each one by the sacramental mediation of the Church. Member and beneficiary of the Church, the Christian shares in its sacramentality: its life in the world in altogether mission and mediation, and it is by it that the Church can make itself present in the vast network of relationships and brotherhood which make up every human life.

IX. Luke
17:11-19
Gospel
Wednesday

This account of the cure of the ten lepers is set against the background of the legislation about lepers in Leviticus 13:45-46 and 14:2-7. When Jesus tells the lepers to show themselves to the priest, he is obeying the requirements of law. Nine of them do go to the priests. The tenth, a Samaritan, is not liable to inspection by the priests in Judea. Consequently he is free to return and express all his gratitude to Christ.

a) This passage also belongs to the dossier of early Christian polemics against the Jews. The law impedes liberty of expression. The non-Jew is in fact closer to true religion because he is free of the law, and thus closer to the only true liberation, that of the cross (Ga 2:19-20; 5:11-16; 2 Co 3:15-18) and gratuitous grace (Rm 5:12-17; 6:14-15). The spontaneous expression of thanks on the part of the delivered man corresponds to the gratuitous gesture of a saving God. Such an exchange would be impossible in the framework of a law where everything is on a "give-and-take" basis. In the order of *faith* it becomes possible: "Go, your faith has delivered you."

b) Leprosy is often a symbol for sin in the Bible. Thus Christ's miracle has more significance than that of a simple cure. It suggests the *salvation* that liberates a man from sin.

We still meet Christians who resemble the nine Jewish lepers. They practice assiduously but are incapable of contemplation.

They take communion frequently but cannot give thanks. Their ethic is narrow, turned inward; scrupulosity and detail bedevil their moral performance. Their God is a bookkeeper. They become incapable of openness to the Other, to gratuity.

The Jewish priests were wont to shut up the healed lepers in the temple, because they alone had the right to declare the disease healed. Our clergy likewise have tended to train the laity in the narrow limits of a legalism that is altogether foreign to true thanksgiving and genuine personal communion with God. These are the people who today find in themselves a growing distaste for the sacraments.

X. Wisdom
7:22-8:1
1st reading
1st cycle
Thursday

This eulogy on divine Wisdom conforms to the laws of this literary genre. In Proverbs 1-9, Wisdom was already personified, present in God from the creation. In Job 28, it was even distinguished from God; in Sirach 24 it came forth from the Most High and guided the history of the people.

The style of this passage is nevertheless superior and the divine character of Wisdom more clearly accented than in the other texts. The author, who wrote a century before Jesus Christ, made use of Greek philosophy without however tying himself to its content or to its precision. If he seems to stress the divine personification of Wisdom, he does not seem to distinguish it from the personality of God.

a) The first part of the reading (vv. 22-24) mention twenty-one qualities of divine *Wisdom*. Most of the attributes are of Greek origin and define both the transcendence and the immanence of Wisdom: it is holy and also the friend of men, unique and also manifold; it is above all the element by which God is present everywhere in all.

b) In the following verses (vv. 25-26) it is not so much the activity and effulgence of Wisdom which are envisaged as its *divine origin*. The images are significant; aura of a power, effusion of a glory, the refulgence of a light, mirror of an activity, image of an excellence. One thinks he is reading a treatise on the Trinity! These traits will be used effectively by the New Testament for the Incarnate Word (Heb 1:3; Jn 1:9; Col 1:15), traits which moreover bring to mind the Spirit as well as Wisdom (cf. Is 11:2; compare Wis 1:7; 12:1; 7:24; 8:1; etc.).

c) Verses 7:27-8:1 describe how the *transcendence* of Wisdom is bound to its *immanence*. Unique, it is present everywhere and renews all things; immutable, it is however moved as events transpire.

It is not only Judaeo-Christian thought which derives from such texts but all of Western thought is influenced by this daughter of the Old Testament. No other culture, no other religion has been able to conceive that the divine transcendence could be expressed in an immanence in man and in the universe. It is true that Christ will accomplish perfectly the intuition contained in this passage in revealing a God very different from the categories which ancient Yahwism and Greek thought believed it could define— more friend of men than of itself, more humble than powerful, more mobile than immutable. The God of Chrisitans is not like other gods, since he thinks that the life of men and even their death are the elements which signify perfectly what he is. This is the Wisdom of God which is even now Folly.

This text establishes the main lines of a theology of the Trinity. Its object is in fact the contemplation of divine Wisdom both in its transcendence and in its immanence. Thus, is the unique and holy God of Israel at the same time the God who shares and saves?

The day on which we understand that the plan of salvation and divinization can succeed only through the hands of a man-God, the mystery of the Trinity will appear as the end of the evolution of monotheism.

XI. Philemon
7-20
1st reading
2nd cycle
Thursday

This is a letter that Paul wrote after his first captivity (61-63) to Philemon, a Christian of Colossae, who was his friend. Philemon had a runaway slave who had taken refuge with Paul's entourage. This was an embarrassing situation for the apostle. It was strictly against the law for Paul to retain a fugitive slave in his service, and furthermore his friendship for Philemon made it impossible for him to conceal any longer the fact that Onesimus was living with him. Then there was the personal embarrassment. How could he adopt a purely legalistic attitude to Onesimus and ignore the personal relationship that had grown up between them?

a) Paul accepts the legal situation of his times and sends Onesimus back to his master (v. 12). However, he does so in a fashion that indicates, from a Christian viewpoint, the inadequacies of the law.

A relationship has developed between Philemon and himself because they share the same faith and above all the practice of the same charity towards the lowly (vv. 5-7). Likewise a relationship has developed between Paul and Onesimus, so that Onesimus has become his very heart (vv. 10-12, 17). A similar relationship can grow between *the slave and his master.* It is true that the slave had given offense to his master (vv. 11, 18). This is however a trivial matter when compared with the boon of brotherhood in Jesus Christ, and citizenship of the Kingdom (vv. 15-16).

Paul does not directly revolt against the law but he sows the leaven that will soon explode it.

b) In describing his relationship with Onesimus he does not hesitate to use the image of spiritual fatherhood which had been prominent in previous letters.

On Paul's lips this is not merely a sentimental phrase. It describes accurately his whole apostolic mission; he regarded his ministry as a real transmission of life. His proclamation of the gospel is the transmission of the message of God, and the Word of God is efficacious, bringing life and fecundity. The one who transmits it is a father in a certain sense (1 Co 4:14-21). And when, as well as giving his message, he lives it in his own person, to the point of suffering (Ga 4:19), the cross and prisons, it is clear that his fatherhood is instrumental, as Christ's life was the instrument of God's fatherhood for men (1 Co 4:15). He can demand filial affection from his disciples, which he is at pains to transmit to his Father, because his fatherhood is vicarious (1 Th 2:7-11).

XII. Luke   We can distinguish three stages in the history
    17:20-25   of these verses and especially verses 10-11b.
    Gospel
    Thursday   a) In uttering the words contained in verses
                20-21, Jesus no doubt wanted to discourage
the disciples who were trying to calculate the date for the Kingdom, and so announces to them the near arrival of the Spirit (cf. Ac 1:7-8: rejects computations and announces the Spirit; Lk 11:13: where the request for the coming of the Kingdom in Lk 11:2 is answered under the form of the gift of the Spirit; and Rm 14:17).

Furthermore, the verb "to carefully watch" in verse 20, designates the attitude of those who were officially instructed with following the phases of the moon in order to determine the exact time for the celebration of feasts. Jesus thus teaches his own to forget about the *arrival of a Kingdom* that is measurable and to be concerned rather about the coming of the Spirit "within their hearts." The Kingdom of God will not be established by messianic tensions or by the legalists of Judaism but by the reception of the Spirit of the new Covenant forseen by Jeremiah 31:31. It is not impossible that Jesus sought at the same time to make relative the discussion of his contemporaries on the date of the Pasch.

b) Another interpretation was given to these verses by the primitive communities when each one insisted on fidelity to the will of God; thus the Judaeo-Christian and the Hellenists (Ac 6:1-7),

Paul and the Twelve (Ga 2), Antioch and Jerusalem (Ac 15). Jesus' words made it possible to appraise conflicts by pointing out that the kingdom does not exist in *observances* or in structures but in hearts converted and enlivened by the Spirit. This appears in particular from the proximity of verses 20-21 and Rm 14:5-17 which is precisely directed towards appeasing the conflicts between Christians of diverse observances.

c) In placing verses 20-21 just before a text with an eschatological bearing (vv. 22-25), Luke certainly wished to determine in advance their interpretation and stay too apocalyptic a commentary. Luke thinks that the Kingdom is already present in the moral life of each man and that it is by being involved with it rather than in waiting passively for events of an apocalyptic type. The example of Christ who lived his fidelity to the very end in his *condition as man* (v. 25) must serve as a lesson: he did not wait in expectation for some extraordinary "day," his day was always his fidelity to daily life.

The kingdom of God is no longer written in the times of the ancients, visibly observable in the signs of nature, but in the time that man himself defines by his involvement in the present.

Until Jesus Christ, man considered time as a fate imposed on him from without. Even the Jew, previously more concerned with a linear and "historical" time, still conceived its unfolding as an exclusive initiative of God. To celebrate time was to come to terms with an evolution the keys to which were unknown. With Jesus Christ, the first man to perceive the eternity of the present because he was the man-God, man himself celebrates his own time to the extent that he seeks it in the very life of God.

Daily life thus takes a step in the unfolding of a preestablished calendar; the meaning of the past and the projects of the future are there only to contribute to the value of eternity contained in the present. There is no longer any waiting for a day beyond history; each day contains eternity for the one who lives it in covenant with God.

XIII. Wisdom   Chapter 13 of the book of Wisdom (1st cen-
13:1-9   tury before Jesus Christ) is one of those which
1st reading   gives the greatest evidence of the hellenistic
1st cycle   influence on the author. Like the Greeks he
Friday   sees a religious value in the beauty of the
    world. (v. 3); like them he thinks that the
dynamism of creation can unveil its Author (v. 4). But he remains thoroughly faithful to the Jewish faith and it is not un-
profitable to note how the two cultures strengthen him in his
faith in the existence of God.

a) *Jewish faith in the existence of the Creator* is marked by the
struggle led by Yahwism against the sacralizing ideas of nature.
For Canaan and Babylon, in fact, nature reveals a God who
keeps it at his mercy by the fecundity which he brings or refuses
to it. Magic rites permit participation in this fecundity; myths
explain it by the mysterious hierarchy of gods and goddesses.

For Israel, on the contrary, the world was created by the free
and loving initiative of God, but was immediately secularized:
the account of Genesis affirms belief in one Creator-God, but at
the same time certitude that the world was confided by God to
man, his vizier. God is indeed the author of the world, but not
in the manner of the creator gods of the Orient who alienate
it in the manner in which they direct it. The creator God of
Israel is more transcendent than the Oriental gods and the religion
has become purer, desacralized and demythologized, it is the
free relationship of the man-vizier to the God whom he knew.
Furthermore, creation is considered by the Jew as the first act of
a God who leads history even to salvation by a series of gratuitous
interventions which presuppose the collaboration of man. The
relation of man to his Creator is no longer commanded by the
natural laws of fecundity and their mythological explanation, but
by the free and gratuitous covenant of God and of his vizier in
the world.

For the Bible, "to ignore God" (v. 1) is not necessarily refusing to believe in his existence but above all refusing the personal and free dialogue which the Jewish doctrine about creation postulates between Yahweh and man.

b) The *notion which the Greeks develop about the world* is rather different from that of the Jews and the author reproaches them for it.

It is not so much idolatry that he condemns—the best of the Greeks did not fall into that abberation—but rather their intellectual speculation. The Greeks are not atheists; they have a sense of the mystery of things and they seek the absolute in their own way. But the author reproaches them for not having known enough to pass from their knowledge of the visible to the knowledge of God (v. 1) and, consequently, for not having completed to the end the road which would have led them to Him. He does not say how they must go about it in order to pass from created nature to God the Creator. His condemnation of Greek thought seems then a slight summary, more especially since certain arguments, like that of the beauty of creation (v. 3), were already known by the philosophers of the epoch who did not necessarily arrive at the notion of a personal and transcendent God. They were, on the contrary, content to extract from it the idea of a demiurge organizing a preexisting matter or that of a principle immanent to creation.

We understand then that the author is proud to owe to his faith the idea of a personal and transcendent God, but he leaves us to our hunger when he affirms the possibility of a natural knowledge of God without showing the way.

XIV. 2 John 4-9   Many exegetes refuse to admit that John is the
1st reading   author of this letter even though there is a
2nd cycle   similarity of thought and vocabulary with the
Friday   first letter of John. The epistle is directed to a
Christian community (the "Lady elect" of

verses 1 and 5), whose charity (vv. 4-6) and faith (vv. 7-9) the author loved to reaffirm.

a) John no longer loses himself in long statements. All of Christian life and all doctrine can be summed up in a single affirmation: *love* (vv. 5-6), love of the brethren and love of God (cf. Jn 5:3; Jn 14:15-21; 15:10).

b) But love of the brethren and service to men will appear as one with the love of God only if the believer maintains his faith in Jesus Christ, *man* and *God*. As soon as one denies the humanity of Christ as certain heretics do (v. 7), one automatically loses an understanding of the unique commandment of love of God in the love of the brethren.

Faith and charity are then inseparable. If Christ is not man-God, he has not loved his fellowmen with the very love which he has from his Father; it makes every religious interpretation of the love of men impossible and it destroys the foundations of the spiritual sacrifice which the liturgy offers to God from the service of men.

XV. Luke
17:26-37
Gospel
Friday

The eschatological discourse reproduced by Luke differs rather obviously from the versions of Matthew and Mark. The third gospel in fact directs the attention of the reader exclusively towards the Day of the Son of Man, whereas the two others freely intermingle it with that of the fall of Jerusalem.

a) Luke produces first of all the comparisons made by Christ between the days which will precede his coming and the days of the *flood* (vv. 26-28). But whereas Matthew sees in this a symbol of the fall of Jerusalem where one will be taken and another left (Mt 24:40-41; cf. Mt 24:19-22), Luke, who wants to make it the symbol for the last days, underscores rather that "all" (v. 17) perished in the flood as all will perish at the end of time. The idea of a Remnant is not even alluded to.

b) Luke extends the image of the flood with that of the *flight* of *Lot* (vv. 29-30 and 32). His vision remains the same: in place of describing the separation of the good and the bad, he shows that "all" are crushed. He thus transforms certain traits of the primitive discourse in order to acknowledge its eschatological character while retaining the description of the fall of Jerusalem, which does not seem very logical. Whence the nuances provided by verse 31 (the flight theme: however, it is not the Day of Yahweh that is being fled!) and verses 34-35 (all the world will be seized on the day of Yahweh, and not only one or two!).

XVI. Wisdom 18:14-16, 19:6-9
1st reading
1st cycle
Saturday

The author of Wisdom draws a parallel between the Egyptians and the Hebrews by contrasting the final plague of Egypt (the death of the first born) with the liberation of the young Moses and by comparing the fate that befell each people during the passage through the Red Sea.

a) Starting with Wisdom 16, the author tries to describe the part which nature plays in the judgment between the Hebrews and the Egyptians. Water, animals, atmosphere, death and the Red Sea intervene for the happiness or misfortune of each. For the author, *salvation* proceeds by *nature* (v. 6; cf. Ws 16:17, 24). There is then a precise reverberation of the salvation of the just on the cosmic equilibrium and vice versa.

b) Chapters 16-19 are strongly marked by eschatology: the events of the Exodus evoke all previous history and particularly the end of time. This amounts to saying that the author thinks, especially in the verses read in the liturgy for today, of the resurrection of the body and of the future in a transfigured world.

This is why he presents the Exodus as the calling forth of the future creation. Thus the Word of God who created all things in Genesis 1 returns to the earth (v. 15) to annihilate his work and to prepare a *new creation*, beyond death (v. 16). The "cloud" thus comes to recover the world as the Spirit over the waters (v. 7; cf. Gn 1:2), the solid earth arises out of the primordial water (v. 7b; cf. Gn 1:9), the verdant plain imagined by the author in the time and place of the desert of the Exodus recalls the creation of plants (v. 7c: cf. Gn 1:11-13). Let us underscore as well the theme of new birth (Ws 19:11) and that of the manna just now unalterable (Ws 19:21; cf. Jn 6) so as to cherish better the beings now immortal.

Without clearly stating the notion of resurrection, the author manifestly wants to affirm that eschatological salvation is a corporeal and cosmic salvation and not a liberation of the soul alone, in the platonic sense. His perspective is that of a cosmos fashioned anew from bodies which henceforth escape death.

In trying to understand the world, man has sometimes distinguished matter and spirit to the point of separating them. He has either chosen a spiritualism which excludes matter or a materialism which rejects the spirit in the realm of ideologies. When he wanted to retain both principles, he opposed them to each other, speaking of dualism or at least of a dichotomy. In certain settings it is good form to swear to the cosmos' final distruction and to believe only in a resurrection where bodies would be transformed into spirits! So long as man is not reconciled with himself, happy with a body made supple to the rhythm of his thought and love, he will not be able to go beyond dualism or dichotomy. As long as modern technology is placed under the sign of the machine, leisure under the temple of eroticism, socialization corresponds with the alienation of the individual, faith in the renewal of the world of man will be only a utopia. But if man succeeds in formulating his liberty in modern machinery, his becoming a person in the process of socialization, then it will be possible to believe in the answerability of man and of the cosmos in the new creation.

Man is answerable for matter and his vocation does not consist in going beyond his existing in the world to a spiritual beyond but in realizing the full personal and cosmic equilibrium demanded by his nature.

XVII. **3 John 5-8**   This final message of John is addressed to a
1st reading certain Gaius (v. 1) and not, as was the custom,
2nd cycle to a community.
Saturday

Gaius, probably the head of an unknown community, seems to have gathered Christians from another community. John asks him to pursue *his beneficence* towards them, for these Christians travel "for the name" of the Lord (no doubt for the proclamation of the gospel: v. 7; cf. Mt 10:8; 2 Co 12:14) and they are worthy of aid in their apostolate in a way worthy of God (cf. 1 Th 2:12; Tt 3:13).

The problem of reward for ministers of the Word was often dealt with in the New Testament. From the discourse on mission, Jesus asks his disciples to procure neither gold nor silver but to give freely what they have freely received (Mt 10:8-10). The minister of the Word is a witness of the gratuity of God; he must then reflect it in his conduct. We are far removed from the mission of the Levites (Ne 10:38-39), charged with gathering in silver and provisions! Nonetheless it remains true that the worker is worth his salary! He freely gives the Word of salvation and those who receive it must, in conscience, give freely to him who gives freely to them (Lk 10:7-8; 1 Tm 5:17-18). To avoid any ambiguity, Paul refused to accept anything at all from these communities (Ac 18:1-5; 1 Co 4:12; 2 Co 12:13; 1 Co 9:15-18) with the exception of the community at Philippi (Ac 16:11-15; 2 Co 11:8-10; Ph 4:10-20). But there is never any question of a fixed reward for ministers of the Word: they give freely; they can then receive only freely. The Word which they proclaim can lead to thanksgiving by the faithful. This can be manifested by a gift of nature or money, but which can never be expected; it will always be received in thanksgiving.

XVIII. Luke This teaching of Jesus on prayer cannot be
18:1-8 understood apart from its eschatological con-
Gospel tent. Note that this passage comes just after
Saturday the statement in Luke 17:22-37, on eschatology, which he completes with an allusion to
the return of the Lord (v. 8). The expression: "not losing heart" (v. 1) is characteristic of the constant and persevering expectation which the Day of the Lord requires (Lk 21:36; 1 Th 5:17; 2 Th 3:13; Rm 1:10, etc.) and which the formula "do justice" that occurs four times in the text (vv. 3, 5, 6, 8) brings to mind, namely the day of "vengeance" when the afflicted will at last receive salvation (Is 61:2).

Thus understood, the parable of the corrupt judge and the persistent widow recall the necessity of praying without ceasing, even if the Lord is slow and seems deaf to every call.

The two figures of the parable are, on the one hand, a judge void of faith or law (v. 2), little solicitous for justice, especially when it involves a being as weak as a widow, an individual so base, who ends in giving the widow justice in order to have peace and avoid a possible bad situation (v. 5) and, on the other hand, a widow, weak but sure of her right and who intends to defend it (v. 3).

Jesus' argument is simple (vv. 6-8): if a corrupt judge ends in yielding to the widow, how much more will God who is just, render justice to his elect, even at the mercy of their adversaries.

The parable also signifies that God will do justice promptly (v. 8a), but only after having *delayed* for a long while (v. 7). Ever since, the Christian must include in his prayer acceptance of the delay which God takes; he will pray "without respite."

Christian prayer is then no longer a call to immediate intervention and to vengeance (as was still the case in Rv 6:10). It espouses the patience of God so that sinners may have time to be converted (2 P 3:9-15).

The prayer of petition does not consist in waiting for God to accomplish what we cannot succeed in realizing: give us bread, give us peace, give us healing. God is not a stopgap! In reality this prayer is a protest: it is not tolerable that war constantly gets the better of peace, that the riches of a small number crush the mass of the poor. It is communion with God who is patient and in that communion the cries of protest gradually give way to action.

THIRTY-THIRD WEEK

I. 1 Maccabees
1:10-15, 41-43,
54-57, 62-64
1st reading
1st cycle
Monday

The anonymous historiographer of the first book of Maccabees (around 100 B.C.) is a loyal partisan of the Hasmonian dynasty. In contrast to the legitimists, favorable to the davidic dynasty, he defends the measures taken by the Hasmonians to defend the country and its laws and is tempted to justify the religious sovereignty with which they are likewise invested.

The general tone of the book is somewhat more "secular" than the other historical books of the Old Testament: laymen are not "under the Spirit of God"; God is barely mentioned and the sacred war itself takes place with very human means, in the military as well as diplomatic sphere. This "laicization" is however very partial, because the author has in mind procuring for the Jews the desired arguments in order to be distinguished from the Gentiles and to reject from their people those who want to reconcile Jewish law with the Gentile culture.

The first two chapters, from which today's passage is taken, describes the two Gentile powers: Antiochus Epiphanes on the one hand, introducing Hellenism into Palestine and abolishing Jewish law, and on the other hand the faithful Jews, gathered around Mattathias and his sons, the founder of the Hasmonian dynasty.

In contrast to Cyrus the Persian, favorable to the customs and religion of subject people (cf. Nehemiah and Ezra), is Antiochus IV Epiphanes who wants to maintain the unity of his vast empire by unifying the laws and customs which are more profane than religious and imposing the worship of Jupiter alone who is even

278

represented with his own characteristics. It is not only the Jews then who are concerned about this measure but all local sects.

It is rather improbable that the rather polemic version of the edict of Antiochus, reproduced in verses 45-49, represents exactly the original text. It expresses rather the way the Jews received and understood it. First of all the decree states a series of clearly antireligious measures: the temple of Jerusalem is to become a pantheon of pagan divinities and the ritual laboriously formulated by the Levites is forbidden in favor of the pagan ritual (vv. 45-47).

Other measures are even more profane but the sacral context of the epoch gives them a religious bearing which simply prohibits the Jews from adhering to it. Thus, the regulation about pork meat (v. 47) has nothing specifically religious and so Christians will do away with it when they desacralize usages of contemporary life. Also the measures taken against the Sabbath (v. 45b) can very well be understood, in a profane context, as simple economic measures, a state being unable to function efficiently if everyone observes the day of rest and feasts of his own religion. In a period so clearly sacralized as that which preceded Jesus Christ, such an imposition of conformity in public life would however have a blasphemous and antireligious flavor and so automatically stir up revolt by the guardians of the strict observance. The same goes for the decisions as regards "impurities and profanations" (v. 45), several of which, however, were clearly reasonable (like the use of certain foods, and contact with blood, etc.). The Jewish law was directed to a small rural people, self-contained; Antiochus Epiphanes wanted to call it to live with others, with the rhythm of a more universal civilization. But he did it in a brutal and antireligious manner which was the cause of the revolt by the Maccabees. But he also called it at a time in history when God had not yet become man and all human activity was surrounded by the sacral to the point that no one could distinguish the political and profane from purely religious obligations.

II. Revelation
1:1-4; 2:1-5a
1st reading
2nd cycle
Monday

This passage contains the introduction to the book of Revelation and the first letter addressed by the author to the Churches of Asia. The construction of this book is artificial. After the letters to the communities one can classify the visions into two intertwining parts. The first is a grouping of the visions which recount the eschatological trials; the second is more orientated to the destiny of the Church (especially starting with Rv 12). But the unity of the book is achieved with the theme of the Lordship of God to which the prologue is precisely consecrated.

a) The first two verses prove that it concerns a revelation made by Christ himself which makes one think that the angel in question in the first verse designates *Jesus Christ*. The description supplied later on by St. John (Rv 1:12-16) confirms this, as well as the tradition that calls the Messiah by the name of angel (Ml 3:1). On the other hand, the doctrine of the apostle presents Christ as the "messenger" (Jn 10:36; 17:18) in order to designate him by this name. After this prologue (vv. 1-3) John "addresses" the Churches of Asia and calls God's blessings on his correspondents according to the practice prevalent in Christians letters of the time.

The formula with which he designates the Father (Rv 1:8; 4:8; 11:17; 16:5) repeats and completes the formula of the Exodus 3:14. The Son is witness (Ps 88/89:28, 38) because he has realized in his person the prophecies of the Old Testament and because he bears the guarantee for the accomplishment of the new prophecies. The author of the new covenant which makes us priests (v. 6, absent in the liturgical period), Christ, is "first born" in this covenant in the sense that he dominates all other heavenly (angels) or earthly powers (Ga 1:15-18; Rv 19:16).

In order to accomplish this role, Jesus appears under the traits of the Son of Man, judge of the nations (Rv 1:6-20), but also as judge of the Churches. This is the meaning we must give to the vision of John who sees Jesus carrying in his hand the seven lamps which symbolize these Churches.

b) The *judgment* of the Son of Man is first of all made on Ephesus: it is objective, with nuances. The community was experiencing the trial of heresy and persecution (vv. 2-3); it is resisting the gnosis of the Nicolites (v. 6), but its charity is softening (v. 4) and it is time that conversion purify a community which, for want of it, would be judged and condemned, thus losing its place on the lampstand (v. 5).

III. Luke | The gospel for this day recounts Jesus' healing
18:35-43 | of a blind man after announcing his Passion
Gospel | and Resurrection; it is presented within the
Monday | context of his ascent to Jerusalem.

The *unbelief of the apostles* is a frequent theme in announcing the Passion and the ascent to Jerusalem. Jesus suffers because of this lack of faith in his own who "do not understand" (Mk 8:31-33; cf. Lk 2:41-50). We could also wonder whether Luke follows the announcement of the Passion by the account of the healing of the blind man in order to supply some instruction on the need for faith. Matthew and Mark place this episode elsewhere, after two other incidents (Mt 20:29-34). Matthew does not even make an allusion to faith and mentions two blind men whereas Luke mentions only one.

Luke's intention appears so much more clearly when he joins the episode of the blind man to the fact that the apostles understand nothing of Jesus' words (v. 34), which he is the only one to point out. He is also the only one to mention "all that has been written by the prophets" (v. 31). What better way of saying that the blindness of the apostles bears precisely on the understanding of the Scriptures about the Son of Man and about his necessary ascent to Jerusalem.

We have a clear replica of this passage in the episode about the disciples of Emmaus where Luke notes that after the explanation of the Scriptures ("wasn't it necessary that Christ endure. . .") and the breaking of the bread: "their eyes were opened" (Lk 24:26-31).

Thus the teaching of this reading is precise. Christ must go up to Jerusalem in order to accomplish the law and the prophets, but to understand this paschal mystery, we must use the eyes of faith and have an understanding of the Scriptures. Human means are inadequate, one must "let oneself be lead" (v. 40) by someone else in order to see the light.

Pilgrimages to Jerusalem occupy a large place in the life of Jesus. To neglect them would cause his public ministry to be incomprehensible. The successive "ascents" of Jesus to Jerusalem are necessary for the understanding of his work. Thus St. Luke conceives his gospel as a progressive ascent to Jerusalem where the sacrifice of the cross will be consummated. For St. John, the pilgrimages of Jesus to Jerusalem form the very substance of the evangelical account (Jn 1:13; 5:1; 7:1-14; 10:20-23; 11:55).

This situation must not astonish us. The historic intervention of Jesus unveils his originality at the heart of the spiritual journey of Israel. Jesus goes up to Jerusalem as a member of the chosen people. For him as for his brothers in Abraham, it involves accomplishing an essential ritual obligation of the Jewish religion. But in accomplishing it as he did, Jesus inaugurates the new religion founded on his person.

Ascending to Jerusalem the Jewish man seeks to express the content of his faith in Yahweh. In this same rite Jesus incarnates his journey of obedience even to death on the cross: he ascends to Jerusalem to die there out of love for men. In giving his life in obedience to the plan of the Father, Jesus founds the religion of universal love; he makes himself the neighbor of all men and attracts them all to himself.

By the same token the rite is made void: fulfilled by Jesus, the pilgrimage to Jerusalem loses its meaning. A new temple is born: the very body of Christ. The regime of the law is finished: here is the era of a religion in Spirit and in truth. Jesus overcomes definitively the pagan solution for "sacred space." From now on no more holy cities. The spiritual center of humanity is the risen body of Christ.

The loving obedience of Christ, even to the gift of his life, inaugurates in him a kingdom which is not of this world. During his entire earthly life he was the pilgrim of the heavenly Jerusalem. Thus also will be the Church, body of Christ. On earth, it is a pilgrim, constantly on the move towards its perfect realization beyond death.

The Church summons each member to be, here below, a pilgrim of the Kingdom. This pilgrimage calls him to give his whole life to building the Kingdom. No holy city awaits him, only the family of the Father. This task requires the Christian to renew his faith and his charity.

To be a pilgrim of the Kingdom is by definition "to follow Jesus." Jesus calls us precisely to follow him in the evangelical passages where it concerns his ascent to Jerusalem. Only Jesus has outlined the way of obedience towards the Kingdom; in following the footsteps of Jesus, the Christian will be loyal to his condition as pilgrim.

During its human journey the Church likes to remind the believing community of its situation here below. The pilgrimage extended to the Christian involves his whole life. It demands first of all theological resourcefulness.

IV. 2 Maccabees The second book of Maccabees is presented
6:18-31 as a resume, written around the year 124, of a
1st reading larger work which we owe to a certain Jason of
1st cycle Cyrene. Even more than the first book, this
Tuesday one envisages the theological bearing of history from which it voluntarily retains pathetic anecdotes.

The martyrdom of Eleazar is the first which Scripture relates with so much precision. The circumstances are rather clear: the hero is invited to take part in a sacred meal with renegade Jews. The organizers of the meal offer the guests meat which is considered impure by the law (Lv 11:7). Eleazar refuses to comply with this custom and rejects the meat which they prepare for him to eat. (v. 20). The renegades then ask him to perform a hypocritical act: to simulate participation in the meal, but to bring his own food (v. 21). The temptation of Eleazar no longer consists of participation in the idolatrous meal but of duplicity.

His death thus sanctions a double attitude of fidelity to the law of God.

The Christian is an ambassador, not the master, of the message he transmits. Hence his intransigency in preserving the purity of the message should not be assessed as fanaticism: it is loyalty to a mission duly accepted. And if casuistry has sometimes tainted the behavior of the Christian in the world, is it not that often they have lost the missionary meaning of their situation in order to preoccupy themselves more with their personal salvation?

V. Revelation	Of the seven letters sent by John in the name
3:1-6, 14-22	of Christ-Judge to the different communities
1st reading	of Asia, the reading for today uses that ad-
2nd cycle	dressed to Sardis (vv. 1-6) and to Laodicea
Tuesday	(vv. 14-22).

The tone of the two letters is rather pessimistic. From the beginning their ardor was seriously weakened: the fall of Jerusalem took place without bringing with it the end of the world; the fall of Rome is on the horizon but the end of the world will probably not depend on it. This means that Christians have lost the key which allowed them to give a religious meaning to catastrophies and persecutions. It was easy to live with faith and hope when one brings together persecutions, the fall of cities and the end of the world. It is more difficult (but more purifying perhaps) to live one's faith in view of events for which one no longer knows the eschatological meaning. One would be willing to die in a persecution when there is hope that it will lead to the new city: but *indifference* arises when it becomes one's daily bread and it no longer appears as a sign of the Kingdom to come.

In this regard the religious situation of the first communities is very similar to the situation which our contemporary churches experience: the usual landmarks of hope vacillate and what one used to interpret in a religious sense suddenly has a purely profane value and significance, a fact which upsets religious minds.

Faith suffers from it, God seems dead. The aim of the book of Revelation is to unveil the religious and mysterious meaning of eschatological events. The modern Christian will place himself then in the school of John to listen to revelation and to get used to the vision of the presence of the resurrected Christ in the heart of every being and in the meaning of events.

VI. Luke 19:1-10   Luke alone relates the Zacchaeus story, the
   Gospel   gospel for today, which fits perfectly in his
   Tuesday   personal view of riches and the reading he
                       makes about the contact of Jesus with sinners.
This text thus appears as a conclusion to a series of teachings which show rather well the privileged class by the parable of the Pharisee and the publican both praying in the Temple, but where we notice that only the publican is heard and justified (an account proper to the Third Gospel: Lk 18:9-14); the incident of the "small" children chased away by the disciples as being unworthy to be a part of the adult group, but who are nevertheless called by Jesus (Lk 18:15-17); the episode of the "rich" man who cannot enter the Kingdom because he is possessed by his possesions (Lk 18:18-27); the healing of the blind man of Jericho, enlightened by faith in contrast to the disciples who "do not understand" the words of the Lord (Lk 18:31-43).

a) The four previous elements are repeated in the account of Zacchaeus; Jericho, cursed city (Lk 18:31-43) shelters Zacchaeus, a rich tax collector (Lk 18:18-27 and 9-14) of small stature (Lk 18:15-17). For Jesus these characteristics are titles for the salvation which he brings to sinners and to the *weak*. The crowd understand this and murmur: "He came to eat with sinners" (cf. Lk 5:30; 15:2).

b) But these still remained an impediment to salvation, at least in the eyes of Luke who considers real poverty a condition for access to the Kingdom: the *wealth* of Zacchaeus: the obstacle that the rich man was unable to overcome (Lk 18:9-14). Now, Zacchaeus brings it up himself: he returns to everyone fourfold and gives half of his goods to the poor. This fourfold restitution occurred only once in the law and in a very serious case (Ex 21:37); the generosity of Zacchaeus leads him then to inflict upon himself a severe chastisement by generalizing this punishment, and this is the gesture St. Luke awaits from all the rich who want to enter the Kingdom, and he will underscore its significance and meaning in Acts.

c) Verse 9 forms the first conclusion of the account, the one that the Lord himself could give: the house of Zacchaeus has received salvation because the conditions have been met. Jesus immediately makes his thoughts concrete by making Zacchaeus a *Son of Abraham,* a title reserved only for the Jews in order to be the only ones benefiting from the promises made to their patriarch (Lk 3:8; Rm 4:11-25; Ga 3:7-29). Now, Zacchaeus is a man marked by paganism even if he is not himself pagan. Thus, Jesus widens the concept, Son of Abraham, by forming the outline of a theme which St. Paul will develop: it is not physical affinity to the race of Abraham that insures the true sonship but only faith truly lived. We thus find here a preview of the great statements of St. Paul on the race of Abraham, the outline of the promise outside the law, the outline of faith outside the law (cf. Ga 3-4).

d) Verse 10 forms a second conclusion, probably brought in by Luke himself. It is rather clearly connected with the lesson of the parables of mercy (Lk 15) which are proper to the evangelist and manifest so well that God comes looking for "whatever is lost" (Lk 15:6, 9, 24, 32). In his mercy God allows all men, whoever they are, to encounter salvation and thus to participate in the privileges of the promise without necessarily calling him to the means of salvation worked up by the law and Judaism.

VII. 2 Maccabees The story of the anonymous mother and her
7:1, 20-31   seven sons probably calls to mind the story of
1st reading   Jerusalem, already represented in Jeremiah
1st cycle   15:9 as a mother with seven sons.
Wednesday

a) The account could be a commentary on the passage of Jeremiah. Whatever men destroy in Sion, God will rebuild; the trial has then meaning, on one condition, that the children of Sion remain at least faithful to the law. What is more, the number seven is always the sign of divine blessing.

The law for which the seven brothers and their mother accept the sacrifice of their lives is that honored by the Pharisees and the account of their martyrdom could serve as a means for diffusing the doctrine of this sect, intransigent in the face of the pagan customs of the time. Salvation is certainly assured but it comes through fidelity.

b) God's salvation here takes the form of a *resurrection* (verses 23, 29). No doubt the author thinks of a restoration of Sion recovering her dead children before the inauguration of the eternal reign.

In Jewish thought, the resurrection of the people of God was only an image: with death designating exile and suffering, life automatically represented the return from exile (Hos 6:1-3; Ez 37:1-14; Is 51:17; 53:10-12). What is new in the book of Maccabees is the faith which is expressed in the individual resurrection of the future citizens of the Kingdom. A resurrection that is still paschal, however, because the impious will be excluded (v. 14).

In reality, this is the idea of retribution, very much fixed in the biblical mentality which engendered this faith in resurrection. The just are promised life, and death cannot deprive them of this benefit; the impious are destined for death and if at any time they seem to escape it, the final combat and trial will cast them into decomposition.

As to the setting for this resurrection, it is still terrestrial: life is a life on earth. This is the main limitation of this passage.

The resurrection is not an idea and the Sadducees are on the margin of reality when they discuss the idea of resurrection (Mt 22:23-33). It arises, on the contrary, from the hope of faith which those possess who are led to lose their life. The gift responds to the gift: one must know how to give his life to believe that one day it is going to be returned. He who has never given should not expect to receive.

VIII. Revelation 4:1-11
1st reading
2nd cycle
Wednesday

The book of revelation is a message given by John to the persecuted and discouraged Churches. The message takes the form of a revelation received from Christ himself, during the sojourn of John on Patmos, perhaps within the context of a Sunday celebration.

Beyond the signs and images, John elaborates a theology of history in which Jesus is the center.

The passage read in the liturgy for today relates the vision of the heavenly court where the mysterious designs of God who directs the history of the world and of men, are elaborated.

a) John portrays heaven and the *throne of God* in conformity with the precedents of his predecessors: Isaiah 6:1-5; Ezechiel 1:4-27 and Daniel 7:9-10. His vocabulary is in great part borrowed from the texts of the Old Testament.

The expression: "He who is sitting on the throne" designates God in his role as universal king and judge. The description of the old man is borrowed from Daniel 7; John fixes their number at twenty-four so that they might represent regenerated humanity. Twelve of them symbolic of the tribes of Israel, and the other twelve, the new Israel. The apostle is probably also thinking of the twenty-four priestly classes of the temple (1 Ch 24:3-19) whose leaders are in fact called "elders" (2 K 19:2). Thus the people gathered around the throne of God are judges of the world with God, and priests of the world for God.

John does not see God; nobody has ever seen him. He simply contemplates, like Moses, the effervescent light coming from the throne (Ex 19:16; Ez 1:13-14). Besides the light: the power of the wind (cf. Ex 19:18) or the breath of God: his Spirit. In order to describe its force, John speaks of seven (perfect number) spirits which are not angels but the vital force of God himself (v. 5). The sea of glass in front of the throne is the dome of the firmament (Gn 1:7) such as the Jewish cosmogeny imagined it to be. The animals holding up the throne are the Seraphim of Isaiah 6 or the Cherubim of Ezechiel 1; they symbolize the cosmic forces and all creation.

b) Around the throne of God there is a solemn *liturgy*. It is made up of two elements: the first, when the whole creation (the four animals) sings the trisagion to the creator; the second, when the chosen people (the ancients) join in with the acclamation of the priestly people to their God.

In the eyes of John, the Christian liturgy has then the greatness of the cosmos and of humanity, the depth of the royal priesthood and the judicature of man saved over the world. But a passage like this one embarrasses the modern Christian who deciphers with difficulty an imagery which he is always in danger of materializing and from which Christ is absent. Here John Judaizes. He certainly does it in order to prepare for the moment when the transcendent God will confide to the Lord the sealed book which will authorize him to guide the history of man (Rv 1-5). But it is regrettable that the lectionary retains only this text where the only concern is the God of Israel.

IX. Luke   The comparison of the version that Matthew
19:11-28   presents of the parable of the talents and the
Gospel   one presented by St. Luke (Lk 19:12-27),
Wednesday   shows divergences which reflect the style and
preoccupations of each evangelist so that we
can affirm that their redactional involvement
was considerable.

In Matthew the parable of the talents, like that of the wise
virgins, retains the moral conclusion of the eschatological discourse (Mt 24) and describes the Christian life in the period that
extends from the glorification of the Lord and the fall of Jerusalem to the final Parousia. Luke is more interested in the events
prior to the Passion.

a) A first essential trait in the account of Matthew was the
theme of delay (Mt 24:19; cf. 25:5), which Luke ignores. The first
evangelist considers the time of the Church, but Luke only that
which separates Christ's death and the fall of Jerusalem (Lk
19:11). People were waiting in fact for the Kingdom to come
immediately, but Christ makes them understand that before its
inauguration there will be a revolt against the King (his Passion)
followed by chastisement (the fall of Sion). Luke, moreover, sup-
ports his arguments with the contemporary example of Archelaus,
off to Rome, looking for his kingship, where he was followed by
Jews intriguing to keep him from receiving it. The horizon of
Luke is limited to the present, that of Matthew involves the "time
of the Church."

b) Another distinction between the two accounts is in the difference between the *servants of the master.* According to Luke,
Christ tells the parable in order to illustrate the attitude of the
people who listen to him. Some believe in him, others appear to
be indifferent or clearly hostile (Lk 19:7, 11). Christ affirms that
all will receive their recompense as soon as the Kingdom is
inaugurated, after his Pasch: to the enthusiastic disciples, power
of jurisdiction will be given (Lk 19:17-29); as for the indifferent
Jews, their privileges will be "taken away" (Mt 24:24; Lk 19:16);

finally for the clearly hostile Jews, chastisement will be allotted, their city will be destroyed (Lk 19:27). Matthew's perspective is different. For him what is involved here is the time of the Church that follows the fall of Jerusalem, and he underscores the extraordinary disproportion between the office exercised on earth in the Church and the promised reward (Mt 25:21, 23, 29). The master distributes his wealth (knowing the benefits of the Kingdom), keeping a record of the quality of each; and here one must not forget that giving one talent to a servant consisted in giving him a fortune! It would then be an error to interpret these "talents" as natural gifts to be exploited. It deals indeed with the concerns of the Kingdom, the wealth of the Lord, of which the Christian becomes the steward, for the Kingdom can advance only with his collaboration.

X. 1 Maccabees 2:15-29
1st reading
1st cycle
Thursday

The first chapter of the book presented one of the two antagonists of the Jewish revolt of the 2nd century, Antiochus Epiphanes. The second chapter presents the other antagonist, that part of the people who remained loyal to the law and gathered around Mattathias.

a) The situation resulting from the occupation of the country is such that some Jews are forced to become an underground resistance movement. Mattathias escapes to the mountains of Juda while many others retreat to the desert with their families and cattle. By choosing either the mountains or the desert, the Jews clearly adopt a means of *resistance*. Modern history confirms the fact that Palestine is, because of its topography, an ideal country for guerilla warfare.

b) A military detachment is immediately sent to chase them on a *Sabbath* day, probably deliberately (v. 32). An ultimatum is given to the Jews: if they "come out" from their hiding, they will save their lives (v. 33). But these Jews are strict followers of the law which forbids them "to come out" of their homes on the

Sabbath (v. 34; cf. Ex 16:29). The assault is carried out at once; the Jews don't even defend themselves because of their strict loyalty to the law (v. 36) and so perish in their caves.

The Jews had not yet discovered that the "Sabbath was made for man and not man for the Sabbath." Their world was still too sacred to permit this idea.

Today, even for the Christian who practices on a regular basis, the Sunday rest no longer has religious value. He is released from the law of leisure which is normally imposed on man.

Does that mean that leisure no longer has any significance for faith? Not at all. Leisure is in fact as indispensable as work. It is during times of leisure that the most fruitful encounters of conjugal or familial love and of friendship take place; reunions for reflection where competency is shared in common, the access to culture which is another form of communion.

If the Church schedules the Eucharist on holidays it is because it can only reassemble around God a people already fraternally united.

XI. Revelation
5:1-10
1st reading
2nd cycle
Thursday

After the majestic opening vision of the throne of God, John goes on to describe the investiture of Jesus as Lord of history.

a) John was inspired with the vision of the book of *history* by Ezechiel 2:9-10. It is closed with seven seals which are the signatures of the seven witnesses demanded by Roman law to authenticate an official document of great importance (v. 1). John laments (v. 4) in the name of the persecuted Church which seeks the meaning of its sufferings. One of the old men, probably the representative of the tribe of Juda (v. 5; cf. Gn 49:9-12), reminds the Church of the prophecy of the old Patriarch Jacob and announces its accomplishment: the lion of Juda, the Messiah, has defeated death and put an end to the determinism of history. This triumphant lion is at the same time a slaughtered sheep (v. 6; cf. Is 53:7), because his manner of triumphing over death consisted of submitting himself in total loyalty to his earthly condition.

Thus, the Son of Man who on earth did not know the secrets of the unfolding of history (Mt 24:36), suddenly finds himself responsible for it by his death and resurrection. The secret of history is the secret of his death.

b) As soon as the Son of Man acquires his new prerogative, the *liturgy* which began in Revelation 4:1-11 with a series of hymns addressed to God, creator of the cosmos (Rv 4:8-9) and of the Church (Rv 4:10-11), is followed by a new hymn, not found in the repertoire of the religions and which is now sung by only one choir, uniting the two previous ones (vv. 8-10).

The new thanksgiving sings especially about the universalism of the new creation: nothing escapes the power of the Son of Man any more and each thing takes on new meaning.

c) We could ask what the *book* offered to the Son of Man by God contains. Many think that it is simply the book of the Old Testament which Christ alone can open if it is to have meaning for Christians. The Jews tried to decipher this Scripture but without success (Is 29:11-12; 2 Co 3:15). John underscores throughout his gospel the lack of understanding in which his contemporaries remained concerning the events of the life of Christ despite their contacts with the Old Testament (Jn 3:9-10).

We understand then the importance of the old inspired books in the redaction of Revelation: John addresses himself to the Jews in order to open their understanding of their own Scriptures, as the resurrected Christ did for his apostles (Lk 24:27).

XII. Luke 19:41-44 *Gospel* *Thursday*	The entry of Christ into Jerusalem is the last stage of the ascent already announced several months ago (Lk 18:31-43). The evangelists have surrounded the entry into Jerusalem with rather disparate events and they do not agree on their sequence. Luke

seems to have arranged them in a way that harks back to Jeremiah 6-7. The first Christians in fact read the life of Christ in the light of the only Bible they knew: the Old Testament, and sometimes they based their ideas on the ancient text in order to put forth a declaration of the Lord.

Jeremiah 6:14: "peace, peace, they say though there is no peace."
—compare Luke 19:42
Jeremiah 6:15: "Hence, they shall be among those who fall; in their time of punishment they shall go down."
—compare Luke 19:44
Jeremiah 6:26: "For suddenly upon us comes the destroyer."
—compare Luke 19:43
Jeremiah 7:11: "A den of thieves"   —compare Luke 19:46
Jeremiah 7:20: "My anger and my wrath will pour out upon this place . . . upon the trees of the field"
—compare the image of the sterile fig tree (which Luke, in contrast to Matthew, did not mention).
And Jeremiah 7:25: "I have sent you untiringly all my servants the prophets."   —compare Luke 20:9-15.

The grouping of facts recounted by the synoptics and especially by Luke, seem then to have been composed as a midraschic reading of Jeremiah 6-7. The events could have happened at different periods in the life of Christ, but their grouping indicates a significant intention. Jeremiah was announcing the destruction of Jerusalem in 587 B.C.; the primitive Church saw there the prophecy of the destruction of Jerusalem in which it had just taken part.

The prophecy put on the lips of Christ (v. 43) is at this point woven through with Old Testament references (Is 29:3; 37:33; Jr 52:4-5; Ez 4:1-3; 21:27; Hos 10:14; Na 3:10; Ps 136/137:9) that it could not have been composed save at the end of a long oral tradition and in relation to midraschic interpretations current in the primitive Christian milieu. If it is impossible to say whether this text was composed before or after the fall of Jerusalem in the year 70, it is, on the contrary, very certain that Christians reread the prophecy of Jeremiah 6-7 after Christ, in view of a *destruction of Jerusalem* even more decisive than that which the prophet had imagined. This destruction is not only material but also spiritual: responsible for the death of Christ, Jerusalem loses its role as religious center and as the city of the Parousia.

A gospel like this has throughout the centuries fostered the antisemitism found among numerous Christians and in the Church itself. The horror provoked by the existence of Nazi camps has undoubtedly put an end to it but we may well ask whether faith has a role to play in this matter. Moved by the dreadfulness of Jewish persecution, Christians perhaps do not consider enough this emotion in view of their faith and the meaning to be given to the permanence of the Jewish people within Christianity.

If it is true that the Church of Jesus Christ is "the Israel of the last days," if it is true that the apostles were all Jews as well as most of the first members of the primitive Christian community, it is equally true that the Jewish people in its representatives as well as in its structure, has rejected the messianic salvation offered by Jesus of Nazareth. Why? Because Israel refused to enter into that supreme conversion which Jesus demanded of it in order to make it the instrument of his universal mission; because it did not renounce its "privileges" as chosen people, or more exactly, the impoverished idea it made of them. Whereas its election was in reality only an election in Jesus of Nazareth, mediator of the salvation of humanity, the Jewish people saw in it a condition for claiming from God a special place in the Kingdom to come. And the observance of the law appeared to it as a claim on salvation, whereas it could only lead to death. The Jewish people rejected Jesus for not having pushed poverty to the point of expecting everything from God as savior, understood as that quality of surety which the Incarnate Word alone could offer.

However, the continued existence of the Jewish people throughout the ages is necessarily going to pose a fundamental problem for the Church's conscience. St. Paul already questions the destiny of this people which is his own; in his letter to the Romans, he expresses his conviction that the Jewish people will be converted when all the nations join the Church. In fact, the entrance of all nations into the Church will make the ecclesial sign of salvation so convincing that a people so proud of its indestructable originality as the Jewish people will surrender before the amplitude of the divine benevolence! But on the other hand, the Church constantly finds itself faced with the need of being fully loyal to its own mystery, which St. Paul defined as that of the reconciliation of the Jews and the nations, acquired in the blood of Christ. The permanence of the Jewish people is for the Church a kind of reminder of this essential loyalty to the law of universal charity. As long as it carries the true face of its catholicity where its manifold diversity is known as such, it is disposed to a real dialogue with the Jewish people. But as the Church turns in on itself and limits its horizons by yielding too exclusively to such or such a cultural world it is cut off from this dialogue and antisemitism grows in it, because the only way to acquire a good conscience is to suppress the embarrassing witness.

XIII. 1 Macca-bees 4:36-37, 52-59
1st reading
1st cycle
Friday

Here we have a full description, summarized in 1 Maccabees 4:36-61, of the purification of the temple and the institution of a feast commemorating the reopening of worship.

The principal objective of the books of Maccabees is the institution of the feast of the *restoration of the temple* among the Jewish people. Precise details are numerous and the solemnity of the feast is raised to the level of the great popular feast of Tabernacles.

There is in the successive restorations and reconstructions of the temple of Jerusalem an implicit avowal of a radical inability to signify the presence of God in the world.

Jews purify their temple each time it is defiled by pagans. Certainly the defilement is often serious; it sometimes implies idolatry or the obligation to worship the emperor; it is the result of aggression. But, restoring the temple, purifying it of the traces of "impure" pagan contact and tightening again the conditions for access, was that reasonable? Would it not be preferable to interpret the pagan aggression as the expression of the right of the pagans to worship the same God as the Jews and to frequent the same temple in the unity of a same faith? Would it not be preferable to reflect on the value of such formal sacrifices? The real restoration of the temple will take place only on the day when Jesus brings to it his own person, accessible to the Jews as to the pagans and offering to the Father worship in spirit and in truth.

XIV. Revelation John imagines his investiture as that of Eze-
10:8-11 chiel (Ez 2:8-3:3) and Jeremiah (Jr 1:10). The
1st reading book which is given to him contains the
2nd cycle prophecies of the Old Testament and he him-
Friday self receives the mission to reveal their significance in the light of the New. In reality
the second part of Revelation can be considered as an explanation of the prophetic content of this book.

The fact that John has to digest the small *book* of the prophecies of the Old Testament in order to understand the significance of the present time reveals that he feeds his visions on the mys-

terious reality of the events to his faith in the unique God, the
guide of history. God makes history and marks it with the reflection of his unicity, a fact which does not mean that he introduces
a fatality similar to that found in nature. History is the product
of the encounter of two freedoms, that of God and that of man,
but God has optimistic views on this encounter, especially since
Jesus Christ was the "yes" of this covenant. What is more, these
events will never be able to question the victory acquired by the
Lord over evil and death. John is full of bitterness after having
swallowed the book, but the after-taste is ultimately one of
sweetness and peace (Rev 21-22). In this respect the Scriptures
really console, not because they unveil in advance the development of events foreseen by God, but because they help to reveal
the deep significance of God's presence in the events which men
live.

XV. Luke   Luke very sensibly simplifies the account of
19:45-48   the purification of the temple (vv. 45-46),
Gospel   probably because his Greek readers would
Friday   not be especially interested in details unin-
                  telligible to them. But he adds two verses on
the teaching of Christ in the temple (vv. 47-48), which are proper
to him.

The account of the purification of the temple is summed up by
St. Luke in two prophetic words which the synoptic tradition
place on the lips of Christ on this occasion (Jr 7:11 and Is 56:7).
They condemn the temple for its exclusiveness and its formalism:
the first prevents the opening of the temple to the nations; the
second prohibits access to it to the poor and the weak.

But Luke contrasts especially *the temple with the Word:* two
expressions from the Word of God are enough to ridicule the
temple and its worship (vv. 45-46); it is enough that Christ re-
establishes the Word at the heart of the temple (vv. 47-48) for a

new type of liturgy based on the Word (cf. Co 12:27-30; Ep 5:26) and his obedience to appear. Thus the episode of the sellers in the temple is practically placed in the background to the advantage of the solemn entrance of the Lord into the temple, that privileged place where he would be able to conclude, and in a brilliant manner, his ministry of teaching.

Christian worship gives primacy to the Word, thus protecting itself from the formalism of the temple. It pays reverence to the essential content of the sacrifice of Christ and the sphere offered to each to rejoin and share it.

But the danger which lies in wait for it is not less than the one which smothered the Jewish cult. The Word can be proclaimed very worthily, even sung; it can feed well-structured homilies; the Word of God proclaimed in the readings is not just any word, not that of the celebrant in his homilies, nor the consecratory words of the Eucharist. But what purpose do they serve if they are spoken by a mere specialist of the "Book," who fails in every way to hear the Word in events and to discover the presence of God in the world.

Certainly the words proclaimed or pronounced in the liturgy are, in their own right, the Word of God. But what echo do they encounter in the conscience of the laity? Why do they seem so esoteric for a great number of them that they do not know either how to obey or to discover the God they sometimes meet and with whom they dialogue in the simplicity of their heart?

The word of God, although inspired, and especially the words of preaching, are not absolute, they are only an interpretation and a commentary on a more profound Word which is the manifestation of God in the event itself. The accounts of the resurrection of Jesus are the word of God, the Passover sermons are too, at another level, but the true Word is the resurrection of Christ itself, the event woven into the life of man and through which God has spoken.

Likewise, all the biblical traditions on the Exodus are not equal, as the Word of God, to the Passover event or the sojourn in the desert, events of human existence in which God has spoken.

The Word of God is then deeply linked with the event; it escapes all formalism to the degree in which it is ceaselessly referred to him. Obedience becomes then communion with God present in life and in history.

XVI. 1 Macca- Several of the details in this account of the
bees 6:1-13 death of the persecutor are certainly histori-
1st reading cal. The biographers of Antiochus preserved
1st cycle the memory of numerous lootings of temples
Saturday which he executed in order to replenish his
treasury. The episode of Elymas (which is not
a city but a region) can then seem likely (vv. 1-2), just as the
pretensions of Antiochus to invade the temple of Jerusalem (vv.
6-7).

The biographers of Antiochus also saw his illness as a kind of
divine curse for his looting of the temple (v. 8), but the author
of the book makes his death result from his failure in Jerusalem
by having the dying make a *confession* which was limited to his
intentions with regard to Jerusalem (vv. 11-13).

XVII. Revelation The vision of the two witnesses takes place
11:4-12 when John measures the new temple which is
1st reading the Church.
2nd cycle
Saturday John is clearly inspired by Zechariah 14:1-3,
11-14 where the two witnesses represent the
political and religious dignitaries of the chosen people, of which
they are the symbols par excellence. John gives the same significance to his two witnesses. Moreover, he does not name them
because they are the soul of the Church in its religious nature
and its political opposition. They are then offered to the two

beasts symbolizing the Roman empire with its political and religious power.

Consequently, the vision of the witnesses, is a way of announcing the opposition between Christians and the empire, the *persecution* resulting from it and the victory promised to those who will "rise" out of the trial by faith in the paschal mystery.

The community of Christians still has at its disposal two witnesses in the contest it wages against the actual empire, that of profit that exploits the individual, power that strangles freedom, force that abusively sacralizes secondary values. It is then not the only one to raise this contest nor to pay at times with its life or freedom for the refusal to obey its power or its police. Christians are "witnesses" in the sense that the combat they lead and the persecution they undergo have a religious meaning, the secret of which resides in the death and resurrection of Jesus.

XVIII. Luke
20:27-40
Gospel
Saturday

Jesus continues his discussion with the Jewish sects by replying here to the Sadducees concerning the resurrection. They regarded bodily resurrection as absurd and cite the case of the widow who successively marries the six brothers of her first husband. Jesus responds by indicating that marriage has nothing to do with life in the Kingdom and affirms the reality of bodily resurrection. The two sentences are quite mysterious, both by reason of their content ("they are as angels"), and the use made of biblical texts that do not seem relevant to the argument.

a) How does Jesus find confirmation for *bodily resurrection* in Exodus 3:6? The text contemplates the God of Abraham, Isaac and Jacob (v. 37) as the God who made a covenant with them and protected them. This God is a God of the living (v. 38) and consequently can hardly be conceived as covenanting with and protecting the dead. God affirms himself the Savior of Abraham. Were Abraham definitely dead, this would be meaningless. Abraham thus, and the patriarchs, will be raised up. What is true of them is true of all members of the chosen people. The covenant must mean that people will enjoy God's protection against the only ultimate enemy, death. It is true that all this can scarcely be found in the text Jesus quotes, Exodus 3:6. What he does is use the text against the background of faith as it had developed in Israel.

b) Jesus' second affirmation is still more mysterious. In excluding conjugal relations from the quasi-angelic state of humanity after the resurrection, he seems to be disregarding needs associated with bodies as we know them. He is not in fact taking any position about the nature of angels. Nor is he saying that the resurrected body becomes angelic to the point of losing corporeity. This would be terminology foreign to Jewish anthropology. His allusion to the angels is meant to indicate that human language cannot describe the nature of the resurrected body.

THIRTY-FOURTH (AND LAST) WEEK

I. Daniel 1:1-6,
8-20
1st reading
1st cycle
Monday

The book of Daniel presents many problems because it contains an important part of the deuterocanonical passages (Dn 3:24-90; 13 and 14) and because the divergences between the Hebrew and the Septuagint text sometimes lead to the belief that there exist two different traditions. The original text itself is ambiguous since part of it is written in Hebrew (Dn 1:1-3, 4 and 8:1-12, 13) and the other in Aramaic (2:4-7:28). Finally, the book was rather arbitrarily placed among the prophets whereas it has a more or less apocalyptic and "midrashic" character. In other words, it is very much concerned with shedding light on the old traditions and with revealing the end of time while preserving a certain halo of mystery. The sources it uses often have a very fertile imagination.

The account of the visions of the book of Daniel probably date from the 2nd century, a fact which places the definitive redaction of this pseudonymous book at the end of this century or at the beginning of the first.

The four characters presented by the account are probably legendary. We find the best indication of this in the fact that they are not given geneologies, contrary to the practice of the inspired writers. The author was able to find their names in the legend of the pagan hero, Daniel (Ez 14:14-20; 28:3) or in the nomenclature of Nehemiah's collaborators (Ne 8:4; 10:3, 24). The chronological details of the two first verses are also unlikely.

The author has, however, tried to create an historical illusion by reproducing the atmosphere of the court of Babylon, not without introducing some anachronisms such as the three years of studies characteristic of later Persian education.

It is, then, not on the historical plane that we should place ourselves but rather on the doctrinal, if we are to understand the message of the author.

a) The author certainly wants to be *universalist*. The four heroes of the account are in fact called upon to become missionaries in pagan territory, a very rare idea in the books of the Old Testament. We find a similar case in the life of Joseph in Egypt and in the forced mission of Jonah to Niniveh. This universalism is particularly interesting because it does not have Jerusalem as the center as with most of the prophets.

b) The life of Daniel has several traits in common with that of Joseph. They both remain faithful to their God in a pagan environment and enjoy the charism of dreams, about which the Old Testament, without denying their value, was a bit suspicious (cf. Nb 12:6; Dt 13:2-6; Si 34:1-7). The book of Daniel opens greater horizons, no doubt under Babylonian influence. But it underscores especially that the dreams of the heroes of Daniel are not due to their knowledge or to some special techniques, or to bodily needs, but to the interpretation of God (vv. 17-20; cf. Gn 41:8, 16, 39).

c) This divine inspiration is, however, felt only in the *most strict observance of the law*. When the Jew lives in pagan lands, the law of cleanness and uncleanness defines a particular position which we still find during the period of Acts (Ac 15:19-21). Though ancient, the prescriptions on cleanness and uncleanness (Dt 14:1-21; Lv 11:20, 25) were, however, literally applied only during the final days of Judaism, as a means of distinguishing themselves from the pagans and claiming special election by God (Tb 1:10; Jdt 10:5; 12:1-4; Est 13:28; 14:17; 1 M 1:62-63; 2 M 6:7-8).

II. Revelation   John has explained that two beasts (paganism
    14:1-3, 4b-5   and the Roman Empire) are opposed to the
    1st reading   reign of the Lamb over history (Rv 13:9-16).
    2nd cycle   The latter dwells on Mount Sion with the peo-
    Monday   ple who constitute a small Remnant, lost in a
world entirely dominated by the two enemy

beasts.

This Remnant is above all composed of virgins (v. 4a; not
found in today's reading); elsewhere John will speak of martyrs
(cf. Rv 7:14). For him, *virginity* is the opposite of idolatry which
is in fact represented in the Old Testament as a kind of prostitution. The hundred and forty thousand elect are virgins because
they have refused to worship the Beast. Virginity, like martyrdom (Rv 7), is the characteristic of the people of God to the degree that it breaks with the worship of false Gods and earthly
powers.

III. Luke 21:1-4   The episode related in this passage completes
    Gospel   the series of discussion that Jesus pursued
    Monday   with the Jewish sects. It is directly bound up
with the curse of the Scribes who rob widows
(Lk 20:45-47). These two texts of the gospel illustrate the eschatological teaching of the following verses (Lk 21:2-36): the leaders of the people are going to be deprived of their privileges and
the direction of the people given to the poor.

The *rich-poor* antithesis reappears frequently in the eschatological speeches of Christ. It uses the method of the beatitudes
where the opposition between the rich and the poor (Lk 6:20-24)
is used to announce the imminence of the Kingdom and the reversal of improper situations. It is less concerned with apologiz-
ing or criticizing an existing social system than with underscoring
the bewilderment which the coming of the last days—those which
participate in God's way of being—will bring to human struc-

tures. The first Christians will often use this method to explain the fact that the Church of the poor took over the place of the leaders of Israel in accomplishing the plan of God.

The widow gave out of her poverty in contrast to the rich who give from their power and privileges, which indicates that she contradicts the proverb which demands that one give only what one has: she, on the contrary, has only what she gave.

Can we see there the image of God? If he gave us from his abundance, he is better represented by the rich than by the widow and we cannot understand the importance which Jesus attaches to the gesture of this latter. And if God, too, gave from his poverty? If we can renounce what a certain theism says of God in order to rest content with the acts manifested by Jesus Christ, would not we then understand that to be God, is to serve and to give, not from what we have but from what we are? Jesus, poor and a slave, is not a parenthesis in the life of God, but the very condition of God; he is not a rich man who came to visit the underdeveloped lands of humanity; he is a slave because his manner of being God is poverty.

IV. Daniel
2:31-45
1st reading
1st cycle
Tuesday

The exegetes often consider chapter 2 of Daniel as prior to the redaction of the book itself and they arbitrarily place it in the first half of the 3rd century. The account reveals the meaning of history conducted by Yahweh in view of the establishment of the reign of God on earth.

Among all the wisemen, Daniel is the only one to understand the dreams of Nabuchadnezzar, because God has revealed it to him, accomplishing in advance the Word of Christ: "You have revealed it to the merest and hidden it from the clever" (vv. 14-19; cf. Lk 10:21-24).

The statue seen by the king represents the kingdoms of earth which succeed each other by mutually destroying each other. They are four, a symbolic number often used by the Bible to designate earthly power (Ez 1:5-18; 7:2; 10:9-21; 14:21; 37:9; Zc 2:1-2; 2:11; 6:1-5; Am 1:3-4; Is 11; 12; Jr 15:2-3). This struggle for power is the cause of a continual decline: gold deteriorates successively into silver, bronze, iron and earth, to the point that a stone thrown at it is enough to destroy the whole statue. This dwindling process is also an idea that is dear to the Bible: a history led by man without recourse to God flows directly to its ruin (cf. Gn 3:1-6, 12).

a) The liturgical reading stops at the description of this destroying stone (vv. 34-35, 45). Thrown against the statue of human empires without the intervention of any hand, it is thus directed by God himself (v. 34). Verse 45 states precisely moreover that it was carved from a mountain, which probably means it comes from God, the mountain often being a divine symbol (Pss 35/36:7; 67/68:16-17; Is 14:13; Ex 3:1). The stone becomes in its turn a big mountain which "fills all the earth," like the glory of God (Nb 14; 21; Is 6:3; Ha 2:14; Ps 71/72:19; Is 11:9 Ws 1:7).

But does this rock designate a personal Messiah or the messianic people?

b) The Old Testament often uses the image of a rock in describing the economy of salvation. Yahweh is a stumbling stone for the tribes of Israel (Is 8:11-15) or a rock of salvation for his faithful ones (Ps 17/18:2-3 and Dt 32:15). The rock referred to in Daniel 2 would then designate Yahweh or more exactly the *monotheistic* Yahwist opposed to the idolatry (the statue) of the great empires, but promised a quick expansion over the whole earth. The perspective of the author is then more apologetic than messianic (cf. the professions of faith in Yahweh to which the different accounts of Daniel lead: Daniel 2:47; 3:24-30; 4:31-32; 6:26-29; 14:40-42).

c) Little by little, however, tradition has imposed a messianic interpretation on the theme of the rock, probably under the in-

fluence of texts like Isaiah 28:16-17; Zechariah 3:9 or Psalm 117/
118:22. This interpretation will be verified in Luke 20:18 (by
osmosis with Is 8:14 and Ps 117/118:22), without knowing, however, if this verse reproduces the words of Christ or a proverb
invented by the primitive community in order to compare the
principal scriptural witnesses with the theme of the rock.

V. Revelation An extract from the second part of Revelation,
14:14-19 this account explains the unfolding of the final
1st reading judgment.
2nd cycle
Tuesday The *judgment* is compared to a harvest (cf.
Jl 3:13; Mk 4:29). The Son of Man appears on
a cloud in order to harvest the just. But since he ignores the date
on which it must take place (MT 24:36), an angel comes out of
the temple (the place where the Father rests) in order to announce it to him (v. 15). Another angel then comes out from
heaven in order to harvest the impious (v. 17) while a third leaves
the altar of holocaust under which moan the souls of the martyrs,
in order to chastise the persecutors (v. 18).

VI. Luke 21:5-11 In this preface to his eschatological discourse
Gospel Jesus gives two categories of signs preliminary
Tuesday to his coming; wars and maladies on the one
hand (vv. 8-11; cf. Mt 24:4-8), persecution on
the other (vv. 12-19; cf. Mt 24:9-13).

a) Matthew 24:5 speaks of false Messiahs. Luke suppresses
this somewhat, as too obscure for his readers of Greek origin. He
alludes to false eschatologies which wrongly predict the end of
the world (v. 8; cf. 2 Thm 2:1-8).

Both evangelists refer to Daniel 2:28, according to whom "it
must be" that wars and upheavals will precede the dawning of

the Kingdom. This phrase should be taken in the sense given to it by Jesus himself when, in justifying his own Passion, he affirms repeatedly that "it must be" that the Scriptures be fulfilled (Lk 9:22, 24; 24:16). There is no question of a *fatalistic necessity*. It is the paschal law, woven into the texture of salvation events, where life emerges from death.

Matthew presents the events in the style of Jewish apocalypse. The earthquakes are reminiscent of the oracles of Isaiah 8:21; 13:3 and Jeremiah 21:9; 34:17. Luke passes this over in silence. His readers were not sufficiently familiar with biblical mentality.

b) Jesus mentions *persecution* at verse 12, as a preliminary sign of the Kingdom. On this point Matthew and Luke differ remarkably. Luke makes use of a passage that Matthew gives elsewhere (Mt 10:17-22). Matthew 24:9-13 contemplates above all the effect of persecution in the community; many dead and much apostasy, many people deceived by false Messiahs, love grown cold. Only a "Remnant" will emerge to be saved. The Remnant for him will be made up of Christians, definitively liberated from Judaism at the fall of Jerusalem.

Luke describes the reactions of Christians to persecution. The faithful will be judged and persecuted by Jews (synagogues) and pagans (v. 12); but they will receive the eloquence and wisdom necessary to answer accusations. In mentioning wisdom, he is thinking perhaps of Joseph or Daniel triumphing over pagan learning (Gn 40; Dn 2). Thus, he is broaching a theology that will be thoroughly developed by John, when he reveals the role of the Paraclete (Jn 15:26-16:15).

By way of conclusion he takes two sentences from another context that are highly optimistic. Thanks to their trust (Mt 10:30) and constancy (He 10:36-39), the persecuted Christians will surmount all trials.

Luke, then, like Matthew, is giving a doctrine of suffering and persecution which stresses the link with the eschatological dynamism of the Kingdom. This is the paschal law. Trial will enable the "Remnant" (Mt) of the "saved" (Lk) who form the Kingdom to establish themselves. The persecuted will be assured of the presence among them of God's Word and Spirit.

VII. Daniel   The author reports the account of the ban-
   5:1-6, 13-14,   quet of Belshazzar in order to strengthen the
   16-17, 23-28   faith of his contemporaries in the approaching
   1st reading   "day" of Yahweh. He has certainly not lived
   1st cycle   to see the event, because he makes Belshazzar
   Wednesday   the son of Nabuchadnezzar whereas he is that
            of Nabonidus.

The purpose of the account is to convince the Jews that the final day is decreed and that the events of the history of man are so many links which accelerate its maturity. There exists then a close connection between the history of man and God's plan of salvation. This salvation does not happen from without but, on the contrary, is accomplished through the very human adventure to which it gives its meaning. The prophet of the end of times will then be the one who lives the events of men in communion with the God of the history that leads them. This means that only one religion of a God of history is able to interpret the events of this last and to disclose the end towards which they move. The religion of the diviners of Belshazzar cannot know the meaning and the aim of history because the God whom they adore is a God of nature.

What is true of the events of history prior to Christ, that they find their significance only in the person of Jesus, the decisive event, is equally true of the events after Christ. The attention that certain Christian centers give to contemporary events and to the "signs of the times" could not dispense from recourse to the fundamental event and to the founder who has the name Jesus Christ.

Between an exclusive biblicism which believes that all is in the gospel and a humanism which acknowledges only the present event, the Christian attitude proceeds simultaneously from the significance of the gospel and the analysis of the lived event, as well as from their mutual confrontation.

VIII. Revelation   The last judgment is here compared to the
     15:1-4   *exodus* from Egypt. While seven angels each
    1st reading   reserve a plague for the impious, the just who
    2nd cycle   have triumphed over the persecutions, find
  Wednesday themselves near the illuminated abode of God
                 and intone their version of the hymn of Moses.

IX. Luke   This gospel has been commented on at the
   21:12-19   same time as that of Tuesday, p. 308.
   Gospel
  Wednesday

X. Daniel 6:12-28 Parallel to the legend of the three children in
   1st reading   the furnace (Dn 3), the account of Daniel in
   1st cycle   the lion's den shows how the persecuted tri-
   Thursday   umph over the trial to the extent that they
               place their confidence in God the savior.

The account of Daniel in the lion's den aims at convincing the Jews, scattered in pagan territory, not to lose the concrete signs of their belonging to the chosen people. Other texts will insist, for similar reasons, on familial piety (Tobit) or the strict application of the law of cleanness and uncleanness (Dn 1).

The reading for this day underscores the necessity of *prayer*, both in its content of faith in the God who will save Israel (vv. 17-24) and in its orientation towards Jerusalem and its fidelity to the three traditional moments of the sacrifice in the temple (v. 14).

The prayer of Daniel is essentially bound up with actual belonging to a given people. For each prayer to God there corresponds a previous fraternity. One must have tried going beyond oneself which every fraternal relation calls for in order to begin to ascend towards God and to dialogue with him. This solidarity with a people is not only a solidarity with other Christians in the Church but with all humanity. The Christian who draws near to God in an act of confession knows that he is bound up with the sins of the world and he will not fail to take into account this solidarity in his prayer so that it is verified in forgiveness. The Christian who addresses a prayer of intention to God knows that other brethren formulate it at the same time—or would be able to formulate it at the same time—by praying for their dead and he freely thinks of all the dead and by praying for the peace of his heart he cannot forget peace in the world. In this way he is part of a priestly people and he verifies in his prayer the universal and unique intercession of Christ on the cross, dying for the many.

The prayer that Daniel recited three times a day was probably the "Schema Israel" which Judaism will impose on its faithful. Christ will propose the Our Father, a prayer which the first Christians also recited three times a day. Could we recite the Lord's prayer with as much care as the people of God as Daniel did!

XI. Revelation 18:1-2, 21-23; 19:1-3, 9a *1st reading* *2nd cycle* *Thursday*   Babylon, a symbol of the Roman Empire, is destined for destruction and its pretensions about procuring salvation for humanity are ridiculed. The cries of praise already burst forth from those who are pleased with the annihilation of the city of evil and the coming of the Kingdom.

a) This *liturgy* is first of all celebrated by a great crowd of angels and saints who express their joy over the establishment of the Kingdom of God by borrowing their acclamation from the psalms and canticles of the Old Testament which tell about the coming of the Kingdom. They praise God for establishing his Kingdom for which a new stage has been bridged by the destruction of the enemy city (vv. 2, 21).

b) The covenant is celebrated here under the appearance of a *nuptial rite* (19:9a) which brings to mind the images and symbols of the Old (Hos 2:16; Is 54:6; Ez 16) and the New Testament (Ep 5:25-32; 2 Col 11:2). Nevertheless the author avoids a too realistic interpretation: he presents the groom but does not mention the bride, and the Church appears only under the traits of guests at the banquet. John proceeds similarly with his account of the wedding at Cana (Jn 2:1-11) and Matthew in the parable of the virgins (Mt 25:1-13). The evangelists probably fear the influence of the pagan hierogamous representations. But if they do not clearly indicate the bride, they do describe rather clearly a Church which faces Christ, whether it is under the traits of the bride or of the guests. This manner of proceeding envisages the Church less as the Body of Christ than as a society distinct from him. In other respects these two concepts are complimentary: the second insists on the dependence of the Church with regard to its Savior, the first considers more the results of grace and the fruits of the Covenant that was made.

The contents of the acclamations of this heavenly liturgy seem at first sight banal: "Alleluia" . . . "always with joyfulness," etc. They "cried," "shouted" (vv. 1, 6) or they resemble the roaring of a violent storm because they were freeing the joy of a crowd.

Our liturgical reunions are only a weak echo of the enormous bursting forth of cheerfulness of the last times. May they at least serve as a prelude in renewing the faith of Christians in the coming of the reign of God!

XII. Luke
21:20-28
Gospel
Thursday

This gospel reading is commented upon at the same time as Luke 21:29-33, the following Friday, p. 318.

XIII. Daniel   Chapter 7 of Daniel is one of the most impor-
   7:2-14   tant apocalyptic pieces in Scripture. It seems
   1st reading   to have been put together according to the
   1st cycle   most ancient traditions. We can discern one
   Friday   source, in prose, which concerns the end of
                    the kingdoms of this world (the vision of the
four beasts; vv. 2-8a and 11b-12). Another, older still, is in verse,
and concerns the Son of Man (vv. 9-10 and 13-14, our reading).
Then comes the angel's interpretation (vv. 17-27) regarding both
the previous traditions, which reassembles doctrinally Daniel 2.
Finally, there are some later interpolations (vv. 8b, 11a, 20, 24
and 25a, 21, 22b and 25b) which are subsequent interpolations,
sometimes fiercely nationalist in tone.

The purpose of the final redactor is fairly clear. He wants to
proclaim the approaching end of the great terrestrial empires, the
last of which in particular tyrannizes over the chosen people. He
is reestablishing confidence in the possibility of a proximate Kingdom of God by a "Son of Man" (v. 13) and a "people of saints"
(v. 18).

Probably the *Son of Man* vision goes back to Ugaritic mythology. The "ancient of days" suggests the title of some ancient God-
sovereign. The "Son of Man" could have been a rival god, whom
Daniel, ignorant doubtless of the mythological background of
these images, reduces to angelic state.

But who is this "Son of Man"? Nothing suggests that he is
thought of as a human being. He is only "like" a Son of Man (v.
13); he comes on the clouds, which is proper to heavenly beings,
and seems to come from the heavens and not from the earth to
present himself before God. We think then more of a heavenly
being than of a man which precludes any messianic and earthly
interpretation. But, in verse 14, the kingship is conferred only on
the Son of Man. In verses 18 and 22, it is likewise for the "saints
of the Most-High" which would make one believe that the Son
of Man represents them or directs them.

The expressions used in this chapter (not to be found else-where): "ancient of days," "Son of Man," "saints of the Most-High" are then ambiguous, but there emerges the idea of a double inauguration of the reign of God, one on the earthly level by crushing the four imperial beasts, the other on the heavenly level, the submission of the heavenly court to the ancient of days.

We are then seemingly in the presence of an important witness of a current of spirituality guiding the soteriological hope of the people towards a transcendent being and no longer towards a davidic messianism.

Jesus will correct this tendency. He was conscious of fulfilling at once three traditions; the transcendent mission of the Son of Man, the expiation of the Suffering Servant and the Messiahship of the Son of David. He modifies considerably the concept of the Son of Man. He sometimes makes the image the sign of his humiliation (Mt 8:20; 11:19; 17:22; 20:28), at others, the sign of his glorification (Mt 26:64; Mk 13:24-27). He retains it for the proclamation of a Kingdom at once heavenly and earthly.

XIV. Revelation Christians believe in happiness immediately
20:1-4, 11- after death (contrary to the Jewish idea), but
21:2 also in a solemn judgment and a final restora-
1st reading tion of creation and of the Kingdom. The old
2nd cycle creation has disappeared after the chaining of
Friday Satan for a thousand years (20:1-4) and his
last incursion to the four corners of the earth
(Rv 20:7-10). The judgment is then solemnly inaugurated (v. 12), the resurrection of the dead is accomplished (v. 13) and the new creation appears (21:1-2).

a) This concept is inherited from Jewish thought. God alone decides events which no longer appear in continuity with an earthly life. He is alone on his throne (v. 11) and no mention is made of those who sit on thrones around him. Even the Lamb is absent from the scene. As for the new city (21:1-2), it seems so unearthly that it descends ready made from God. The first Christians lived then with two ideas that they did not perfectly integrate: one which underscores that eternal life is at work in the life of the baptized, the other which makes of it an event left to the *good pleasure of God*. Verse 12 of this reading allows this tension to appear clearly: during the meeting for judgment we open all together the books which report the actions of men and the book of life which contain in advance the will of God for each one of them.

But this opposition between two concepts of eschatology is not contradictory and everything is harmonized to the degree that one is willing to grant to the earthly life of the baptized a significance which is already heavenly. Thus, the city which descends from heaven among men is not only reserved for beyond death (Rv 21:3); it is already built in each heart (Jn 14:23). Thus, this future Jerusalem will be "heavenly" (v. 2) in contrast to Babylon, the city made by human hands (Rv 18). But are not believers henceforth in heaven (Col 3:1-3) and can they not take part in the construction of this holy city? Finally, even if God has transmitted his own beauty to the fiance of his son (v. 2, cf. Ez 16:14), this latter is however a liberated humanity which was able to accede to the distinction of bride only in freely accepting the beauty God gave her.

b) Within the context of chapter 21, the description of the *new Jerusalem* is made in three parts, each inaugurated by: "And I saw . . ." (Rv 21:1-8) or by: "And he showed . . ." (Rv 21:9-17; 22:1-5).

Each subdivision starts with the description of the heavenly city in an apocalyptic style (Rv 21:1-3, 5-6ab; 21:9-23; 22:1-2), is followed by a prophetic oracle based on the vocabulary of the Old Testament (Rv 21:3c, 4, 6, 7; 21:24-26; 22:3-5) and is completed by a curse on sinners (Rv 21:8, 27; 22:15).

The first part, the only one represented in our reading (vv. 1-2) presents the new Jerusalem in terms which clearly recall Isaiah 65:17-19, a text which belongs to the prophecies of the messianic transfiguration of Jerusalem (theme of the appearance of the new world and the destruction of the old, and the new manifestation of Sion). This description recalls Isaiah 61:10 on the theme of Jerusalem, the espoused.

We can however pick out some differences between Revelation and Third-Isaiah. The latter had thought of only one image by saying that we "should forget" the ancient world. Revelation confers on it more reality by affirming that the ancient world "will vanish." Moreover, John adds a new trait: the city will descend from heaven, not from the cosmogonical heaven (because it will have been destroyed with the ancient world), but from a mysterious region, from "God's realm." The Jews had already imagined an ideal city in heaven, of which that on earth would be only a replica (for example for the tabernacle: Ex 25:9-40; 36:30; 37:8; Nb 8:4). Elsewhere, after the fall of Jerusalem, in 70, the Jewish apocalypses will in fact announce a miraculous intervention of God for the reconstruction of Jerusalem. But this action is always a reconstruction of the old city, and if one sometimes makes an allusion to the descent of a heavenly Jerusalem, it is only to assure in a miraculous manner (because the people cannot realize it) continuity with the ancient city. The Jewish perspective is then to assure a revival of the destroyed city, although the perspective of Revelation is quite different: it is indeed a new city to come and its continuity with the old is less important than the recognition of its transcendence and unique character.

Why then does John preserve the Jerusalem theme if it involves such a different reality? It is because for him it still remained the center of the Covenant, the concrete figure of the people of God. To present a new Sion amounts then to putting in concrete form the new people's election and the conclusion of a new type of Covenant in a city.

c) It involves moreover a *new type of Covenant:* a new marriage between God and the city (v. 2b) inspired by Isaiah 54:1-6;

62:4, 12; 66:7-9; the election of a new people (v. 3b) according to a formula inspired by ancient covenant formulas of the Old Testament: "I shall be their God and they will be my people." This new type of covenant brings new privileges: the guarantee of God's presence in it (this is the dwelling: Rv 21:3; a text inspired by those which speak of the tent in the Old Testament: Ez 43: 4-5; 2 M 2:8), intimacy with God who will heal every ill (Is 25:8), inheritance and adoption as sons of God (Rv 21:7).

XV. Luke
21:29-33
Gospel
Friday

This passage should be replaced in the difficult context of prophecy concerning Jerusalem's fall. Using the terminology customary in Jewish apocalypse and eschatology, the Lord makes the event assume the dimensions of an ending for the last days.

a) Today's reading immediately follow the description of the siege of Jerusalem (vv. 20-24). The city's fall is seen as the result of a *cosmic catastrophe*, which will unhinge even the stars and plunge men into the greatest confusion (vv. 25-26). Jewish apocalypses always describe the destruction of a city, or the "Day of Yahweh," in terms of cosmic catastrophe (Is 24:10-23; 13:6-10; Jr 4:23-26). Like Babylon, Samaria, Gomorrha and many another pagan city, Jerusalem herself now undergoes the chastisement of the "Day of Yahweh." In illustrating with images of a cosmic order (more conservatively though than the parallel passage in Mt) his description of Zion's fall, Luke does not necessarily proclaim the end of the world. What he does is present the fall as a decisive stage in the establishment of Yahweh's reign in the world.

The implication of all creation in the city's fall was a typical biblical approach. The messianic kingdom tended to be presented as a "new creation" which would reverse the fundaments of the old (Jl 3:1-5; Hg 2:6; Is 65:17). Hence, Jerusalem's fall seemed to be the dawn of a new creation.

b) Having alluded to the cosmic significance of the collapse, Luke goes on to announce the *coming of the Son of Man in a cloud* (v. 27). This is obviously a reference to the mysterious judge of nations. As he sees it, the manifestation of the Son of Man, Lord of nations, begins precisely at the moment of the temple's fall. It was considered the place of the nations' great assembly under the rule of Yahweh (Is 60); but Christ had transferred the prerogative to "he who comes" or "he who comes in the cloud" (Mt 26:61-64; 23:37-39). "Coming in the cloud" was a phrase used of someone haloed with divine glory, and the Christians had no difficulty in applying it to the risen Christ. Until the end of time he is the "one who comes" (Rv 1:7; cf. Rv 14:14), since the moment of his resurrection, and more actually still after the fall of Zion, constitutes then the "coming of the Son of Man."

c) When the account is finished the gospel goes on to moral applications. Luke invites his contemporaries (vv. 31-32) to see a "sign" of the proximity of the Kingdom (vv. 27-31) in the fall of Jerusalem. Proximity not of a temporal order as if the end of the world were imminent, but ontological rather. The Kingdom is in a state of becoming in each event of human history and of salvation history, as we must endeavor to discern it there. Watchfulness is a virtue precisely of the man who concerns himself with the Lordship of the Son of Man, and who watches it germinate in each person and "in all things."

A stage in the coming of the Lord on the cloud was marked by the fall of Jerusalem, because it forced the Church to open her ranks irrevocably to the nations, and to shape a spiritual cult purified of the temple's particularism. Every stage then in the evangelization of the world, linked to all the stages in the humanization of the planet, is also a stage in this coming of the Son of Man. Each conversion of heart by which man opens himself to the action of the Spirit of the Risen One, and relies a little less upon the "flesh," is a new manifestation of the coming. Every eucharistic assembly, united "until he comes again," is the recipient of the glory and power of the Son of Man on the cloud, and is indeed the stage *par excellence* of this coming.

XVI. Daniel
7:15-27
1st reading
1st cycle
Saturday

The commentary for this reading is the same as that for the first reading, the first cycle of the previous Friday, p. 314.

XVII. Revelation
22:1-7
1st reading
2nd cycle
Saturday

John terminates the description of the heavenly city (vv. 1-5) and begins the epilogue of his book (vv. 6-7).

John here takes up again the most ancient images of the Old Testament, those of paradise: trees of life, river, the definitive victory of day over night. Thus, all the history of humanity was truly in the hands of God; the alpha and the omega are rejoined.

XVIII. Luke
21:34-36
Gospel
Saturday

Luke brings to the eschatological discourse of Christ a personal conclusion which extols vigilance.

From verse 31 Luke underscores the necessity of *vigilance*, because of the "proximity" of the Kingdom. Now he takes up again the same image, but more in detail (vv. 34-35) and replaces the theme about the proximity of the Kingdom in the suddenness of the judgment of the Son of Man (v. 36). No doubt this passage is early, for it contains a great number of biblical references (Is 24:17-20; Ec 9:12; Gn 7:23) and reveals a rather primary concept of the judgment of the Son of Man. Undoubtedly it is only after several years that the primitive communities understood that this proximity was not of the temporal but the ontological order: the proximity of the Kingdom and the coming of the Son of Man are present in each event of the history of salvation. Vigilance consists in revealing this presence.

TABLE OF READINGS